# Global Pirates

## THE NORTHEASTERN SERIES ON
## WHITE-COLLAR AND ORGANIZATIONAL CRIME

*Edited by* KIP SCHLEGEL and DAVID WEISBURD

# GLOBAL PIRATES

*Fraud in the Offshore Insurance Industry*

ROBERT TILLMAN

NORTHEASTERN UNIVERSITY PRESS
*Boston*

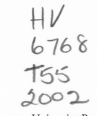

HV
6768
T55
2002

Northeastern University Press

Library of Congress Cataloging-in-Publication Data

Tillman, Robert.
Global pirates : fraud in the offshore insurance industry / Robert Tillman.
p.   cm. — (Northeastern series on white collar and organizational crime)
Includes bibliographical references and index.
ISBN 1-55553-505-4 (pbk. : alk. paper) — ISBN 1-55553-506-2 (cloth : alk paper)
1. Insurance crimes.   I. Title.   II. Series.

HV6768.T55   2001
364.16'3—dc21                    2001030812

Designed by Gary Gore

Composed in Adobe Garamond by Coghill Composition in Richmond, Virginia. Printed and bound by The Maple Press Company in York, Pennsylvania. The paper is Sebago Antique, an acid-free sheet.

Manufactured in the United States of America
06  05  04  03  02     5  4  3  2  1

*For A.M.T., who made it all worthwhile*

# CONTENTS

# Global Pirates

# INTRODUCTION

On Father's Day 1991, Diane Collras and her husband were driving their new Pontiac Trans Am to church in the San Fernando Valley of California when they were broadsided by another car, hurling Mrs. Collras twenty feet from her vehicle. She left the hospital a week later, burned and scarred. "But the hardest scar came when I went home," she later told a legislative panel.[1] Once home, she tried to get in touch with her insurance company but got little response. Gradually she began to realize her claims were never going to be paid.

> You've been calling almost every day. You get a machine or you get somebody who's very, very funny who says, "We'll have him call you back. He's on another line; he's out, he's this, he's that . . ." And then all of a sudden phones start being, "This line is disconnected. We have no new service."[2]

The Collrases' problem was that they had unknowingly purchased their car insurance from an offshore company, Union Pacific Fire and Marine, based in the British Virgin Islands. Their insurance broker, whom they had found in the yellow pages, neglected to mention where the company was located or the fact that it was not licensed by the state when he took their check for $2,000.

Afterward, with her Trans Am still sitting in a wrecker's yard, Mrs. Collras explained her situation to a group of California legislators:

> We're paying on two cars. The lady who hit us, she wants to take our house. We've got two teens, teenagers, that want to go to college. We're losing part of our lives because you don't tell anybody what these companies even are, and then when you ask about them, you can't even get a straight answer from the Department of Insurance, the Surplus Lines Association, or even your own state Senator. . . ."[3]

The Collrases' plight was likely not weighing heavily on the minds of Union Pacific Fire and Marine owners when they fled to Costa Rica with $4 million in premiums collected from their policyholders.[4]

Mrs. Collras was aware that there were many other victims like herself, but she was unlikely aware of the fact that the problem went far beyond California and unscrupulous auto insurance scam artists. In fact, she and her husband were just two of thousands of victims of a global con game. Like characters in an old *Twilight Zone* episode, they had unwittingly stumbled into the often surreal world of the offshore insurance industry, a world in which sophisticated white-collar criminals operate beyond the reach of government regulators to set up elaborately orchestrated scams that drain illegal profits out of the $3 trillion U.S. insurance industry.

Congressman Ron Wyden, who in 1990 was a member of a congressional committee investigating offshore insurance crooks like the infamous Carlos Miro, likened the situation to the mythical land of Oz.

> This whole Carlos Miro empire of phony companies and bogus insurance reminds me of these fairyland kind of stories. The obstreperous lawyers are like the strawmen in the *Wizard of Oz* and the agents are just a bunch of tinmen without hearts. They go out and try to pave a yellow brick road with policyholders' money across the sea to Mr. Miro's magical land of Oz in the Caribbean, Ireland and London, and the fact is the state regulatory system has been like the cowardly lion without the courage to prevent or punish this continuing farce. All the while, you've got Mr. Miro hiding behind the smoke and the screens and the mirrors in effect to take advantage of the huge loopholes in today's regulatory process for his own personal enrichment.[5]

With a strong dose of sarcasm and cynicism, Congressman Wyden's analogy succinctly summarizes the elements of an extraordinarily complex set of white-collar crimes that emerged in the 1980s and continue to plague the United States and other countries today. Congressman Wyden's committee had discovered the existence of a large network of criminals who were in the business of setting up insurance companies offshore, in places such as Antigua, Barbados, and Ireland, where financial regulations are minimal and restrictions on outside access to insurance companies' books are high. These offshore companies would then sell insurance policies and other products to American citizens to whom they had no intention of honoring their obligations. Congressman Wyden's committee would come to the conclusion that "[t]he combination of easy money based on easy promises makes the insurance industry an irresistible target for *financial knaves and buccaneers*"[6] (italics added).

This is a book about these "financial knaves and buccaneers"—their schemes and the larger forces that made them possible. While it is a book that describes specific groups of white-collar criminals and their crimes, it is also a book about the changing nature of society, to wit, globalization and its criminal consequences. At one level, these criminals are simply old-fashioned con artists using tried and true techniques such as Ponzi schemes. At another level, the knaves and buccaneers are individuals who have taken advantage of rapidly changing financial markets and the regulatory environments that surround them. In this sense, their crimes are the white-collar crimes of the future—crimes that combine the traditional elements of clever salesmanship and gullible victims with elements drawn from the "new economy," an economy that is more information based, less geographically bound, and much more volatile than in the past.

To explain these events, a broader theoretical argument will be advanced that can be summarized as follows. The process of globalization has generally led to deregulatory policies in which governments have ceded their authority to regulate commerce. This liberalization of regulations has created "regulatory voids"—industry niches that are largely ungoverned. These conditions, in turn, create opportunities for white-collar criminals to hatch schemes that take advantage of the absence of regulation. This is not an iron law. Globalization and deregulation can occur without criminal consequences. Nonetheless, the fact that the process can be observed, as we shall see, not only in the offshore insurance industry but also in the banking and securities and other industries, suggests a broader pattern that needs to be explained.

## The Problem Emerges

Concerns over problems in the insurance industry increased in the late 1980s as policy makers who were just becoming aware of the debacle that was taking place in the savings and loan industry were worried that the insurance industry might have been facing a similar crisis. One of the problems was the growing number of insurance company insolvencies. In the sixteen-year period between 1969 and 1984, a total of 187 property/casualty insurers were declared insolvent; in the five-year period between 1985 and 1989, that number soared to 205.[7] Several congressional committees held hearings to examine the sources and extent of problems in the industry and found that, while there were significant problems among licensed, domestic insurers, the problems were even more glaring among unlicensed companies operating in the United States from offshore bases.

In the House, hearings were held in February 1990 by a committee headed by Representative John Dingell of Michigan. Dingell's committee focused its attention on several large insurance companies that had recently failed, result-

ing in billions of dollars in losses that would ultimately be paid for by taxpayers.[8] In its report, *Failed Promises*, the committee compared problems in the
savings and loan industry with emerging problems in the insurance industry.

> The driving force behind [the savings and loan crisis] was management
> greed and incompetence, accompanied by self-dealing, conflicts of
> interest, lavish life-styles, violations of laws and regulations, and out-
> right fraud . . . The same patterns of industry and regulatory conduct
> have emerged from the Subcommittee's recent investigations of insur-
> ance company insolvencies.[9]

One of the insurance company failures that Dingell's committee dissected
was Transit Casualty, whose losses were estimated to total between $3 billion
and $4 billion, leading the committee to refer to it as the "Titanic of insolven-
cies." A key actor in the Transit failure was a Cuban-born, U.S. resident named
Carlos Miro. After abandoning Transit's sinking ship, Miro started his own
company, Anglo American Insurance, that was licensed in Louisiana, a state
where three successive insurance commissioners wound up being indicted on
corruption charges. Miro would later testify that among his many crimes he
paid bribes to the insurance commissioner, at the suggestion of former gover-
nor, Edwin Edwards, who was on Miro's payroll and who would later be convicted on federal charges that included insurance fraud.[10] Between 1986 and
1989, Anglo American took in over $56 million in premiums. Investigators dis-
covered that Miro had illegally diverted over $20.8 million from the company,
which "was nothing more than a name, with no employees, no payroll, no
office space or equipment, and no expenses."[11] The money was used to fund a
lavish lifestyle, that included a chauffeured limousine to transport Mr. Miro
around Dallas, where he lived, charter Lear jets, stay in the finest hotels in
London and Dallas, and a $1.4 million condominium.[12]

*Failed Promises* was groundbreaking and controversial. It alerted the public
to major fault lines in the insurance industry that threatened to bring it down.
However, the most detailed examination of fraud in the offshore insurance
industry came in a series of hearings held by a Senate committee headed by
Senator Sam Nunn of Georgia. On April 24, 1991, the committee opened hearings that focused on the operations of a network of insurance companies operated by a British citizen and former Lloyd's of London broker, Alan Teale.
What the committee and its investigators found can best be described as a
series of Chinese boxes, in which one set of fraudulent organizations and scams
revealed the existence of another set, which led to another set, and so on. An
investigation of a health insurance scam, for example, pointed to a network

of Teale-connected offshore reinsurance companies, which in turn provided evidence of a ring of white-collar criminals who were engaged in scams involving government securities (see Chapter 1).

The committee also heard testimony from a remarkably diverse array of victims that ranged from professional football players such as Joe Montana to a Taco Bell employee from South Carolina. Senator Nunn succinctly summarized their common plight:

> Whether it is health insurance or professional disability insurance, what all of these individuals have in common is that they were sold a promise, a promise that there would be something to fall back on when the hard times hit, a promise which turned out to be empty. It is in this sense that insurance scams are the cruelest hoax of all.[13]

## Offshore Insurance Fraud: Basic Elements

Offshore crooks, like Alan Teale, who actually resided in the United States, take advantage of a number of fundamental elements of the insurance industry in general, and the structure of the U.S. regulatory system in particular. First, they exploit the nature of transactions in the insurance industry itself:

> Unlike other industries that produce tangible products or provide immediate services to customers, the business of insurance essentially involves the *selling of promises*—"promise(s) to pay all or a part of the costs associated with some future event." In some cases the consumer may rarely use the services being paid for. Moreover, transactions in the industry are characterized by a *long tail*; that is, a long period of time often elapses between the date when a customer begins paying for future services . . . and the date that those services are actually demanded. . . . In the interim, unscrupulous insurance company owners and operators have ample time to abscond with their clients' premiums[14] [italics in original].

A second feature of the insurance industry that makes it particularly conducive to fraud has to do with the layered nature of insurance coverage itself. Insurance, in all of its forms, is fundamentally about risk. From a consumer's point of view, insurance is a means of protecting oneself against the consequences of unforeseen events, such as an automobile accident, illness, or earthquake. Insurance companies make money by virtue of the fact that, for any single individual or company, those events are largely unpredictable. However,

in the aggregate, for large numbers of individuals or companies or other entities, the likelihood of such events are relatively predictable and thus their costs
known. Hence, risk can be commoditized—bought and sold. Insurance com-
modities can be chopped up, repackaged, and resold to many other insurers,
far beyond the original company that agreed to provide an insurance policy to
an individual or a company. An individual who purchases an automobile policy, for example, may be unaware that his/her policy has been, in effect, resold
to another company, called a reinsurance company, which has, in turn, sold a
portion of the obligation to pay claims to other companies, known as retrocessionaires. Thus, the risk may be spread out among large numbers of entities
that may be located within the United States and in foreign countries. One of
the consequences of this distribution of risk is that it makes it very difficult
for regulators to keep track of all the companies involved in every insurance
transaction and to verify the solvency of those companies. This inability to
regulate creates an ideal situation for white-collar criminals who set up complex chains of insurance, reinsurance, and retrocession in what are, in effect,
houses of cards that are destined to collapse, but not until after millions of
premium dollars have been collected.

Third, offshore insurance crooks often take advantage of regulatory loopholes that have allowed certain segments of the insurance industry to operate
outside of the government regulations that cover much of the industry. As shall
be discussed, many of these loopholes were the result of legislative efforts to
deregulate portions of the industry, to intentionally allow them to "self-regu-
late"—often with disastrous consequences.

Fourth, these schemes often take advantage of the fact that many countries,
particularly small Caribbean countries, actually encourage foreigners to establish insurance companies in their countries with minimal requirements for
assets and guarantees of secrecy, as long as they do not sell policies within the
country itself. At the same time these companies sell their products in the
United States but evade the scrutiny of U.S. authorities by hiding behind the
sovereignty of the country in which their firm is officially domiciled. Even if
American regulators suspect an offshore company of dubious dealings, they
can have a very difficult time verifying the company's vital statistics.

Finally, offshore insurance crooks often market their products to consumers who find it difficult to obtain insurance from legitimate companies.
Included here: inner-city merchants whose neighborhoods have been redlined
by insurance companies; small-business employees, or the self-employed who
have a hard time obtaining health insurance; and automobile and truck drivers
with bad records who have difficulty finding affordable auto/truck insurance.

In other words, these white-collar racketeers prey on people who are most vulnerable and who have the fewest means to defend themselves.

## Trends in the Insurance Industry

Like air, insurance is all around us, enveloping us in an invisible shield against the unexpected. Insurance policies cover our cars, our homes, our businesses, our health, and our lives. More than that, insurance is used in virtually every type of business transaction, small to large. The legs of professional athletes and ballerinas, the success of Hollywood movies, the safe arrival of cargo ships, the safety of those who attend rock concerts, the reproductive capabilities of championship bulls . . . all are protected by insurance.

The insurance industry is divided into two main sectors: life/health and property/casualty. The life/health sector provides individual coverage in the form of life insurance and health insurance as well as annuities and other investment opportunities. Property and casualty insurers provide coverage for both individuals and companies against losses of property or injury. Some of the more common types of property/casualty coverage are auto insurance, malpractice insurance for doctors, workers' compensation, and homeowner insurance. At the end of 1999, U.S. insurance companies held assets worth over $3.8 trillion.[15]

Despite its size, there is no federal regulation of the insurance industry. Instead, regulation is spread throughout the fifty states where insurance companies, brokers, and agents are licensed and supervised by state insurance commissions or insurance departments. The limited authority and resources of state regulators has frequently been cited as a major problem in the pursuit of fraudulent offshore insurers. Annual expenditures on insurance regulation by all fifty states combined amount to less than one-third of what the federal government spends each year to regulate banks.[16] Nonetheless, efforts to impose federal regulation on the industry have been beaten back by coalitions of state regulators and the insurance industry.

Beginning in the 1970s, major changes in certain segments of the insurance industry led to several "insurance crises" in which demand for insurance far outstripped supply, leading to what is sometimes called a "capacity problem." The response of government officials and politicians to these crises was to attempt to open up the markets by creating or giving greater freedom to noninsurance companies that sold insurance products and were allowed to operate outside the regulatory requirements imposed on traditional insurance companies. The effects of these moves was to "deregulate" or "under-regulate" these segments of the industry by either creating exemptions for these entities or by not creating new regulations governing their behavior. One of these sectors was the small business health insurance market.

By the early 1980s, small businesses in the United States were encountering severe difficulties in obtaining health insurance for their employees. A combination of events, including the tendency of large corporations to set up their own insurance programs for their employees together with a shift by many health insurers to highly competitive underwriting practices that drove down profits, led to the departure of many large insurance companies from the market. Those that remained offered group policies to small businesses at rates so high that few could afford them. In response, in 1983 Congress passed the Ehrlenborn Amendment, which expanded the provisions of an earlier law, the Employee Retirement Income Security Act of 1974 (ERISA), which allowed small businesses to pool their resources by forming "multiple employer plans." These plans were intended to give employees of small businesses access to the same affordable health insurance as the employees of large firms, by allowing employers to "pool" their employees for insurance purposes. Pooling arrangements bring down rates by creating a mix of high-risk and low-risk participants whose costs balance one another out, as well as producing economies of scale that reduce administrative expenses.

Importantly, under ERISA, "multiple employer plans" were exempt from state insurance laws that impose on insurance companies such requirements as minimum funding standards, mandated benefits, and contributions to a guaranty fund. Most states require all licensed insurance companies to contribute to "guaranty funds," based on premium taxes that can range from 2 to 3 percent of all premiums. These guaranty funds are used to cover the costs of unpaid claims from insolvent insurance companies. These exemptions granted under ERISA were intended to give multiple employer plans advantages that would allow them to compete with large companies for health insurance.

The Ehrlenborn Amendment created a new entity, Multiple Employer Welfare Arrangements (MEWA), that also allowed small employers to band together to form groups for the purpose of providing health insurance to employees at reasonable rates. While the law's creators envisioned that MEWAs would be formed by trade associations and similar employer groups, the Ehrlenborn Amendment allowed third parties to organize these associations. This third-party organization of MEWAs would open the door to crooks who saw MEWAs as the ideal vehicle to perpetrate frauds. Although the law was designed to fill some of the regulatory loopholes in ERISA that had allowed con artists to fleece small business employees, it actually created more ambiguity over the role of state versus federal authorities in overseeing these new entities. This ambiguity often paralyzed state regulators who were forced to sit back and watch as crooks set up bogus MEWAs, took in millions of dollars in premiums from unsuspecting employees who desperately needed medical coverage for themselves and their families, and then skipped out leaving their policyholders with expensive medical bills. Many of the victims of these scams not only suffered financial setbacks, but also physical harm. Once their health coverage disappeared they often found themselves with medical conditions that legitimate insurance companies deemed to be "pre-existing conditions," thus rendering them ineligible for coverage, and they were forced to forego medical treatment because of their inability to pay for treatment and to obtain replacement insurance.

Problems in the MEWA industry became so severe that Senator Nunn's committee held hearings on the subject in May 1990, which were opened with a statement by the senator: "Unscrupulous [MEWA] promoters . . . are literally playing with people's lives."[17] In a 1992 study, the General Accounting Office (GAO, Congress's research arm) estimated that, between 1988 and 1991, fraudulent MEWAs left more than 400,000 individuals with $133 million in unpaid medical claims.[18]

A similar series of events occurred in the property/casualty industry. In the late 1970s, small businesses were having a difficult time obtaining product liability insurance, after large insurance companies either refused to sell them policies or charged exorbitant rates for that coverage. In 1981, Congress passed the Product Liability Risk Retention Act. The legislation created risk retention groups that operated in the product liability market in many of the same ways that MEWAs did in the health insurance market. Small businesses engaged in similar or related business activities were given the right to band together to form risk retention groups in order to self-insure their liability risks through the formation of trusts or pools that, as with MEWAs, enabled them to provide the same coverage to their members that large corporations could obtain from insurance companies. It also allowed for the formation of risk purchasing groups in which small business groups could purchase insurance directly from licensed companies. Importantly, neither risk retention groups nor risk purchasing groups were subject to the same regulations imposed by states on licensed insurance companies.

In 1986, the provisions of the Risk Retention Act were expanded to cover all commercial liability coverage when Congress passed the Liability Risk Retention Act that expanded the provisions of the 1981 law. Once again, the legislation was enacted in response to the needs of owners of small businesses, like daycare centers, who complained of the inability to find affordable insurance. When President Reagan signed the bill he called it a "marketplace solution" whose "goal is accomplished without imposing any new federal regulations or expenditures."[19]

In an effort to reduce regulatory red tape, the law required that risk retention groups be licensed in only one state but allowed them to sell insurance in all other states. This meant that the operators of risk retention groups could shop around until they found a state with lax regulatory requirements, obtain their license there, then sell their products nationwide. Like MEWAs, risk retention groups were also exempt from contributing to state insurance guaranty funds, which gave them an economic advantage over licensed insurance companies, but also meant that, when they became insolvent, policyholders were left with no place to turn to have their claims paid.

After the passage of the 1986 Act, risk retention groups were formed among groups who had previously encountered difficulties in obtaining liability insurance, including physicians who, in the 1980s, had seen their premiums for malpractice insurance skyrocket. Into this void came not only legitimate risk retention groups but also con artists who took advantage of both the new law's regulatory loopholes and physicians' lack of knowledge about the insurance industry.

One high-profile case involved a Louisiana-based group known as Physicians National Risk Retention Group. The group was founded in 1987 by a group of prominent Louisiana lawyers and businessmen who obtained a license from the Louisiana insurance commissioner, Sherman Bernard, who would later be convicted in an unrelated case for taking bribes in exchange for licenses (see Chapter 3). Physicians National embarked on a highly successful campaign to sell malpractice insurance to physicians nationwide, eventually signing up 4,500 doctors in thirty-five states, many of whom were in hard-to-insure specialties like anesthesiology. A big factor in their success was the fact that the premiums were as much as 60 percent lower than policies offered by traditional insurance companies. Physicians National was able to offer these cut-rate prices for the simple reason that it never intended to pay most claims. After taking control of the company in 1991, Louisiana regulators claimed that the principals behind Physicians National had siphoned over $7.7 million from the company, in part by moving some of the money to a Bahamian reinsurance company. Ultimately, Physicians National would leave unpaid bills totaling over $40 million.[20]

Another mechanism for dealing with capacity problems in insurance markets is the surplus lines market. Many states allow insurance carriers that are not admitted (licensed) in their state to sell insurance as "surplus lines carriers." Insurers that are licensed somewhere, either in another state or in a foreign country, may be allowed to sell policies if licensed insurers are not meeting insurance needs in some part of the market.

States vary in the requirements they place on surplus lines carriers, with some demanding that they go through an application process similar to licensing and others allowing them to market their products after filing only minimal documentation. As we shall see in Chapter 2, the failure to adequately monitor and regulate offshore insurers operating in California's surplus lines market in the late 1980s and early 1990s led to disastrous consequences. Hundreds of fraudulent offshore insurance companies flooded into the state to take advantage of tremendous demand for auto and small-business insurance and an "open door" policy by the state's insurance commission. In one year alone, state officials estimated, offshore insurance crooks operating in the surplus lines market defrauded California policyholders for $200 million.[21]

Another major source of problems in the insurance market has been the reinsurance industry, specifically, the offshore reinsurance industry, which was never so much "deregulated" as it was simply never adequately regulated. Reinsurance may be defined as "a form of insurance for insurance companies—a way of spreading the risk more widely."[22] In many ways, reinsurance allows a primary insurer to do what bookies often do. When a bookie wants to take in more bets than he can handle given the cash he has available to cover payouts, he will often "lay off" the bets with other bookies, taking a percentage of the amount wagered. Similarly, reinsurance allows primary insurers to write more policies than their cash reserves would allow, by enabling them to "lay off" a portion of the risk with reinsurers. As mentioned earlier, these reinsurers may in turn cede some of the risk to other reinsurers, known as retrocessionaires.

While states regulate insurance companies directly through licensing requirements, the oversight of reinsurers is largely indirect. The primary mechanism for controlling reinsurers is by setting standards for primary insurers regarding the credit that they receive for placing reinsurance as an asset on their books. One of these standards concerns the amount of capital held by the reinsurers with which the primary insurer has ceded risk. However, these standards are difficult to enforce, opening the door to abuse. These abuses led Senator Nunn's committee to conclude that the offshore reinsurance industry was "dangerously underregulated."[23]

Offshore reinsurers account for a large portion of the U.S. reinsurance market. Many of these companies are located in countries like Antigua and Barbados, where requirements for obtaining a charter are minimal and controls over the disclosure of financial information to outsiders are tight. As we shall see in Chapter 1, these conditions were open invitations to people like Alan Teale to set up shell reinsurance companies in Caribbean island nations with inflated if not worthless assets and then use those reinsurance companies in complex schemes to defraud American policyholders and companies.

Probably the best known provider of reinsurance is Lloyd's of London. Begun as a coffee shop in London in the 1680s where merchants gathered to pool their resources to insure the safe passage of ships, today Lloyd's takes in just under 3 percent of all insurance premiums worldwide. Lloyd's does not function as an insurance company but rather as a network of syndicates consisting of a limited number of individuals and groups, known as Names, who invest money to be used to underwrite various risks. Unlike corporate executives whose personal assets are shielded in most transactions, Lloyd's members are liable "down to their cufflinks" to pay claims on business they have underwritten.[24]

One of the most significant changes in the U.S. insurance market in the last several decades has been the growing presence of "offshore" companies— insurers whose primary market is the United States, but who are officially domiciled in foreign countries and thus not fully subject to American regulatory and tax standards. By 1994, 10 percent of all U.S. insurance premiums went to foreign insurers. In certain segments of the industry, the percentage was much higher. For example, by 1995 one-third of all reinsurance premiums paid in the United States went to foreign companies.[25]

The economic advantages of locating offshore is well illustrated by the recent move of a number of insurance companies to the increasingly popular destination of Bermuda. This small island in the Atlantic Ocean, almost 800 miles southeast of New York, has in the last two decades become the home of a number of major players in the global insurance industry. A number of property/casualty insurers have moved their headquarters there in order to take advantage of the fact that Bermuda places no tax on corporate profits, whereas American-based companies must pay as much as 40 percent in state and federal corporate taxes on the profits earned from their investments (the major source of profit for most of these companies).[26] This gives an enormous advantage to Bermuda-based companies over their U.S.-based competitors.

## The Globalization Debate

On November 30, 1999, the normally peaceful streets of Seattle were turned into an urban battleground as protestors smashed shop windows and set fires in trashcans, while dodging rubber bullets and avoiding tear gas canisters fired by National Guard troops. The object of the protestors' rage was not the promoters of an unjust war or the suppressors of free speech as they might have been in an earlier era, but a heretofore noncontroversial international organization, the World Trade Organization (WTO), that was holding meetings in the city. The protests brought together an odd amalgam of union members, environmentalists, and old-fashioned anarchists, who were united in their opposition to an organization that represented, to them, the force that was behind many of the world's problems. That force, in a word, was "globalization."[27]

The events in Seattle gave a human face to a debate that had, up to that point, largely been taking place in intellectual circles. Unlike other debates, however, that focus on a single issue, globalization, includes a wide range of trends and movements whose consequences are sometimes apparent and sometimes not, that impact different groups in different ways, and whose desirability or undesirability often depends on the part of the globe from which one is observing them. While a full review of all the issues in the globalization debate lies beyond the scope of this book, a brief discussion of some of these issues is necessary because, as will be argued within, they are directly related to the problems that have plagued the insurance industry.

Academics have observed that countries around the world have been economically linked in a "world system" for some time.[28] However, the current global economy represents something new. A useful definition is provided by Manuel Castells who has written that a global economy is "an economy with the capacity to work as a unit in real time on a planetary scale," the best example of which is found in financial industries where "capital is managed around the clock in globally integrated financial markets working in real time for the first time in history."[29] Both sides of the debate generally agree that one of the major factors that has led to the emergence of the global economy is the rapid change in telecommunications, notably the proliferation of cheap computers and the Internet.

Advocates of globalization, who include many prominent political figures and business leaders, generally see its results as benefiting everyone, albeit with a few initial bumps in the road for some. For them, the many positive results of globalization include: rising prosperity for all citizens of the world; the spread of democracy to countries where it had never before been practiced as the mass media makes information about Western democratic ideals available even in the remotest of areas; reduced inequality as entrepreneurs from all classes use new technologies to acquire and create wealth; and a reduced threat of war as countries find it in their interest to compete with one another economically, not militarily.[30] Some proponents of globalization display an almost evangelical zeal for the concept. In their book, *A Future Perfect*, John Micklethwait and Adrian Wooldridge write:

> Globalization is helping to give birth to an economy that is closer to
> the classic theoretical model of capitalism, under which rational indi-
> viduals pursue their interests in light of perfect information, relatively
> free from government and geographical obstacles. It is also helping to
> create a society that is closer to the model that liberal political theorists
> once imagined, in which power lies increasingly in the hands of indi-
> viduals rather than governments, and in which people are free, within
> reasonable bounds, to pursue the good life wherever they find it.[31]

They acknowledge that "globalization is often a brutal and chaotic process"
that tends to create "winner-take-all" societies, but argue that, overall, the posi-
tives of globalization outweigh the negatives.[32] While those at the top of the
new global order may have made it big, "we are all winners several times over
as consumers" as "globalization has brought us better, cheaper cars, computers
and holidays. . . ."[33]

Critics of globalization have argued that its many destructive consequences
include: the growing inequality between rich and poor within and between
countries; the further degradation of unskilled labor; the concentration of
power in the hands of an increasingly small circle of corporations and individuals; the destruction of fragile ecosystems; a sharp reduction in democratic institutions and processes; and a general Americanization of world cultures, as
indigenous cultures are destroyed by the overwhelming advance of American
mass media and restaurants, stores, and products into every corner of the
globe.[34]

Critics and advocates agree on at least one fact: Globalization has
unleashed a tremendous amount of capital that is moving around the world at
unprecedented speeds in search of new investment opportunities. Having been
freed from its geographical limitations by high-speed computers, fiber optic
cables, and the Internet, trillions of dollars in capital is now moved across the
globe in a matter of seconds, all day, every day. While agreeing on this fact,
the two sides of the debate see its implications very differently. Critics of the
global economy see a sinister side of this development. Where globalization
advocates see new sources of capital for entrepreneurs in third-world countries,
they see "hot money,"[35] "stateless money,"[36] and "money without a home"[37]
that exists outside the regulatory purview of any sovereign country. In this
world, there are few ways to distinguish "clean money" from "dirty money."[38]

The transformations wrought by globalization have not impacted all segments of the economy alike, but have been most evident in certain industries,
notably, financial industries. In contrast to manufacturers who are often limited by physical demands for space, materials, and access to transportation,

commercial banks, investment banks, and insurance companies have traditionally operated largely "on paper," as their principal activities consist of recording, storing, and disseminating information about accounts and transactions.
In the insurance industry, computerization of their basic processes, including
claims processing, has made companies even more mobile as "there is no
longer any need for a physical, central office located in proximity to the clients."[39] As a result, "insurance companies' work has become highly decentral-
ized and mobile, and a company's various offices may be located in different
parts of the country and even the world."[40]

As shall be discussed below, this mobility in the industry as a whole made
possible the rapid development of the offshore insurance industry, which consists of companies that are legally chartered in places like Antigua and the Cayman Islands, but whose clients are largely located in the United States and
whose actual operations may be conducted from anywhere in the world.

## Globalization, Deregulation, and Financial Crime

Both sides of the globalization debate also agree that one of the consequences of the emergence of the global economy has been an erosion of the
power of the state over the economic sphere.[41] Variously referring to the
"retreat of the state,"[42] the "powerless state,"[43] the "transformation of the
state,"[44] many writers have pointed to the declining ability of the state to regulate economic activity in an era of globalization. A principal indicator of this
new limited state authority has been a trend toward the adoption of deregulatory policies. As used here, deregulation simply means that "governments are
relinquishing their regulatory powers, getting out of the business of trying to
control business."[45] This is most commonly understood to occur when existing
policies or laws are removed or repealed. However, it should be recognized that
the same result is achieved when governments fail to impose adequate regulations on industries, creating *under-regulated* industries and markets.

While the extent of deregulation has been a matter of debate,[46] many contemporary analysts would likely agree with Saskia Sassen's assessment:

> Global markets in finance and advanced services partly operate through
> a "regulatory" umbrella that is not state centered but market centered.
> More generally the new geography of centrality is transnational and
> operates in good part in electronic spaces that override all jurisdic-
> tion.[47]

In 1997, for example, 102 nations signed a World Trade Organization pact that
opened their markets to foreign banks, insurance companies, and securities

firms. The *Wall Street Journal* referred to the agreement as "a sweeping accord . . . to deregulate the global financial-services industry."[48]

Despite widespread consensus regarding the trend toward deregulation in the financial industries, there are sharp differences among commentators on the consequences of these policies. On the positive side are those who argue that deregulation and "market-centered" forms of governance have greatly increased competitiveness and efficiency in financial industries. More than simply accept deregulation as inevitable, they argue, we should actively promote it as a policy, as a means for maintaining a competitive edge in the global economy. This argument emerged repeatedly in the recent debate over legislative efforts in the United States to repeal the Glass-Steagall Act, the landmark Depression-era law that required a separation of banks, securities brokers, and insurance companies. Strong support for this "reform" legislation came from Federal Reserve Chairman Alan Greenspan, who stated his position in a 1998 speech that "the pace of technological change, of globalization of markets, and of the pressures for deregulation can only increase. . . . However, many of our regulated financial institutions find themselves unable to respond in the most efficient and effective way because of outdated statutory limitations."[49]

On the other hand, globalization critics have described the many deleterious consequences of deregulation. William Grieder, for example, has referred to the trend toward deregulation as the "politics of escape," in which transnational companies have sought to evade the rule of law in financial markets and labor markets, while at the same time promoting laws that protect private property.[50] Richard Barnet and John Cavanagh warn of an "anarchic world of high-speed money," and admonish us to consider the consequences of deregulation: "[T]he history of deregulation is littered with scandals and financial foolishness for which a handful of bankers, but mostly millions of taxpayers and depositors, have paid a heavy price."[51]

A diverse group of academics, journalists, and politicians have argued that the emerging global economy and the breakup of the old Soviet regime have given rise to new organized crime groups that operate transnationally. Manuel Castells writes about the emergence of a "global criminal economy" whose wide acceptance worldwide may signal the "cultural breakdown of traditional moral order."[52] Claire Sterling has written about "a new underworld order" dominated by Russian crime organizations.[53] U.S. Senator John Kerry of Massachusetts has described a "global criminal axis" composed of "the Italian Mafia, the Russian mobs, the Japanese *yakuza*, the Chinese triads, and the Colombian cartels."[54] Louise Shelly points out that while crime was once local in nature, "today, thanks to computer and communications technologies, crime and corruption are no longer limited by geographic boundaries."[55]

All of these works alert us to the important fact that, with the rise of the global economy, the nature of crime has fundamentally changed. But these writers tend to focus on traditional organized criminal activities—illicit drug manufacturing and distribution; smuggling; extortion—rather than white-collar criminal activities. Those that do touch on financial crimes tend to concentrate on money laundering, and do not adequately consider the role that deregulation has played in the opening up of markets to other forms of white-collar crime.[56]

Globalization and deregulation have also led to the emergence of new organized white-collar crime groups that operate in deregulated and under-regulated "criminogenic" markets. The term criminogenic market has been used to refer to markets whose organization and structure facilitate and encourage criminal activity.[57] One element of this structure is the regulatory environment surrounding the market.

Saskia Sassen has argued that deregulation does not mean that nation-states have abandoned the exercise of any legal authority over financial industries. Rather, what has emerged is an "interstate system" of legal agreements (such as the WTO pact referred to earlier) that "guarantee the global rights of capital."[58] In addition, "the ascendance of international finance has produced *regulatory voids* that lie beyond not only states but also the interstate system"[59] (italics added). The new global white-collar criminals, such as those to be described in this book, exploit these regulatory voids to promote their schemes.

The connection between deregulatory policies and white-collar crime within domestic markets has been made by several writers. Henry Pontell and Kitty Calavita have shown how deregulation transformed the savings and loan industry, "precipitating its demise, and opening up opportunities both to those seeking windfall profits from high-risk investments and to those who used the industry as their personal 'money machine.'"[60] In an earlier book this author demonstrated how the creation of MEWAs operating in an under-regulated environment, led to widespread fraud in the small business health insurance industry.[61] On the basis of a case study of a large gas producer operating in the western United States, John McArthur demonstrated how deregulation of the American natural gas industry led to antitrust violations.[62] The connection between deregulation and white-collar crime is even stronger in global markets where criminals can operate in a world without borders and hide behind the protective shield of national sovereignty.

The schemes described in the book involve insurance companies that sell their products in the United States, but are based in locales like the Cayman Islands, Barbados, and Antigua, many of which have been designated as "offshore financial centers" (OFCs). These OFCs have become important components of the global financial industry, as geographer Susan Robertson has written:

> Contemporary capitalism is characterized by the ongoing development of an enormous and unprecedentedly complex international financial system. . . . As the international financial system has grown in sheer size and sophistication it has secreted new and dynamic geographies. Mapping these new geographies shows that a new type of financial center has arisen: the offshore financial center. These are new regulatory spaces through which the new financial markets and institutions operate.[63]

An essential feature of "regulatory spaces" in many of these OFCs is that they allow companies to conduct business abroad, but not in the host country. Many of these countries encourage the charter of what are known as "International Business Corporations" (IBCs)—"a corporation with anonymous ownership which can do no business in its own country of incorporation."[64] Among other things, IBCs have become major tools in the international money laundering trade.

A number of Caribbean countries grant to insurance companies charters that require those firms to possess little or no minimum capital reserves to cover claims, as long as the companies do not sell policies within the home country. Among these countries is the Turks and Caicos islands, a British dependency located southeast of the Bahamas, whose thirty cays and islands have a combined land mass of just 166 square miles and a population of 17,500. In 1993, the islands were home to a total of 1,488 licensed insurance companies.[65] Another is the Cayman Islands, a British crown colony that consists of three islands located in the western Caribbean. Despite the fact that the resident population of the country was only 33,000, in 1992, the Cayman Islands was home to 372 offshore insurers.[66]

One of the features that attracts insurance operators to these Caribbean locations is the ease with which IBCs can be set up. The official Web site for Antigua and Barbuda, a former British colony, boasts that an IBC can be formed with "minimal compliance procedures" within twenty-four hours and can be completed by a local accountant or attorney, so that the principals need not set foot in the country.[67] In 1997, the tiny Caribbean island-nation of Dominica enacted an Exempt Insurance Act, which enabled foreigners to obtain an insurance license by filing documents showing "evidence of availability of minimum Paid-up Capital of US $100,000," and a registration fee of $2,500, with the important provision that "the risks and premiums of Exempt

Insurance companies registered in Dominica must originate outside Dominica."[68]

The abuse of these offshore entities creates serious problems for law enforcement and regulators. Investigator Jack A. Blum, in a congressional testimony describing international financial fraud, has succinctly summarized the problem:

> The problem is, who has the authority to investigate? Whose job is it to police the international financial system? And, in the end, how will you ever bring any of the perpetrators to justice or recover any of the money? One difficulty is this: Where was the crime committed? There was the "European Union Bank" of Antigua, which operated on the Internet on a license from the corrupt government of Antigua. The computer server that handled the bank was in Washington, D.C. The man who was operating the computer server was in Canada. And under Antiguan law, the theft of the bank's assets was not illegal. So now the problem is, where is the crime committed? Who committed it? Who is going to investigate it? And will anyone ever go to jail?[69]

In a nutshell, the statement captures an essential conflict that lies behind not only fraud in the offshore insurance industry, but a host of other white-collar crimes and cyber crimes. In a global economy, financial commerce easily transcends national borders, but regulators and law enforcement officials remain largely restricted by geopolitical boundaries. As a result, one increasingly finds crimes being committed in "the space between laws,"[70] in a legal no-man's-land where geography has lost its relevance.

## Overview of the Book

The theoretical issues described above are useful inasmuch as they help one to make sense of the empirical materials presented in the following chapters. The case studies described in those chapters are not presented in an attempt to provide proof of the theoretical argument proposed. Rather, the theories help to locate these events in a broader sociohistorical context and show their commonalities with other events. John Walton has nicely described the relationship between case studies and theory:

> Cases come wrapped in theories. They are cases because they embody causal processes operating in microcosm. At bottom, the logic of the case study is to demonstrate a causal argument about how general

social forces take shape and produce results in specific settings. That demonstration, in turn, is intended to provide at least one anchor that steadies the ship of generalization until more anchors can be fixed for eventual boarding.[71]

The case studies presented here, then, may be thought of as an initial anchor to a theory that awaits further anchoring.

Chapter 1 takes a detailed look at the "godfather" of offshore insurance fraud, Alan Teale, and the fraudulent empire he created. The chapter will trace Teale's criminal career, beginning in the early 1980s in Florida where he headed an organization called the Insurance Exchange of the Americas through the late 1980s and early 1990s when he was the "shadow boss" behind a remarkable number of insurance and reinsurance companies and brokerage firms that were linked in complex webs of fraudulent schemes. Along the way he collaborated, directly and indirectly, with a diverse array of white-collar criminals: from securities scam artists to former savings and loan crooks to phony Indian chiefs. Many of those collaborators, as we shall see, would go on to their own successful careers in insurance crime.

One of the places where Teale and his associates were very successful was California. Chapter 2 shows how in the late 1980s and early 1990s the auto and small-business insurance markets in that state had become "criminogenic markets." The confluence of several events, including state policies that effectively deregulated the surplus lines industry and the departure of legitimate insurance companies from these markets, opened the door to offshore insurance crooks who poured into the state, stealing millions of dollars from consumers. One company, First Assurance & Casualty Company Ltd., symbolized all that was wrong with the surplus lines industry in California in the early 1990s. The rise and fall of First Assurance is described in Chapter 2, along with a description of some of the firm's many victims.

The evolving nature of offshore insurance fraud is illustrated in Chapter 3. In the mid-1990s, after many states enacted measures to close the loopholes that had made offshore insurance fraud so easy and profitable in the 1980s, a number of the individuals who had been involved in those schemes changed their modi operandi and joined forces with white-collar criminals involved in securities scams. These scams involved the sale of promissory notes, mostly to elderly retirees looking for safe investments, issued by a wide variety of little-known companies, and whose payment was guaranteed by surety bonds issued by offshore insurance companies. In these schemes, the insurance companies were but one component in complicated Ponzi schemes that linked local insurance agents, real estate developers, Texas oilmen, securities brokers, members of organized crime groups, and, in one case, an exiled financial guru.

The basic premise behind locating a fraudulent insurance company in a foreign country that asks few questions before handing out a charter is to create a shield against the scrutiny of U.S. authorities. In Chapter 4, we will see how offshore criminals have taken this logic one step further, eliminating the need to find a friendly country by simply creating their own countries. Once created, either on disputed areas of terra firma or platforms in the ocean or completely in cyberspace, these "countries" can not only issue charters for insurance companies, but also license banks, issue bonds, sell passports, and even declare war. This chapter will examine a number of these "fantasy islands" and the fraudulent, often imaginative, schemes their creators have perpetrated. These phony countries and their schemes can be seen as a form of postmodern fraud.

The broader implications of these cases are considered in the final chapter. There, the discussion will return to questions of globalization and its consequences for white-collar crime. One of these questions concerns the ways that deregulated markets—both in the countries of origin and in the countries where business is conducted—create criminal opportunities. Another question concerns the role that globalization plays in the formation of white-collar, organized, transnational crime groups. Finally, the discussion will turn to questions of policy: What steps can governments take to protect their citizens from these global crimes?

# 1

# The Alan Teale Empire

In April 1994, a sixty-four-year-old British native named Alan Arthur Teale died of heart and kidney failure after contracting pneumonia while serving a seventeen-year sentence in a U.S. prison for insurance fraud. Thus ended the life and career of one of the most remarkable con men in history. Teale's involvement in the American insurance industry lasted less than a decade, but in that period he established a labyrinth of companies and individuals that would eventually defraud consumers for millions of dollars. How the son of a London bus driver whose formal education ended at high school could have gone on to become the mastermind behind what would be called "the Super Bowl of insurance fraud" is a story not only of individual ambition and malice but also of the vulnerabilities of the insurance industry itself to fraud and deception.[1] For Teale and his many associates were masters at seeing the loopholes and legal ambiguities that surround the industry and exploiting them.

Most of the Teale schemes took advantage of two of the weaknesses in the insurance industry discussed in the Introduction. First, there is the inherent difficulty of establishing the value of the assets that guarantee that insurance companies are capable of paying claims; a condition that is exacerbated when the companies are located offshore. As we shall see, in a variety of schemes Teale used bogus government securities and other forms of "fictitious capital" to convince regulators of the financial wherewithal of his companies. He took advantage of a number of "regulatory voids" in the insurance industry that allowed him to operate insurance companies largely outside the scrutiny of state regulators.

Teale's crimes were so serious that they merited a series of congressional hearings headed by Senator Sam Nunn, held in 1991, nearly two years before Teale was indicted. Senator Nunn, and other members of the committee, were concerned that the entire insurance industry was on the brink of collapse, just as the savings and loan industry had come close to a meltdown. Everywhere they looked they saw insolvent companies, millions of dollars in losses, and the hand of Alan Teale. In the course of those hearings, the committee's investigators discovered a "vast network" of white-collar criminals whose operations were "global in nature" and whose activities went far beyond insurance to include crimes committed in the securities and banking industries.

Before coming to the United States in 1981, Alan Teale had spent nearly thirty years in the European insurance industry, establishing an unremarkable, but also unblemished, career. During that period in his life he was, in the words of a reporter who knew him, "the archetypal pin-striped grey man, whose horizons extended no further than the string of worthy committees on which he sat."[2] It was only when he emigrated that he discovered, like so many before him, the potential fortunes to be made in the "land of opportunity." And, in the early 1980s, one of the best places to discover those opportunities was Miami.

## The Insurance Exchange of the Americas

In the late 1970s, William Sadowski, a Florida legislator, had a vision: to create a new Lloyd's of London in south Florida that would become a gateway to the Caribbean, providing insurance to the growing corporate interests of that region as well as to South and Central America. While not formally affiliated with Lloyd's, Florida's version would be modeled on the venerable English institution. As such, it would not be an insurance company per se but would be comprised of various syndicates in which investors pooled their funds to take on a variety of risks. In 1979, the Florida legislature passed a bill enabling the creation of Sadowski's vision and giving it a name: the Insurance Exchange of the Americas (IEA).

The key to IEA, and what set it apart from insurance companies, was that it would not be regulated by the state, but instead would be "self-regulated." According to Sadowski, who would become IEA's counsel, "this system wouldn't work with a lot of regulation."[3] This was the beginning of the 1980s, a time when deregulation was not only a catchy buzzword, but also a philosophy embraced by politicians and business leaders alike. In 1980, Ronald Reagan was elected President, having campaigned on a platform that stressed deregulated markets and, specifically, the withdrawal of government from key financial industries. In that same year, the first of a series of laws were passed that loosened restrictions on the nation's savings and loan institutions. The disastrous consequences of that legislation would only fully be appreciated a decade later.[4] It is not surprising, then, that in this environment the concept of a "self-regulated" insurance market would have been seen as the way of the future.

In May 1981, Alan Teale, formerly the director of the British Brokers Association, the brokers organization for Lloyd's of London, whose résumé also listed several stints as a university professor and as an "adviser to several governments," was appointed as director of the IEA. One of the reasons he was appointed was because of his knowledge of the Lloyd's system and his perceived ability to transplant the Lloyd's model to south Florida. Another was his salesmanship. "In the formative years of the exchange," one IEA official would later say, "[W]e needed a used-car salesman with a British accent. And that's just what we got."[5]

On April 4, 1983, IEA opened for business operating out of a 30,000-square-foot facility in downtown Miami, with the blessing of most of the city's public officials and $50,000 from the Miami Chamber of Commerce.

According to the enabling legislation, while the state Department of Insurance would not directly regulate the IEA, it was responsible for reviewing the applications of those who applied for membership to the IEA and, in the words of its former head, to make sure that everyone involved "has clean hands."[6] In hindsight, the state was less than completely diligent in inspecting the hands of all the IEA's members, as many of them had questionable histories when they joined, and many more, who may have had clean hands when they joined, went on to get their hands very dirty indeed.

> Stephen Arky was the first elected chairman of the IEA board of governors. Arky committed suicide in July 1985 while he was being investigated for his connection with a firm, ESM Securities, that was at the center of a scheme that resulted in a crisis in the Ohio savings and loan industry.[7]
>
> Another investor in IEA was Fred Carr who would later gain notoriety for his role in the failure of Executive Life, a fiasco that resulted in $3 billion in losses, after the junk bonds Carr had purchased from Michael Milken turned out to be nearly worthless.
>
> Soon after the Interamerican syndicate was approved to write business on the IEA, one of its principals, Jose Pina, was accused by the state of defrauding 112,000 persons who held policies from his Universal Casualty Insurance Co.[8]

Then there was Peter Cameron-Webb, the lead underwriter for the Usher
syndicate, who arrived at the IEA after a long career at Lloyd's that
ended when Lloyd's uncovered evidence of his involvement in what
came to be known as the "missing millions scandal," in which Cameron-Webb and another underwriting manager, Peter Dixon, along
with twelve colleagues, allegedly misappropriated $53.2 million from
syndicates under Cameron-Webb's control.[9]

When the IEA opened for business in April 1983, it had four syndicates
and a total capitalization of $6 million. In its first year and a half of business
IEA did very well. By the end of 1984, the fifteen syndicates operating on the
IEA took in $100 million in premiums.[10] In May 1984, Teale was forced out as
head of the IEA, though that did not end his involvement. IEA's financial success continued for the next couple of years; in 1986, the IEA took in $200
million in premiums.[11]

Despite these outward signs of success, trouble for the IEA soon began to
develop. In the spring of 1986, Omaha Indemnity Company, a unit of Mutual
of Omaha, filed a suit against the Royal American Managers (RAM) syndicate,
alleging fraud. Rumors began to surface about other syndicates being in trouble and, by March 1987, seven were under court-ordered rehabilitation. After
several attempts to revive it failed, in January 1988 IEA was placed into receivership by a state judge. When regulators finally got around to cleaning up the
IEA mess they discovered some $200 million in liabilities, which they ulti-
mately settled for about five cents on the dollar.[12]

How an organization that was launched admid such high hopes and ambitions could have sunk so quickly was the subject of an inquiry by a Florida task
force. In its report the task force cited a number of factors that led to the
demise of the IEA, but focused its attention on the failure of self-regulation.
Not only did the IEA fail to regulate itself, but "the apparent genuine belief
by DOI [Florida Department of Insurance] that the IEA was self-regulating
prevented aggressive oversight of the IEA by DOI."[13] Another factor, was the
extensive "incestuous relationships" among the members of the board, including the fact that "many people who owned management companies were on
the Board of Governors . . ."[14]

Other critics pointed to the inherent instabilities of the markets in which
IEA was involved. Despite the fact that the IEA was created as a vehicle for
targeting expanding Latin American and South American business, it entered
the business during a "soft" period in the market, meaning that there were
more insurers offering products than there were consumers to purchase them.

As a result, the IEA's members were forced to take on riskier and less predictable fringe business. The syndicates on the IEA, which often specialized in certain types of coverage, took on a wide variety of highly risky business in which potential claims, and thus losses, were very high. For example:

> The syndicate led by Peter Cameron-Webb underwrote 50 percent of a New Jersey racetrack's offer to pay $2 million to the owners of a Kentucky Derby winner if their horse continued its winning streak in New Jersey. When the horse crossed the finish line ahead of the field, the syndicate lost $1 million.[15]

> An IEA syndicate headed by Richard Lehman, a Miami attorney, took the lead in providing nearly $1 million in coverage to a championship Angus bull. The animal, whose estimated market value was $5.5 million, was thought to be the most expensive bull in the world. At the time Lehman commented, "We all took a little piece of the bull. We figured the bull's semen will probably double in value if he dies, so we can't be hit too hard."[16]

> The IEA was one of the participants in a $57.5 million policy that insured Universal City studio against injury or illness of Tom Selleck during the taping of his television series, *Magnum, P.I.*[17]

While the state's task force did not explicitly cite fraud, it was well known that several of the syndicates had become ensnared in allegations of criminal wrongdoing. The most prominent of these scandals involved the RAM syndicate and the Omaha Indemnity Company.

Among other things, the RAM scandal revealed the inherent dangers posed by Managing General Agents (MGAs) in the insurance industry. As a means to expand their client base, insurance companies often enter into arrangements with MGAs—individuals or firms—in which the MGA is given the power to underwrite business in the name of the company, to handle claims, and to arrange reinsurance. In a 1990 report to Congress on insolvencies in the insurance industry, a committee headed by Representative John Dingell cited unregulated MGAs as a factor in many of those insolvencies. As Representative Dingell's committee pointed out,

> [t]here is an inherent conflict for MGA's [*sic*] between writing quality business and earning commissions on the volume of business written. MGA's [*sic*] are not insurance companies, and their activities are not generally regulated by state insurance authorities.[18]

The RAM/Omaha Indemnity case illustrates just how dangerous this conflict can become for companies that, in insurance industry parlance, "give the pen" to MGAs without carefully monitoring their activities.

In 1982, Omaha Indemnity, a wholly owned subsidiary of the well-known Mutual of Omaha Insurance Company, signed an agreement with World American Underwriters, an MGA based in Missouri, in which World American would do underwriting and arrange reinsurance, primarily low-risk property/casualty policies in Omaha Indemnity's name. World American was managed by James Wining and Willie Schonacher. Soon thereafter, Wining and Schonacher left World American to form Royal American Managers, which controlled two syndicates on the IEA, and they convinced Omaha Indemnity to allow RAM to act as an MGA for the insurance company.

Officials at Omaha Indemnity had expected that RAM would write a relatively low volume of business and would provide reinsurance through their IEA syndicates. At first, things seemed to be going well. After the first fifteen months, RAM reported taking in $7.9 million in premiums. However, as Omaha Indemnity would soon learn, this was only a small fraction of the business RAM was actually writing. By 1986, RAM had actually taken in $193 million in premiums, while reporting only $61 million to Omaha Indemnity. Of the total amount, Omaha Indemnity would later claim in a lawsuit, Wining and Schonacher pocketed $34.6 million. Messrs. Wining and Schonacher accomplished this feat by chartering "a complicated network of interrelated companies in the United States and offshore to take a cut of Omaha Indemnity's premiums at every step of the insurance and reinsurance process."[19]

How could they write such a high volume of business in such a short period of time? The answer was fairly simple: They took on high-risk, low-profit business—including insurance policies for taxicab companies, long-haul truckers, and restaurants—that other insurers did not want, and offered cut-rate prices. And why not, since as MGAs they were not responsible for paying any of the claims these policies generated? They then reinsured many of the policies through their own reinsurance company, Fielding Reinsurance Limited, of the Turks and Caicos, where both Wining and Schonacher maintained beachfront homes, and diverted a substantial portion of those premium dollars to themselves.

In 1986, Omaha Indemnity filed a suit against RAM, Wining, and Schonacher, claiming that they had lost hundreds of millions of dollars as a result of their deceit. The next year the two RAM-controlled syndicates on the IEA were placed into receivership. In 1989, Omaha Indemnity was awarded $225 million in its suit against RAM, although officials at the company recognized that the likelihood of their ever seeing a substantial portion of that award was slim. Ultimately, Mutual of Omaha was forced to contribute $250 million to keep its subsidiary afloat.

As the Omaha Indemnity lawsuit dragged on through the courts, Wining and Schonacher were not idle. While they were being investigated for their misdeeds in connection with RAM, the entrepreneurial duo embarked on new insurance scams. In 1987, operating out of their Missouri headquarters, they formed Laramie Insurance in Wyoming and transferred assets to the company from their offshore company, Fielding Reinsurance Limited. By 1989, Laramie Insurance was in serious financial difficulties, leaving millions of dollars in unpaid claims.[20]

One might wonder how two individuals who were already under a cloud of suspicion for insurance fraud were able to obtain a license to start an insurance company, particularly one that had questionable assets. Simple: Like several other crooked insurance owners who moved their businesses to Wyoming during the period, Wining and Schonacher bribed the state's insurance commissioner, flying him to a family reunion aboard their corporate jet and putting several of his and other state officials' relatives on their board of directors.[21]

In March 1992, Wining and Schonacher were finally convicted on federal charges in connection with the RAM/Omaha Indemnity scheme and for filing false financial statements for Laramie Insurance. Amazingly, despite having been convicted of crimes involving the theft of $20 million from Omaha Indemnity and $5 million from Laramie's policyholders, Schonacher received a prison sentence of two years. James Wining, after pleading before the court about the need to take care of his mentally handicapped son, was given a sentence of five years' probation. In explaining his sentence Judge Dean Whipple stated: "What I really did was sentence Wining to care for that boy for the rest of his life, gave him a life sentence."[22] The light punishments Wining and Schonacher received did not escape the notice of the press. One newspaper editor opined:

Judge Whipple's leniency is appalling. It's no wonder some people have lost confidence in the justice system. An unemployed breadwinner could go to jail for writing bad checks to feed his kids. So could an uneducated kid who tries to earn money for child support by running drugs. But a James R. Wining can work several years setting up a scheme to rip off a major insurance company, paying himself $450,000 a year in money he had no right to lay his hands on . . . Then, when the law catches up to him, he avoids jail time by reminding the court of the obligations of parenthood.[23]

For many of those involved with it, the IEA was a launching pad for numerous projects, legitimate and illegitimate; Wining and Schonacher, for example, were able to use the money they stole from Omaha Indemnity to start Laramie Insurance. It was also a great place to make contacts that would pay off in the future. Alan Teale, who left the IEA in 1984, was able to use the contacts he made there to create an incredibly elaborate network of insurance companies, reinsurance companies, and brokerage houses that he would use to bilk millions of dollars out of individuals and companies in the years to come.

## The International Underwriting Association

For the ever-resourceful Mr. Teale, his forced departure from the IEA wasn't the end of his career, but an opportunity to start anew. He remarried, to Charlotte Rentz, a former vice-president at the Universal Insurance Group in Florida, a company run by the brother of IEA member Jose Pina.[24] The couple moved to Atlanta, Georgia, and began putting together a series of new business enterprises that would end up making insurance fraud history.

Operating out of a suite of offices in an Atlanta business park, Teale's operation housed dozens of supposedly independent offshore insurance companies, reinsurance companies, managing general agents, and consulting firms, many of which operated under the umbrella of an organization called the International Underwriting Association (IUA). By 1988, the IUA consisted of thirty ostensibly independent insurance and reinsurance companies, many of which held charters in foreign countries: fifteen in the Turks and Caicos islands; two in Barbados; one each in Panama, Belgium, the British Virgin Islands, and Cypress; two in Canada; and the rest in the United States.[25] With the exception of Canada, what these foreign jurisdictions had in common was very lax regulation on insurance companies chartered on their soil but that did business elsewhere.

Over the next five years these companies figured in numerous insurance scams all over the United States in what appeared to be an epidemic of white-collar crime. Investigators working for Senator Nunn's committee collected detailed evidence on a number of these schemes. But it was not until Teale was arrested in 1993 that federal prosecutors began to put together all the pieces of the IUA puzzle in which all the signs pointed ultimately to Alan Teale.

In their indictment of Teale and his colleagues, prosecutors sketched the outlines of what was a massive fraud, involving hundreds of individuals and scores of companies that operated in dozens of countries. First, Teale and Rentz would use other con men to front as legitimate insurance brokers and agents to form a national and international network ("network") of companies represented to be insurance companies, when . . . the "network" and its companies were merely vehicles for fraud and part of a con game designed to defraud consumers who were tricked into believing that they were buying insurance.[26]

Second, an essential part of this "network" was that many of the companies were "formed in foreign countries such as Belgium, the Turks and Caicos Islands (British West Indies), the Republic of Ireland, and the Bahamas, to avoid licensing and auditing procedures required of American insurance companies."[27] Third, the various schemes, in essence, involved the following:

> [T]he defendants would issue and cause to be issued insurance policies promising to pay claims, when, as the defendants well knew, they had diverted the flow of premiums out of the United States to offshore foreign bank accounts to be used for their own personal benefit and the benefit of others and to the detriment of policy holders and potential claimants.[28]

The companies were run as Ponzi schemes in which Teale and his associates "would pay some claims to avoid early detection by state insurance regulators to allow the defendants and others to defraud more consumers who were tricked into believing they were buying insurance."[29] Fourth, in order to keep the Ponzi schemes going long enough to generate huge profits, Teale and colleagues employed a number of techniques:

> [W]hen consumers attempted to have the defendants and their co-conspirators pay claims, the defendants and their co-conspirators would claim that the consumers were to blame for their losses or that claims adjusters, insurance agents, attorneys and others were to blame, when as the defendants well knew, consumers were not being paid because they had diverted the premium payments of the consumers to the personal benefit of themselves and others, and because their companies were worthless.[30]

> [O]nce the defendants' companies were shut down by state insurance regulators, the defendants and their co-conspirators would start new companies under different names, and would continue to operate under the newly named companies.[31]

[D]efendants would create the illusion that Alan Teale was not involved in the network of companies by setting up multiple addresses and telephone numbers, when, the defendants well knew, those addresses and telephone numbers were controlled by the defendant Alan Teale and his co-conspirators.[32]

In other words, these scams were elaborate shell games in which the dollars paid by policyholders in insurance premiums were channeled through a series of brokers, insurance companies, and offshore reinsurance companies, each of which siphoned off significant proportions of the original premium dollars, and in the end, when claims were submitted, there were no funds left to pay claims and all of the people involved in the insurance chain pointed their fingers at each other claiming that they, too, were victimized. What the real victims often did not know was that these entities were not in fact independent but were part of an organized network with Alan Teale at the center. By the time regulators could piece together the entire scheme, the players had moved on and started new companies. This process was well illustrated in a series of insurance scams that were headquartered in the unlikely location of Mobile, Alabama, but that operated on an international scale. The major players in this high-stakes game were: Teale and his wife, Charlotte Rentz, who operated behind the scenes; Stephen Coker, the owner of a Mobile insurance brokerage firm; and Gary Cowan, a southern California insurance broker.

According to a federal indictment, in February 1988, Coker purchased British and American Casualty Co., Ltd., a surplus lines carrier chartered in Tortola, British Virgin Islands. Coker then went about looting British and American through an elaborate money-laundering scheme. First, he set up a "bogus" reinsurance agreement with one of his own companies for $1 million and made sham loans to himself and others. He then moved the money out of Mobile and into bank accounts in the Cayman Islands and Nassau, Bahamas. Then he smuggled cash from the accounts back into the United States. Finally, to avoid paying claims, he put British and American into liquidation.

In the spring of 1989, Coker moved into the insurance fraud big leagues when he accompanied Teale on a trip to Brussels to charter a reinsurance company, American and Southern Compagnie de Belge (American Southern Belge) that was funded with $30,000 from the looted money in his account in the Bahamas, and that listed Coker as the owner. In preparing financial statements, Coker showed that American Southern Belge owned $5 million in "marketable securities." These "marketable securities" turned out to be worthless penny stocks that Teale arranged for him to "rent."

Teale's decision to locate his reinsurance company in Belgium was a calculated move to evade regulation. Under Belgium law, a reinsurance company that does not act as a primary insurer does not fall under the country's insurance regulations.[33] This allowed Teale to establish companies there with very little capital.

With the offshore reinsurance end of the scheme in place, all Coker and Teale needed was a source of revenue. In the late 1980s, one of the best places to find that kind of money was in the California auto insurance market. As will be described in detail in Chapter 2, at the time many California automobile owners were desperate to buy insurance after new laws forced the departure of many insurance companies from the market. Among the many disreputable offshore companies that moved in to fill this gap in the market was U.S. & Continental Reinsurance Co. (US&C), a Teale-owned, Belgium-based insurance company that sold auto policies in California through Gary Cowan's brokerage firm. Coker set up a reinsurance agreement in which American Southern Belge would reinsure policies sold by US&C. In 1991, US&C wrote $51 million in premiums in California.[34] Between March 1990 and December 1991, American Southern Belge received $4.1 million of those premiums. The arrangement proved very lucrative to Teale as well as to Coker, who was paid $1.4 million from 1990 to 1992.[35]

In the summer of 1992, the California Department of Insurance tried to shut down US&C after discovering that the company did not own but merely leased the securities listed on its book and had missed payments on the lease.[36] However, when US&C offered to deposit $4 million in a Beverly Hills bank, a Los Angeles judge quashed the state's attempt to prevent the offshore insurer from selling policies in California. Almost immediately after the judge's ruling, US&C began wiring money out of the account, leaving virtually nothing to pay future claims.[37] In December, the order was reversed and US&C was out of business for good.

In 1993, Coker filed a civil lawsuit against Teale claiming that Teale had defrauded him when he put worthless securities on US&C's books without his knowledge. Federal prosecutors were not fooled and, in 1994, Coker was indicted in Alabama. Coker, however, was not available to answer the charges since he had fled to Portugal. In 1996, he was extradited and returned to the United States where he was convicted and sentenced to sixty-three months in prison. In a separate case, Cowan pleaded guilty to federal charges and was sentenced to a term of thirty-three months.

## Victoria

The California auto insurance market was just one of the many opportunities that Teale saw in the American insurance industry of the 1980s. Teale had learned from his years at Lloyd's that there were considerable profits to be made in smaller niche markets, by covering risks that other insurers would not handle. These markets were particularly lucrative if one had no intention of paying claims. One of these markets was insuring athletes—both professional and amateur—against the possibility of injury.

In August 1986, Delaware authorities received an application from a company calling itself Victoria Insurance Company for a license to operate a property/casualty insurer. James E. Charge, an Australian resident, was listed as president and director. Also, included in the documentation was a former Lloyd's brokerage house employee, Paul Yorke-Wade of London. The application proposed to capitalize the new company with a $500,000 loan from a group known as the Arab American Trust Fund (AATF). The Delaware Insurance Commission rejected the application and almost immediately the group filed for a license to operate in Georgia. The Georgia application listed Paul Yorke-Wade as president and sole stockholder, Alan Teale as the executive vice president, and Teale's wife, Charlotte Rentz, as the secretary and treasurer. The licensing process in Georgia usually took two to six months. Victoria's application was approved in four weeks. The fact that James Bentley, a former Georgia Insurance Commissioner, was listed as a director of the company may help to explain why Victoria's application was approved so quickly.[38]

Victoria was only in business for eighteen months before the state of Georgia shut it down, but in that short period the company

> wrote liability policies covering attorneys, nurses, certified public accountants, asbestos removal contractors, child care centers, insurance agents, limousine companies and even police departments through the country . . . [I]t wrote casualty policies on race horses and disability policies on professional and college athletes and sports teams, both in this country and in Europe.[39]

While Victoria was licensed to sell insurance only in Georgia, its policies were sold in states across the country through risk purchasing groups. Recall that according to the Risk Retention Act, these groups can sell insurance policies in states where they are not licensed. Ultimately, Victoria would be the insurer for twenty-seven different risk purchasing groups.

The short history of Victoria reveals how easy it was in the late 1980s to start an insurance company with little or no real assets, take in huge amounts of money in premiums, move that money overseas, and then shut down the whole operation, leaving the policyholders with worthless claims.

In order to obtain its Georgia license, Victoria was required to put $1.5

million in a bank account before it could start business. Within three weeks of establishing the account, $1.2 million was transferred to accounts in London, controlled by Paul Yorke-Wade. As a result, the company was technically insolvent from its very beginning.[40]

Where Yorke-Wade got the money to start Victoria was never entirely clear, but regulators surmised that it came from a group that operated under the name Arab American Trust Fund (AATF), which, according to regulators, was controlled by the Kuwaiti Royal Family (though, representatives of the Royal Family later denied this). Fairly early on, AATF apparently demanded that Yorke-Wade repay their money. When he was unable to do so, they moved to take control of Victoria. In November 1988, Yorke-Wade was ousted from control of Victoria, and another Englishman, Charles Gordon-Seymour, was named as CEO, and Bharat Shah was named Chief Financial Officer. According to Georgia regulators:

> The clear and obvious purpose of placing these two men in charge of Victoria's operations was to siphon off from Victoria whatever profits it made in order that AATF . . . could recoup the advance they had made to Yorke-Wade. However . . . the amount of monies they extracted from Victoria far exceeded whatever was allegedly loaned to Yorke-Wade initially.[41]

In other words, they stripped Victoria of all its assets.

One of the first actions taken by the new owners of Victoria was to "terminate the services of Alan Teale."[42] Nonetheless, it appears that Teale continued to be involved in selling the organization's policies after his formal termination. In November/December 1987, Charles Gordon-Seymour began transferring large amounts of money out of Victoria's accounts in Atlanta and into accounts at Lloyd's Bank in London. Eventually, these transfers totaled $10.8 million. The source of these funds was premiums remitted to Victoria by policyholders. From the Lloyd's Bank accounts the money was transferred by an AATF associate, Anthony Dyson, to Swiss bank accounts.[43]

In the summer of 1988, Georgia regulators conducted a routine examination of Victoria's books. According to those books the company had assets of $20 million, including $16 million in U.S. zero coupon bonds. The problem was that these assets were not located in the state of Georgia, as required by state law, but instead were purportedly held on deposit with a firm known as Goldman Dollar Securities in Paris, France (no relation to Goldman-Sachs in the United States). When the regulators demanded that those assets be moved to the United States, Victoria's operators stalled. Later, it was discovered that there was no Goldman Dollar Securities and the address given was for a "mail drop" in Paris. In September 1988, the state of Georgia obtained a cease and desist order against Victoria.[44]

After Victoria was shut down, regulators discovered that the firm had $20 million in unpaid claims, but only $691,000 in assets.[45] So, where did all the money go? Here the story gets a bit hazy, but regulators suspected that a significant portion of those funds ended up in accounts at the notorious Bank of Credit and Commerce International (BCCI).[46]

Victoria specialized in "high risk" liability and casualty policies. Among their most popular programs were disability policies sold to professional athletes. Operating through an insurance wholesaler in New York, John G. Whittier, and a series of brokers across the country, Victoria issued over 200 policies to professional athletes in the United States and around the world. Among the professional football players who purchased policies in the United States were Kenny Flowers, a running back for the Atlanta Falcons; Jim Kelly, quarterback for the Buffalo Bills; John Elway, quarterback for the Denver Broncos; Brian Bosworth of the Seattle Seahawks; and Bo Jackson of the Los Angeles Raiders. All of these players paid between $60,000 and $115,000 for policies from Victoria, which were to pay them as much as $3 million in the event that they sustained a career-ending injury.

Victoria enjoyed quick success in this niche market because, at the time (1987), the primary writer of such policies was Lloyd's of London, but Lloyd's was very restrictive about the type of policies it would write, having recently been hit with major claims from well-known athletes such as football players Marcus Dupree, Billy Simms, and Jack Lambert. Lloyd's would only write policies for athletes below the age of twenty-seven, for one-year periods and the premiums were very high. Victoria offered relatively less expensive policies to athletes that Lloyd's would no longer insure.[47]

Once brokers arranged for a policy to be sold to an individual, the premiums went first to John G. Whittier & Associates, the wholesaler in New York. Whittier kept 25 percent, keeping 10 to 15 percent for himself and giving the remainder to the broker. The remaining 75 percent went to Paul Yorke-Wade in England, who deducted 10 percent for his commission and then was to have forwarded the rest to Victoria, in Georgia. Teale took another 6 percent. Thus, of the millions of dollars being given to Victoria by the holders of disability policies, 41 percent was skimmed off the top in commissions and fees.[48]

With their high salaries and entourages of agents and publicists, professional athletes may not at first appear to be hapless victims. But recall that in the mid-1980s many of these athletes were not paid the astronomical sums they are today, and when their careers ended suddenly they could find themselves in desperate financial straits.

One of the athletes defrauded by Victoria was Kenny Flowers. In April 1987, during his senior year in college, Mr. Flowers was drafted to play football for the Atlanta Falcons. That summer his agent advised him to purchase a disability insurance policy from Victoria as a measure of protection in the event of an injury. Mr. Flowers took that advice and sent a check for $7,380 to Whittier and Associates for a policy that would have paid him $230,000 in the event of an injury. In August 1988, in a preseason exhibition game Flowers sustained a serious injury that resulted in surgery that involved inserting seven screws into his knee. He was out for the entire 1988 season and was eventually released by the Falcons. He then filed a claim with Victoria, but never received any payment. In testimony before the Nunn committee, Flowers described his situation:

> I have not played football since my release from the Atlanta Falcons. Prior to my release, I had done some work in the community with the handicapped and homeless, so I went to work last year in a private hospital near Atlanta doing rehabilitation work with the elderly patients. I earn $6.35 an hour. At that rate it would take me more than 15 years to earn what my disability policy was supposed to pay me due to my injury.[49]

Another one of Victoria's victims was J. Craig James, a running back who played with the New England Patriots from 1987 to 1989. Through his agent he learned about Victoria's disability plan, which for a premium of $40,575 per year would provide him with up to $2 million in payments in the event of a career-ending injury. Convinced, in September 1987, James sent in his first premium check for a year's worth of coverage. In October 1988, during a game with the Green Bay Packers, James was hit from the front and sustained an injury to his shoulder. The next June he learned from his doctor that his injury was so severe that he could no longer play football. The next month he learned that Victoria was out of business and that he would never receive the $2 million that was due him. As he later told the committee:

> For me, as an athlete, I knew my professional career would be limited in terms of years. So as I signed my second contract, I sought out a policy that would protect my earnings. My thoughts were simple. If I stayed healthy I would earn my salary. If I had a career ending injury then I would collect my salary through an insurance plan. Well, when

that happened, I obviously came face to face with reality. My whole financial plan was built around my contract and/or insurance.[50]

Mr. James was more fortunate than Mr. Flowers. He was able to reach a settlement with the insurance agent who sold him the policy.

The Victoria story ended with regulators trying to clean up the mess, congressional committee members shaking their heads, and professional athletes left holding the bag. But it was not the end of the story for many of those behind Victoria. Several of them—James Charge, Paul Yorke-Wade, Charles Gordon-Seymour— went on to illustrious careers in insurance fraud.[51]

## Stealing from the Disabled

With its focus on disability insurance for professional athletes, Victoria was taking advantage of a niche market. But, in doing so it generally ignored a much larger market: liability insurance for high-school athletic programs. While Victoria may have ignored this market, Alan Teale did not, and Teale's connection to the market was primarily through one individual: Douglas Ruedlinger.

In the late 1970s, directors of high-school athletic programs became concerned over the increasing number of lawsuits filed by students who had been injured in school-sponsored athletic programs. In particular, a judgement against a Seattle high school in 1981, which awarded a former high-school football player $6.3 million for injuries, far more than the school system could pay, alerted many school administrators to their own liability. Up to this point, most schools' insurance policies covered accidents like falls in hallways, but did not provide catastrophic coverage.

To fill this gap, Kansas native and college drop-out Douglas Ruedlinger emerged with a new program: the Scholastic Extra-curricular Liability/Lifetime Medical Policy, or LifeCat as it was popularly known, a program that would provide catastrophic coverage for all student athletes for only $1 per student.[52] The plan covered all injury-related costs that exceeded $10,000, including not only medical and rehabilitation bills but also the costs of refurbishing homes and outfitting vans to make them wheelchair accessible, and even provided $300 per week over the injured's lifetime to cover lost earnings.[53] To receive these benefits the injured athlete simply had to agree not to sue the school. Eventually, 18,000 schools across the country signed up for the LifeCat program. To many, the program seemed too good to be true. In fact, it was too good to be true.

Ruedlinger's success was due in large part to his longtime friendship with the head of the National Federation of State High School Associations (NFS-HSA), a nonprofit organization that set the rules for high-school athletic programs across the country. In 1983, NFSHSA created a trust, funded by the association's dues, part of which was used to purchase insurance from a legitimate firm, All American Insurance. Ruedlinger was appointed to administer the trust via a risk purchasing group he had set up called Fund Administrator's Association (FAA). The NFSHSA also agreed to market Ruedlinger's LifeCat program. This apparent conflict of interest—NFSHSA's head sat on the board of one of Ruedlinger's insurance companies—was of no concern to Ruedlinger. "Hell, yes, it's a conflict, but it's done every day," he was quoted as saying.[54]

The specifics of the arrangement were as follows: FAA was to procure $1.9 million in liability coverage from United International Insurance Company (UIIC), a licensed insurance company based in Rhode Island and owned by Ruedlinger, and $3 million in coverage from Fund Insurance Co., another Ruedlinger company, based in Bermuda. Both firms were subsidiaries of Wheatland Group Holdings, Inc., a Kansas holding company owned by Ruedlinger.[55]

UIIC then signed contracts with a number of reinsurance companies, seven of which had direct or indirect connections with Alan Teale. In 1986/1987, UIIC had reinsurance treaties with IEA (which Teale had formally parted company with in 1984), and with Lloyd's U.S., a Dallas-based reinsurer founded by Teale after he left IEA, and where he was briefly employed as a "consultant." In 1988/1989, UIIC entered into reinsurance agreements with American Transportation Insurance Company, Ltd.; Northern Commercial Fire and General Insurance Company; American Trust Insurance Company; American Marine and General Insurance Company; and Old American Insurance Co.[56] All were offshore insurers domiciled in the Turks and Caicos and all were created by Alan Teale.

Ruedlinger's legal troubles started in 1989 when it was discovered that many of Teale's reinsurers were not paying claims. Eventually, the five reinsurers would fail to pay $2.3 million in claims to LifeCat policyholders.[57] In 1992, Rhode Island officials declared UIIC to be insolvent and appointed a receiver to liquidate the firm's assets. Payments to LifeCat claimants immediately stopped at that point. Rhode Island regulators estimated that the company's assets were so depleted, in part because $2 million of those assets were used to purchase stock in another Ruedlinger company, that there was no way the insurance company could cover the $12.5 million that was necessary to pay the lifetime medical expenses for injured athletes holding LifeCat policies.[58]

In 1993, Ruedlinger and his attorney Edwin Carpenter put Wheatland Holdings into bankruptcy. Using an argument made famous by savings and loan owner Charles Keating, Ruedlinger claimed that UIIC's demise was the fault of the regulators. "Why didn't they shut the company down in 1989? It's a zoo up there. What did Rhode Island say in 1989? Not a damn thing." In public statements, he would claim that he and his companies were victimized by sophisticated insurance thieves, like Alan Teale.

Federal prosecutors took another point of view. While acknowledging the crimes of Teale and his reinsurers, they pointed out that Ruedlinger siphoned off money from the companies to fund an extravagant lifestyle that included a private jet, a million-dollar home in Florida, a condominium in Vermont, and annual salaries of as much as $1.4 million.[59] In June 1996, Ruedlinger was indicted in Kansas.

Unlike some of the victims of the Teale-related schemes, such as businesses that suffered pure monetary losses, Ruedlinger's victim's were young people who had suffered devastating injuries only to find that their medical needs would not be covered. Regulators estimated that the collapse of Ruedlinger's companies would leave 160 injured high-school students, 68 of whom were paralyzed or brain damaged, without medical coverage.[60]

One of those victims was Jeff Gadwah. He described the day in 1987, when he was practicing football with his high-school team in North Carolina:

> We were starting a blocking drill. Two of us would line up, roughly 10 yards apart, and then you hit, recoil, hit, recoil, hit, and go to the end of the line. We hit, and the next thing I can remember is waking up, looking at a blue sky, and I couldn't move.[61]

Gadwah had broken his neck and would be paralyzed for life. At least, his mother thought, his medical bills would be covered by the high school's insurance policy. Only later did she learn that the policy was issued by one of Ruedlinger's companies and would pay them nothing. Six years later, in a televised interview, Jeff Gadwah explained how he felt when he learned the news:

> I wanted to kick the [censored] out of somebody. You know, all of a sudden I do—I'm being taken care of, and then all of . . . all of a sudden they say, you know, "Too bad; sorry; catch you later." You know, it made me very angry.[62]

Another one of Ruedlinger's victims was John Avila, a former high-school football player from Virginia who suffered brain damage after he was hit in the head during a game. Six years later he was still bedridden and semicomatose in a nursing home. Despite the fact that his policy was to provide him with lifetime benefits, when the company went bankrupt he stopped receiving any payments. His father, a cabinetmaker, was forced to work two jobs to pay for his son's treatment and his mother had to quit her job in order to care for her son.[63]

In late 1992, as his business was collapsing, Ruedlinger took several measures to insure that, even if his victims were suffering, he could continue his comfortable lifestyle. First, he had himself "terminated" from his position at Wheatland Holdings, thereby triggering severance pay of between $300,000 and $400,000. He then had himself designated as a "consultant" to the company in a contract that specified that he would be paid $50,000 a month, a contract that contained an unusual clause that his services should not "require a major or substantial portion of his time."[64]

In 1993, after UIIC had failed and had stopped paying claims, Ruedlinger was down but not out. In that year he started a new plan for high-school athletes with insurance provided by his Bermuda-based Fund Insurance Co. He even went so far as to send letters to high schools that had been left with worthless LifeCat policies suggesting that if they signed on to his new plan, their coverage might be applied retroactively to cover old LifeCat claims. According to Ruedlinger, the solution to John Avila's problem, and those of others in his situation, was simple: "All those kids could be receiving benefits today," he said, if only their high schools would have signed up his new plan.[65] Not surprisingly, few schools took him up on the offer.

In April 1997, Ruedlinger was convicted on federal charges in Kansas. Prosecutors estimated that losses to the victims of his crimes exceeded $20 million.[66] After his conviction, numerous relatives and friends of Ruedlinger wrote letters on his behalf, urging the judge to show mercy when he handed down his sentence. His attorneys wrote:

> [Ruedlinger], a once proud businessman, active in the community has been shamed by the indictments, the jury's verdict, and his confession of guilt in the second case. He has been financially devastated and faces significant jail time. He is separated from his wife and young child. Mr. Ruedlinger has redeeming values to society . . . He has a small child, Morgan, who he loves deeply, and for whom he seeks to pay his debt to society, and then rebuild the family life and unity they had together.[67]

His son wrote:

> He has lost all his material possessions and is a bankrupt man. But emotionally and spiritually, he has realized that while material things

come and go, his family has remained strong and true. It has given him time to ponder his mistakes and rearrange his priorities. His family and his God are now number one.[68]

A friend who lived in the same Florida town as Ruedlinger wrote that he had "devoted his time and made generous contributions to civic causes in our community . . . [and] maintained his property in top condition at all times . . ."[69]

Not surprisingly, few of those who wrote on his behalf mentioned the pain and suffering he had caused his numerous victims. Whether or not the judge was influenced by these letters is not clear, but in March 1999 he sentenced Ruedlinger to serve seventy-eight months in prison, four months less than prosecutors had recommended.

## International Forum of Florida

At the heart of many of Teale's schemes was a ploy to place bogus securities as assets on the books of insurance companies and reinsurance companies in an effort to mislead regulators. In doing so, Teale colluded with other white-collar criminals whose principal business involved "rent an asset" schemes that used various forms of securities. Two of these schemes involved MEWAs, Multiple Employer Welfare Arrangements, the under-regulated health insurance pools described in the Introduction.

In December 1987, four years after Congress passed the Ehrlenborn Amendment that created MEWAs, the state of Florida gave a certificate of authority to the International Forum of Florida Health Benefits Association to establish a multiple-employer welfare arrangement in the state. IFF, as it came to be known, was created for the primary purpose of providing health insurance benefits to small employers in Florida. Two of the principals behind IFF were: John L. Gazitua, who had previously operated a failed Miami health plan and George Doherty, who was reportedly nearly broke and living in his car on the Florida Turnpike when the association was created.[70]

Given the lack of availability of health insurance plans for small businesses, IFF was able, in a very short period of time, to enroll hundreds of small employers into its program. Despite the fact that Florida law prohibited MEWAs from selling their plans to the general public, IFF sold its health insurance plans to anyone willing to pay the premiums. The plan enrolled garage mechanics, restaurant workers, and beauticians, and eventually covered over 40,000 individuals.

Despite the volume of its revenues, by the end of 1988, a little more than one year after IFF started business, its books showed a net deficit of $786,000.

By March 1989, that figure had increased to $1.7 million.[71] It would later be discovered that the main reason why the trust was running such high deficits was that most of the premium money that should have been used to pay claims was being skimmed off by the association's principals and their colleagues. In addition to being compensated in the amount of $57,000 per year as a trustee to the IFF trust, Gazitua was also paid $56,000 a year as a "consultant" to the association.[72] IFF also paid large amounts of money to various firms that served to market the health plan and to firms that administered the plan, collecting premiums and processing claims. In its short history, IFF paid over $6.8 million to marketing firms, including $387,000 to one whose director was Doherty, and $719,00 to another firm of which Gazitua was president.[73] It also paid, in 1989 alone, over $3 million in commissions to sales agents.[74]

By May 1989, Florida authorities were aware that the health insurance provider was deeply insolvent, yet they failed to shut down IFF. In fact, in August of that year, the head of the state's department of insurance wrote a memo "assuring IFF members that the plan [was] in good standing," but noting that they, the policyholders, might have to help cover any losses incurred by the plan.[75] The state had recently passed a bill that made MEWA participants themselves responsible for any losses incurred by the health plans in which they were enrolled.

To shore up its standing with Florida regulators, IFF's operators did two things: First, they signed an agreement with three reinsurers to provide reinsurance to the health insurance plan; and, second, they informed the Department of Insurance that they had eliminated the trust's deficit by putting $3 million in government securities on its books. The regulators were satisfied that IFF was on solid footing. They could not have been more mistaken.

The three reinsurance companies with which IFF signed contracts were offshore firms controlled by Alan Teale and operated through Teale's reinsurance brokerage firm, World Re. The three firms were Northern Commercial Fire and General Insurance, registered in the Turks and Caicos islands; Euro Reinsurance Company, licensed in Ireland; and Compagnie de Reassurance des Etats Units et Continentale, a Belgium firm. These firms were to cover claims that exceeded $250,000, and up to $1 million.[76] What the state regulators did not know was that these offshore firms were shell companies whose operators had no intention of paying off claims.

In September 1989, Florida Department of Insurance informed IFF that in order to eliminate the deficit on its books it would need to secure more assets. In short order, the trust's principals contacted Alan Teale, who was by then in Atlanta, and explained their dilemma. Teale assured them that he could help them obtain the necessary assets. He put them in touch with people in Texas who were in the business of "renting" assets, specifically, what they claimed were government securities, to insurance companies that were financially "on the ropes." Included in this group was Terry Lozelle, who, in 1988, had pleaded guilty to the charge that he had allowed his airplane to be used to smuggle drugs. In 1989, Lozelle was operating a firm known as Tartan Investments. Another member of the group was a man named Ralph Ben-Schoter, who operated the U.S. Monetary Fund (USMF). Ben-Schoter also had an interesting background. In 1976, he was prohibited from dealing in securities for violating securities laws and in 1979 he was sentenced to five years for committing securities fraud.[77]

In late October 1989, IFF officials signed agreements with Tartan Investments and USMF to "lease" government securities, specifically, Government National Mortgage Association securities, known as Ginnie Maes, for an initial payment of $46,000 and monthly payments of roughly $16,000 (later increased to $50,000 and $25,000). Importantly, IFF did not own the securities, but merely rented them. On October 31, 1989, IFF sent a letter to Florida insurance regulators informing them that they had $3 million in government securities in a Florida bank, along with supporting documentation. Upon receiving this information, the Department of Insurance halted its plan to place IFF into receivership and allowed the MEWA to continue to market its plan and to collect premiums under the assumption that the securities could be used to cover future claims if problems arose.

What the Florida regulators did not know was that not only did IFF not own the securities, but neither did the persons from whom they had allegedly purchased them. Florida regulators might have been more suspicious had they checked into the background of some of these individuals. If they had, they might have discovered that the securities deal with IFF was only one of a series of scams perpetrated by a ring of crooked brokers and securities dealers in which bogus securities were rented to ailing insurance companies across the country who used them to deceive regulators.

Ginnie Maes are securities issued by the U.S. Treasury through the Government National Mortgage Association. The securities themselves represent blocks of mortgage loans made by lenders. Because they are government-backed they are regarded as highly trustworthy and they are also very liquid. At this time, when individuals wanted to purchase Ginnie Maes they contacted Chemical Bank in New York, which often did not transfer the securities themselves, but rather kept them in its vault and issued a statement to the buyer indicating his or her ownership of the securities and, importantly, the identification number assigned to those securities, a CUSIP (Committee on Uniform Security Identification Procedures) number.

In the early 1990s, government investigators discovered a ring of individuals who were renting what were essentially nothing more than lists of these CUSIP numbers corresponding to Ginnie Maes that they did not own, to insurance companies that were experiencing financial difficulties so that the companies could put them on their books at the full face value of the securities. State regulators, as in the case of IFF, accepted these assets because of the high regard in which Ginnie Maes are held. Two of the principal players in this ring were Ralph Ben-Schoter and his partner David Lloyd. Ben-Schoter (who ran USMF) and Lloyd obtained lists of CUSIP numbers from brokers corresponding to $200 million in Ginnie Maes. They then began contacting insurance companies and letting them know that they would be willing to rent these assets to the companies for a fee. In some cases the insurance companies knew the lists were phony, and in other cases they didn't bother to ask. The scheme worked very well. Government investigators found that among insurance regulators, "generally little or no investigation of Ginnie Mae assets is conducted . . . As a rule, regulators do not verify the ownership of the Ginnie Mae securities claimed on an insurance company's financial statement."[78]

Ben-Schoter, Lloyd, and their confederates leased these securities to at least seventeen companies.[79] In addition to IFF, other Teale-connected offshore insurance companies put the bogus assets on their books. One of these was Promed, a company based in the British Virgin Islands that sold its products primarily in California on a surplus-lines basis. In 1992, Promed took in nearly $3 million in premiums in California.[80] In its May 1990 financial statement, Promed listed over $5 million in Ginnie Mae securities as assets. California regulators later filed a cease and desist order against the company. Another Teale-connected firm that leased Ginnie Maes was World Life and Health Company of Pennsylvania, which eventually reinsured all of its health insurance policies through Teale's offshore companies (see page 50). According to congressional investigators, in late 1989, Worlco, World Life and Health's parent company, signed an agreement to pay $8,333 per month to the USMF to place $1.17 million worth of Ginnie Maes on its books. Eventually, Worlco had to write off the entire investment.[81] In 1989, Central Insurance Company, incorporated in the British Virgin Islands, showed $5.3 million in Ginnie Mae securities on its books. Those securities were obtained from the USMF and Tartan. Central's owner, Richard Adeline, was, not coincidentally, the former accountant for IFF, and he had conducted several audits for Teale-related companies.

A September 1990 financial statement filed in California by Standard Indemnity Co., Ltd., of the British Virgin Islands, showed among its assets $10 million in Ginnie Maes. California regulators disallowed the assets.[82] Standard

Indemnity was shut down and its owner, Charles Clover, was later convicted and sentenced to prison, after the company was one of dozens that failed to pay claims following the riots in Los Angeles in 1992 (see Chapter 2).[83]

Palisades National Insurance Co., chartered in the British West Indies, claimed $19 million in Ginnie Mae securities among the assets listed in its June 1990 financial statement. A statement issued six months later showed that those Ginnie Maes had been replaced by Indonesian war bonds, valued at $72 million. Using this as an example of problems in the offshore insurance industry, California insurance commissioner John Garamendi later noted, "[E]ven if the company had owned these securities, bonds issued by a Third World country to finance war materials does not qualify, in our view, as a sound investment."[84] One of Palisades' owners was the son-in-law of the infamous savings and loan operator, Don Dixon, who defrauded the U.S. government out of $1.3 billion when he looted Vernon Savings and Loan in Texas.[85] This was one of several connections between the Ginnie Mae scam artists and savings and loan crooks. In 1990, David Lloyd agreed to lease $17.2 million in Ginnie Maes to a company called Oxidyne Corp., a Dallas company that was purportedly developing techniques for disposing of hazardous wastes. One of Oxidyne's various owners was Edwin "Fast Eddie" McBirney, former owner of Sunbelt Savings, another infamous Texas thrift that went bust in the 1980s after McBirney and his confederates stole millions of dollars from its coffers.[86]

Meanwhile, back in Florida, in April 1990, Florida insurance regulators learned that the Ginnie Maes that IFF claimed to own were worthless and took over the health plan.[87] To make a bad situation worse, when the regulators made a demand on World Re, the manager of the three Teale reinsurers, to pay the portion of IFF's claims they had reinsured, World Re refused, claiming that the fact that IFF had listed bogus securities among its assets invalidated the reinsurance contract. Ironically, it was Teale, the behind-the-scenes mastermind of World Re, who had played a major role in putting those securities on the books in the first place.[88]

After combing through IFF's files, Florida authorities were shocked to discover the magnitude of fraud and abuse at the health insurance provider. Final estimates indicated that 40,000 policyholders would be left with $34 million in unpaid medical claims.

One of those 40,000 policyholders left stranded was Stanley McNeal, who described in a newspaper interview how he learned of his situation:

> I'm standing in the doctor's office. He has just read my X-rays and said that I have a tumor of the colon, I need surgery and it could be cancer. Then his nurse walks in and says she hates to be the bearer of more

bad news, but they've just received a letter announcing that my health insurance company no longer exists.[89]

Within six months, Mr. McNeal's bills for costly treatments totaled over $32,000, about half of which the state eventually returned to him from the remaining IFF assets. But worse, after being diagnosed with cancer, the fifty-four-year-old McNeal was unable to buy another health insurance policy because he now had what insurance companies refer to as a "pre-existing condition"—an ailment that he would have to disclose on any application for insurance and that insurers would view as making him too expensive to cover. As a result, future medical expenses for his condition came out of his pocket.[90]

To add insult to injury, after IFF failed, the state of Florida sued many of the victims of the scam, many of whom had already lost money from unpaid claims, under the state's 1989 law that made MEWA participants liable for losses from bankrupt MEWAs. The state took the position that people who signed up for the program should have been aware of the state law and the possibility that they would be "assessed" to cover losses. Yet, to obtain that information policyholders would have had to have read the fine print at the bottom of page twelve of their contracts.[91]

In November 1992, two of the principals behind IFF—Gazitua and Doherty—were indicted by federal prosecutors. Gazitua eventually was sentenced to eight months and Doherty to twenty-two to eighty months in prison.

## World Re

The idea of operating a health insurer as a Ponzi scheme, with phony assets and bogus reinsurance policies, was a strategy that Teale would use again and that other insurance swindlers would imitate. In the late 1980s and early 1990s, the demand for health insurance, particularly among the employees of small businesses, soared, as legitimate health insurers left the market. Multiple-employer welfare arrangements were created as a means to help fill this gap, without the cumbersome baggage of state regulation. This situation—high demand and little government oversight—created the ideal situation for con artists like Teale to take in millions of dollars in premiums (as they did in the IFF case), funnel the money through a series of brokers and reinsurers, and leave the policyholders high and dry when the claims started coming in. Teale-related entities—operating as primary insurers, reinsurers, or brokers—showed up in a variety of health insurance scams, but one case in particular epitomized the complexities of these frauds, a case that combined numerous forms of white-collar crime and ultimately resulted in the indictment of a dozen individuals, including Teale himself.

The story that follows is complicated, but boiled down to its essentials involves four key entities: (1) a licensed life insurance company, World Life and Health, that provided health insurance for (2) four different health insurance plans, with policies that were reinsured through (3) a series of Teale-related reinsurers, which Teale ultimately controlled, and (4) a group of securities brokers who set up accounts with bogus securities that were intended to give the insurance company the appearance of being backed by substantial assets. These elements came together in a far-reaching scheme, orchestrated by Teale, the goal of which was to defraud thousands of workers and their families for millions of dollars.

World Life and Health Insurance Company of Pennsylvania, a partially owned subsidiary of Worlco, Incorporated of Delaware, sold life insurance, group and individual accident health coverage, and pension annuity plans in seventeen states and the Virgin Islands.[92] Despite the scope of its activities, in the mid-1980s, the company was losing money and its executives decided to focus on health insurance. In 1989 and 1990, World Life and Health signed agreements with four group health plans, at least two of which were MEWAs, to provide insurance to their members. World Life then set up a "fronting arrangement" in which 100 percent of the responsibility for claims from the policies was assumed by reinsurers.

World Life was shut down by Pennsylvania authorities in 1991, after regulators discovered serious problems in the assets listed on the company's books. When the house of cards collapsed, policyholders were left with over $8.6 million in unpaid medical claims. Eventually $2.2 million was disbursed to policyholders from World Life's assets and the Pennsylvania Guarantee Fund, a state-run fund to which licensed insurance companies contributed to cover the costs of insolvencies, was forced to pay the remaining $6.4 million.[93]

In the aftermath of World Life's collapse, congressional investigators from Senator Nunn's committee began examining the company and its close affiliate, World Re, a reinsurance brokerage firm ostensibly run by a Matthew Bonar, but that had the same address as Teale's operation in Atlanta, and that was for all intents and purposes controlled by Teale.

> The staff attempted to examine the financial soundness of the reinsurance companies used by World Life and Health. In doing so, the staff confronted what we can only conclude is a regulator's nightmare: a massive web of brokers, financial intermediaries and companies, many of which were located offshore and far beyond the jurisdiction of state

regulators. The staff found that premium income from World Life flowed through this network to fund a host of commissions and fees to these intermediaries, leaving only a few cents on the dollar to protect policyholders. Moreover, the money was channeled into a vast array of accounts, both domestic and foreign, making it nearly impossible for regulators to accurately determine the amount or whereabouts of the funds.[94]

Teale and his associates used two basic schemes that allowed them to delude regulators long enough to take in millions of dollars before World Life collapsed. The first was a rent-an-asset scheme in which Teale rented securities from a brokerage firm named Forum Rothmore. With these assets on its books, World Life appeared, at least temporarily, to be financially viable. The second scheme involved transferring liability for the policies from World Life to a number of Teale-created offshore reinsurance companies, which were also backed by overvalued if not worthless securities.

### The Rent-an-Asset Scheme

Because the World Life reinsurers were neither licensed in Pennsylvania nor on a list of acceptable unlicensed insurers, state law required that assets be placed into an escrow account to be used to cover claims in the event that the reinsurers became financially impaired. This meant that World Life was required to put $6 million in an escrow account. To meet the requirements, in May 1990, Matthew Bonar, the titular president of World Re who took his orders from Teale, placed stocks from five firms into a bank account with a combined value, according to World Life's financial examiners, of $4.3 million. The remaining $1.7 million listed in the account came from various other sources, including cash.[95] A later investigation by examiners at the Pennsylvania Department of Insurance determined that the actual value of the assets in the account was not $6 million but just under $600,000.[96]

In fact, World Re did not even own the stocks, but rather "leased" them from another firm, Forum Rothmore, a securities brokerage firm operated out of Utah. In exchange for monthly fees (that totaled $1.3 million over a 14-month period), Forum Rothmore's principals and their associates performed financial sleights of hand that artificially inflated the prices of their leased stocks.[97]

One of the stocks placed in the account was 100,000 shares of a company called the Independent Business Alliance (IBA) with an estimated value of $700,000.[98] Based in Texas, IBA was supposedly in the business of offering discounts and rebates on various goods and services to member business, although in the two-year period ending in 1992 it had no revenues and no earnings and no members. Pennsylvania regulators differed with World Life's estimate of the IBA stock; rather than $7.00 a share, they estimated that it was worth $.013 per share, contributing a mere $1,300, not $700,000, to the account.[99]

IBA stock also showed up on the books of a number of other questionable insurance companies. In 1991, 175,000 shares of the stock, valued at $2.5 million appeared on the books of Old Hickory Casualty Insurance Co., a Louisiana insurer owned, in part, by Marvin Lewis, a principal in the notorious First Assurance & Casualty Company, Ltd. (see Chapter 2).[100]

Also in the escrow account were 160,000 shares issued by the Ecotech Corporation. Ecotech was a Utah-based company purportedly in the mining business, though its only significant asset was an inactive gold mining leasehold in California. It had no business operations, no operating capital, and produced no revenue or earnings.[101] Despite these facts, the Ecotech shares placed in the escrow account were valued at $1 million.[102] World Re's estimate of the value of the Ecotech stock was confirmed by an outside auditor whose opinion on that stock was greatly influenced by a letter produced by Forum Rothmore from an offshore company Europe and Transpacific Mercantile Insurance Company, S.A., stating its commitment to invest $1.5 million in the stock and its willingness to finance its mining operations. What the auditor didn't know was that Transpacific was a Teale shell company on whose board sat two of Forum Rothmore's principals.[103]

Then there was the 400,000 shares in American Family Services, a North Carolina company that supposedly provided "financial, management and development services for a single non-profit organization called American Association of Parents and Children."[104] Despite the fact that it had minimal assets, no revenues, and virtually no membership, its shares were ascribed a value of $650,000.

A total of $723,355 of the $6 million in the escrow account came from 186,667 shares in Omega Power, Inc., which turned out to be a small business in Salt Lake City, Utah, that "reconditioned used, discarded and surplus power company equipment for resale."[105] By January 1992, the company was out of business.

One of the most interesting stocks in the escrow account was U.S. Card Investors, a small company located in Boston that purported to trade in sports cards and other sports memorabilia. How such a firm could have its stock end up on the books of an insurance company, or even issue stock at all, is an interesting story in itself.

In 1990, David Yeaman, who operated a small firm in Salt Lake City that specialized in incorporating small companies, and who had a long history of securities violations, met David Grossack, a Boston lawyer who wanted to create a company that sold sports cards and other sports related novelties on cable-TV home shopping programs. By merging Grossack's company, U.S. Card Investors, with a shell company he controlled, Yeaman was able to give the company tradeable shares. Despite the fact that U.S. Card's only asset was Grossack's father's baseball card collection, valued at $44,000, Yeaman was able, through a series of stock swaps, to inflate the company's assets to $1.2 million (on paper). By 1991, U.S. Card had 24 million shares outstanding worth, again, on paper, $1.50 per share.[106] Yeaman then rented 466,667 of these shares to World Re, which then placed them into the World Life escrow account showing a value of $816,667, an amount that was twenty times the value of the company's only real asset.[107]

Fundamentally, Teale, Forum Rothmore, and the others were perpetrating a stock fraud using what are known as "penny stocks" or "micro-cap stocks." Micro-cap stocks are companies with low capitalizations; that is, the total value of the company's stock is relatively small. These stocks are traded "over the counter" (OTC) and are not required to file reports with the SEC as are larger public companies. As a result, the value of these firms' stock is much more difficult to assess.[108] Their value is often determined by what are known as "market makers"—brokers who buy and sell these OTC stocks. The principals at Forum Rothmore were able to manipulate the value of the stocks they rented to World Re, by buying and selling small amounts of the stocks themselves through a series of these market makers. Through this technique they were able to perform a sort of financial alchemy in which virtually worthless stocks were magically transformed into valuable securities, at least for the purpose of being listed as assets on World Re's books.

### The Bogus Reinsurers

The four health insurance plans that were insured by World Life and Health were eventually 100 percent reinsured by five offshore reinsurance companies. On paper these firms were run by different individuals, but were in fact operated by Teale, and most were backed with nearly worthless assets. These offshore reinsurers were principal components of the Teale empire, and were central to the World Life and other swindles. The five reinsurers were: Helensburgh, Ltd., of Dublin, Ireland; Trelawney Insurance, Ltd., also of Dublin, Ireland; Euro Am Re, registered in the Netherlands; Compagnie de Reassurance des Etats Unis et Continentale (United States and Continental Reinsurance Company), a Belgium firm; and United Southern Insurance Company, Ltd., of the Turks and Caicos islands.[109]

Helensburgh and Euro Am Re were owned by two Dallas residents, Dallas Bessant and Jerry Tidmore, whose operations would later receive considerable scrutiny from congressional investigators as well as federal prosecutors. Bessant was a native of England who had moved to Texas originally to work in the real estate industry, but later became involved in the insurance industry after he made the acquaintance of several infamous white-collar criminals. Tidmore was a Texan who had previously been involved in loan frauds. Both came to the insurance business with little knowledge of reinsurance but a great deal of experience in financial frauds.

According to congressional investigators, Bessant and Tidmore met in the mid-1980s when they both worked at a private trust company in Texas called Dominion Savings and Trust, which later ran afoul of the Texas Banking Department after it had "developed a reputation for selling bonds and/or letters of credit without sufficient financial backing, consisting of, allegedly, little more than worthless penny stocks."[110] After that venture failed, in February 1988, Bessant and Tidmore started U.S. Dominion Financial Corporation (USDFC), with an initial capital investment of $1,000. According to one of the company's brochures, USDFC "offers a full line of financial services which include consulting, insurance underwriting management, reinsurance intermediary services, risk bearing facilities, risk group formation and associated administrative services . . ."[111] As investigators would come to suspect, and Bessant himself would later admit,[112] the real business of USDFC was to run "advance loan fee scams." In these schemes, offers are made to secure loans for individuals in exchange for an "advance fee"; the fees are collected but the loan never arrives. Tidmore would later admit that of the 110 people who paid USDFC fees the number who had "received an actual loan from a bank based on USDFC taking their proposal and submitting it to a lender" was exactly zero.[113]

In July 1988, Bessant and Tidmore decided to branch out and chartered their first reinsurance company, American Indemnity Assurance Group (AIAG) in the Turks and Caicos islands. The company was created with two main assets: $50 million in gold futures certificates issued from an Arizona company known as Shell Mining; and an entity known as the Strasshoff Estate, with assets estimated at $231.03 million. In fact, AIAG did not own the estate, whose assets were never actually verified. The gold futures were in reality worthless and Shell's owner was ultimately indicted for selling bogus gold mining debentures.[114]

Neither Bessant nor Tidmore knew much about the operations of the reinsurance company and "were interested in reinsurance because there was money to be made there and that offshore reinsurance was attractive because it was unlicensed."[115] While Bessant and Tidmore were the ostensible owners of AIAG, the company was controlled from behind the scenes by Alan Teale. In April 1990, Teale advised Bessant to reincorporate the company in another country because of recent changes in the insurance law of the Turks and Caicos. In a letter to Bessant, Teale wrote:

> I believe that the disallowance of Real Estate under the law will otherwise cause difficulty in retaining status in Turks . . . Monserrat is probably the place to go. We then, after redomicile, register it as a Branch in Belgium. The new Turks and Caicos law is pretty tough but it will take some 6–9 months before it is fully operative.[116]

Bessant and Tidmore's second venture into the reinsurance industry was with a company known as Euro Re. Bessant initially obtained the company from the legendary insurance swindler, Carlos Miro, but the circumstances of that transfer of ownership are a matter of dispute. Miro's infamy resulted from his involvement in several large-scale insurance company failures that resulted in losses of hundreds of millions of dollars, including the collapse of his own Anglo American Insurance (see Introduction).

Bessant claimed that Miro, who lived a few blocks away from him in Dallas, gave him the company in exchange for some overvalued penny stocks and worthless bonds that Miro wanted to use to bolster the assets of his Anglo American Insurance.[117] Miro's version of events is somewhat different. According to Miro, his first encounter with Bessant ended quickly when Bessant "tried to peddle some outlandishly bogus treasury bonds . . ."[118] Miro described their second meeting as follows:

> I told him to go away, but, he was nothing if not persistent, as well as obnoxious, so, namely to get rid of him I told him I'd "give" him one of the companies (he liked the name Euro Re, the "United States of Europe" in 1992 and all) if he'd just reimburse me the £5000 or so I'd spent on incorporation. Bessant's reply was that he didn't have that kind of money, but, he'd get it shortly after I gave him the company. (I was sure he would.) Once again, I told him to get lost.[119]

Later, in the summer of 1989, Miro recalled, "Bessant now turned up on my doorstep in London, with a glossy Euro Re brochure . . . [Bessant] became quite angry with me when I still wouldn't 'give' him the company, and, he stormed away to find a place to stay since, he'd flown over presuming I'd put him up for the night."[120]

Either way, in October 1990, Bessant and Tidmore transformed Euro Re into Euro Am Re, incorporating it in the Netherlands. Soon thereafter, Euro Am Re was reinsuring approximately 20 percent of World Life and Health's liabilities.[121]

In April 1990, Bessant and Teale incorporated Helensburgh, Ltd. in Ireland, specifically for the purpose of providing reinsurance to Teale's World Re clients, one of which was World Life and Health. The entrepreneurial pair put up no assets to start the company other than $25 million in bogus bonds (see page 57). Helensburgh was quickly listed as a reinsurer for 25 percent of World Life and Health's plans.

### The Sovereign Cherokee Nation Tejas

When congressional investigators working with the Nunn committee began investigating the Teale reinsurance network, they noticed that the main asset claimed by both Euro Am Re and Helensburgh was $25 million worth of "treasury bonds" issued by the Sovereign Cherokee Nation Tejas (SCNT), whose treasurer was a man known as Chief Wise Otter. When the investigators called the offices of SCNT they "found themselves talking to an individual who called himself Wise Otter but who spoke with a very distinct British accent. This individual . . . we now know to be Dallas Bessant . . ."[122] Coincidentally, SCNT's offices were located at the same address as Bessant and Tidmore's USDFC in Dallas.

According to the "tribe" 's purported leader William Fry, a.k.a. Bear Who Walks Softly, "the 'Nation' was created by an 'act of God.' " Skeptical investigators determined that the nation was actually created by a retired U.S. Air Force colonel, Herbert Williams, who in the mid-1970s had an idea that put him ahead of his time. He claimed ownership of a sandbar in the channel of the Rio Grande river, a 154-acre plot that he allegedly purchased in 1974 for $20,000 after the "island" was created by hurricane Beulah. He would assert that this new land was neither part of the United States nor Mexico and he therefore claimed it as an Indian nation and, despite his lack of Native American heritage, gave himself the name Little Bird on the Shoulder.

The purpose of the new "nation" was clear: to create a haven for financial ventures free of U.S. regulation. SCNT's lawyer Chief Screaming Eagle, a.k.a. Gary Derer, told the congressional investigators "that he and the SCNT would seriously consider any business deal, including casinos, offshore banking, vessel registration, etc."[123] Among the ventures that they looked into was the creation of an airline chartered by the "nation," which would allow it to circumvent Federal Aviation Administration licensing requirements.[124] When Bear Who Walks Softly was interviewed by Senator Nunn's committee staff he told them that the organization's primary purpose was to "help indigenous Indian people." When asked to give examples he stated, "Well, we sponsored Tammy Billy when she was a candidate for Miss Indian World, which she won."[125]

Investigators would learn that SCNT's primary business, like that of its office neighbor USDFC, was advance-fee loan schemes. Part of the scam involved claiming ownership to false or inflated assets. Among the assets listed on SCNT's 1990 financial statement was $25 million in industrial development bonds issued by the Cherokee Business Council, an offshoot of SCNT, and a plaster of paris "life mask" of Marlon Brando, with an estimated value of $1.5 million. The bonds were worthless and the Brando mask could never be found. Despite claiming total assets of over $80 million, SCNT had trouble paying its day-to-day bills. The organization's application to lease two Lincoln town cars was turned down by a local car dealer, and it was refused a request for direct billing from Motel 6.[126]

In its report, Senator Nunn's staff concluded that "the group of individuals who call themselves the Sovereign Cherokee Nation Tejas is neither sovereign, nor Cherokee, nor a nation . . . it is a sham, run by a group of 'white' or 'Anglo' Americans for the sole purpose of self-enrichment."[127] The potential for fraudulent profit presented by the fact that real Indian tribes can legitimately operate some businesses outside of government regulations was immediately seen by Alan Teale. In a letter to Bessant he wrote:

> I believe that the possibilities arising from your privileged position [as treasurer to SCNT] are many. For example, on the basis that the Nations are free of the many bureaucratic interferences in trade others suffer, highly favorable proposals can be devised for: Medical covers PHI Travel Possessions Liabilities at the least. The numbers involved would all be capable of producing good income.[128]

As we shall see in Chapter 4, the idea of creating fictitious countries to license financial enterprises that could defraud investors with impunity was also understood by other individuals, some of whom had connections to Teale, and would be greatly refined in the future.

### Retrocessionaires

To make matters more complicated, the five reinsurance companies also ceded some of the liability for World Life and Health claims to other reinsurance companies through a process known technically as retrocession. "Retrocession is simply the ceding of premium and liability from one reinsurer to another."[129] One of these retrocessionaires was American Indemnity Assurance Group, the Bessant/Tidmore reinsurance company discussed above. Another was a London-based firm, Dai Ichi Kyoto Re. Despite the fact that officials at Dai Ichi Kyoto denied any involvement with World Life and Health, the firm had signed a contract in 1990 that made it responsible for reinsuring 25 percent of one of World Life's health plans.[130] Dai Ichi Kyoto was a mysterious organization that would show up again and again in a variety of global insurance scams.[131]

Backed by the five reinsurance companies and their bogus assets, an undeterminable number of retrocessionaires, and an escrow account containing nearly worthless securities, World Life and Health was in no position to cover unforeseen medical expenses from the members of the MEWAs to whom it had written policies. Moreover, given the way that premium monies were siphoned off at every stage in the complicated, multilayered scheme, there were few funds left to pay even expected medical expenses. Out of every dollar the policyholders paid for health insurance, only between 46 and 66 cents was even available to be used to pay claims, even if the reinsurers had been legitimate.[132]

## The Fall of the Empire

The demise of World Life and Health spelled the beginning of the end for Alan Teale and his empire. On January 19, 1993, Teale and Rentz were arrested at their home in suburban Atlanta. Indictments were filed in Alabama and Pennsylvania charging the pair with numerous crimes, including mail fraud, money laundering, and operating an ongoing financial crimes enterprise. Both were eventually convicted in federal court and sentenced to prison, Teale for seventeen years and Rentz for six-and-a-half years. Other members of their gang were soon rounded up and sent to prison. Bessant (a.k.a. Chief Wise Otter), Tidmore, and Matthew Bonar received sentences of six months in prison, twenty-six months in prison, and probation, respectively. Six of the people involved in the World Life and Health rent-an-asset scheme were indicted in federal court in Philadelphia. All were convicted and received sentences ranging from probation to sixteen months in prison. However, as we shall see in the chapters that follow, many of Teale's confederates and affiliates escaped punishment and went on to commit more white-collar crimes.

While the exploits of Alan Teale and his associates were reported by the press, the articles often appeared in industry periodicals; or, if they were published in major newspapers, they wound up on the back pages. It may be that the cases were too complicated and the schemes too opaque to make them easily explainable to the average reader. Or, it may be that editors felt that, after the insider trading scandals on Wall Street and the savings and loan debacle of the 1980s, the public had simply grown weary of financial scandals. Either way, Teale never gained the public recognition that other infamous white-collar criminals, such as Charles Keating and Michael Milken, did.

Despite the lack of public attention to international insurance fraud, revelations about the scope and consequences of Teale's schemes opened a window on the vulnerabilities of the insurance industry to large scale fraud. First, the very structure of the industry—with its reliance on the goodwill of insurers to back their policies with real assets—facilitates the ease with which white-collar criminals can set up these scams. As one of its investigators told the Nunn committee during one of its hearings, "Basically, anyone in this room could be a billionaire if they followed the example of Bessant, Tidmore and the Indians. You basically get some bond paper and a typewriter." With those materials, he explained, Tidmore and Bessant created what he called "Dallas Paper," worthless bonds that could be used to create offshore reinsurance companies.[133]

Second, Teale's exploits revealed the utter inadequacy of regulations governing the reinsurance industry, which the Nunn committee referred to as "grossly unregulated by the current U.S. regulatory system," noting that, "World Re, a reinsurance broker, answered to no one, yet handled tens of millions of dollars of policyholders' hard-earned premium money."[134] Because their jurisdictions end at their states' borders, state insurance commissions "cannot possibly investigate the type of vast international networking and money flow that the Subcommittee found in its investigation."[135]

The crimes of Teale and other international insurance swindlers also revealed how easy it was for them to exploit the limitations of sovereign laws in foreign countries while selling insurance on the global market. In particular, they were keenly aware of the fact that many countries lightly regulate insurers and reinsurers as long as they do not sell their products domestically. When Carlos Miro testified before Representative John Dingell's committee he was asked why he chose to set up Anglo American Reinsurance in Ireland. He explained, "They [Irish regulators] absolutely did not regulate anybody who was incorporated in Ireland, but insuring other than Irish risks. As long as you weren't messing around with the Irish people, they didn't care what you did."[136] For the same reason, many of Teale's reinsurance companies were registered in Ireland. Teale also showed that he was aware of the importance of paying attention to changes in foreign regulatory laws when he wrote to Bessant advising him to redomicle one of his reinsurance companies in Belgium because of changes in the law in the Turks and Caicos islands.

Finally, inquiries into Teale's activities revealed the existence of networks of financial criminals who operate globally, who form temporary alliances with other criminals, and incorporate different forms of white-collar crime into their schemes. Investigators from Senator Nunn's committee stated:

> We have merely exposed the tip of an iceberg of international white collar criminal syndicates. We found also that the individuals involved in these insurance scams were equally willing and able to work other fraudulent activities involving advance fee schemes, stolen counterfeit securities, tax evasion, and money laundering. In sum, insurance fraud may also be just the tip of the criminal iceberg, too.[137]

As we shall see in later chapters, what they had found really was the tip of the iceberg as insurance frauds have, since those words were spoken, become part of much larger schemes that involve investment scams, bank frauds, and the activities of organized crime groups.

# 2

# Opening Up Those Golden Gates

When Alan Teale and his Alabama confederates began selling low-cost auto insurance in California in the late 1980s, they were in the vanguard of a virtual army of insurance con artists who would move into the Golden State. There the convergence of several conditions—legal and economic—had opened the door for widespread fraud in California's lucrative insurance market. In 1992, the state's insurance commissioner summarized the situation:

> We are, in California, in the middle of several insurance crises. . . . Thousands upon thousands of Californians are being ripped off every day, by shady, unlicensed insurance companies who swoop into town, take in millions of dollars of premiums and then head back to some island in the Caribbean with their booty in hand. Policyholders are usually left holding an empty bag, or to be more accurate, thousands of dollars in unpaid medical bills, or a car they can't get out of the repair shop because the insurer won't pay the bill, or a business burned down, as we're going to see in the recent Los Angeles rioting, that won't be rebuilt because the insurance was fictional."[1]

The door to easy money in the California insurance market was opened by two changes that took place in the 1980s. First, there was a movement of licensed insurers out of inner-city neighborhoods. Through a practice of "redlining"—whose existence was only halfheartedly denied by industry officials—licensed insurance companies would refuse to write auto, home, and commercial policies in low-income, often minority, neighborhoods where losses were deemed to be too high to make the business profitable.[2]

The impact of the second factor was more sudden. In 1989, California voters approved a referendum (Proposition 103) that forced insurance companies to reduce their rates by nearly 20 percent. In response, many large insurers simply withdrew from the California market, leaving a void that financial predators quickly moved to fill.

The primary vehicles for these schemes were "surplus lines" carriers. California insurance laws, like the laws in many other states, allowed certain brokers to sell policies from nonadmitted insurers, companies not licensed in the state and not subject to full state regulation. Many of these carriers were chartered in places like Antigua and Barbados where financial requirements were minimal.

Thus, by the end of the 1980s there was a very strong but unmet demand for reasonably priced auto insurance across the state and commercial insurance in inner cities. At the same time there was a loophole in the law that allowed unregulated insurers to sell their products in those markets. There existed, in other words, a situation that was ripe for people like Alan Teale to exploit to their own advantage.

## Proposition 103

Throughout the 1980s, auto insurance rates in California increased steeply, so that by 1988 an average couple, living in Los Angeles, with good driving records, could find themselves paying $2,500 a year to insure their cars.[3] The insurance industry claimed that these sky-high rates were the result of the hefty settlements they were forced to pay out by juries sympathetic to plaintiffs in lawsuits filed against them.[4] Supporters of Proposition 103, whose backers included Ralph Nader, disagreed. In their view insurance companies were simply gouging the public, raising premiums in order to increase profits.[5]

On November 8, 1988, California voters went to the polls and overwhelmingly approved Proposition 103. Many of them undoubtedly favored one of the new law's critical components: a requirement that insurance companies roll back their rates to 20 percent less than their 1987 rates. Before the vote, a number of insurance companies had warned that they would leave the state if Proposition 103 was enacted, and, after the law was passed, many did exactly that. Less than two weeks after the vote, insurance giants Geico, Travelers, Liberty Mutual, and TransAmerica stopped writing new policies in California.[6]

With insurance companies refusing to sell them policies, many Californians turned to the California Automobile Assigned Risk Plan (CAARP), an industry-sponsored pool that served as "an insurer of last resort for high-risk drivers."[7] The pool was originally intended for motorists with poor driving records, but post–Proposition 103, many good drivers began utilizing the pool because of its lower rates. When industry officials realized that good drivers, the low-cost drivers they wanted to insure, were leaving them, they pressured CAARP into tightening up its eligibility requirements and to double their rates.[8] As a result, the number of drivers receiving insurance from the fund declined from 1.2 million in 1989 to 140,000 in 1992.[9]

## The Surplus Lines Industry

In the wake of Proposition 103, the sale of policies by unlicensed offshore insurers increased dramatically. In 1988, Californians paid just $54 million in premiums to unlicensed offshore insurers. Three years later, that number had increased to $261 million.[10] The number of complaints filed with the state's Department of Insurance against these insurers also grew: from a mere 22 in 1988 to 2,303 in 1991.[11] To understand how these unlicensed insurers were able to move so quickly into the California market and to steal so much money, one has to understand the nature of the surplus lines industry and the regulatory bodies that were supposed to govern it.

Rather than being overseen by the California Department of Insurance, as licensed insurance companies are, surplus lines carriers were primarily monitored by a private organization, the California Surplus Lines Association (CSLA). In 1991, CSLA represented 425 surplus lines brokers who, by law, had the exclusive ability to sell policies from insurance carriers not licensed to do business in the state, otherwise known as "nonadmitted carriers." Even more peculiar, the association and its member brokers—not state regulators—had the primary responsibility for examining the financial statements of offshore companies to determine if they had the wherewithal to pay claims. In other words, for this segment of the industry, a private organization, one with direct ties to members of the industry, was given the role of watchdog over the industry. Ultimately these financial statements were sent on to the California Department of Insurance, which retained the right to prohibit companies from doing business in the state, but the process was slow and, in the meantime, rogue insurance operators could pull in millions of dollars in premiums.

According to state law, insurance agents could not directly write policies from nonadmitted insurers. Rather, they had to go through surplus lines brokers who were allowed to write policies from nonadmitted carriers only after they filed an affidavit stating that the broker was unable to place the insurance with admitted insurers and that the policy was not being placed with a nonadmitted company simply to obtain a lower premium.[12]

Despite CSLA's conflicting roles as regulator and trade association, historically the system had worked reasonably well with the association conducting internal reviews of unlicensed companies and passing their findings on to the Department of Insurance. However, in the mid-1980s, a new insurance commissioner, Roxani Gillespie, a former insurance company executive, instituted a new policy. In 1988, she told an insurance conference:

> The culture is an open market culture. We are there only to take care of the exceptions, to take care of things that might go wrong. Other states believe that they should tell insurers how to run their businesses. We do not believe that at all.[13]

This change in policy had serious consequences. As a former insurance department official stated, "[F]rom that day forward . . . it was Katie bar the door. Everybody knew you could go to California and nothing would happen."[14] Financial examinations conducted by the CSLA of offshore insurers were cursory and little scrutiny was given to the documents the companies submitted to the organization. Any questions about the veracity of the people behind the companies were left in the association's files and were not passed on to state regulators.[15] As a result of the new "open door" policy, unscrupulous promoters operating out of islands in the Caribbean flooded into the state.

In the wake of Proposition 103, California motorists found their options for auto insurance greatly diminished. Thousands of them were forced to turn to offshore insurance companies, although many did not realize that the ultimate backers of their policies were located outside the United States. Unscrupulous brokers who sold policies from offshore companies advertised heavily on late-night television with ads that promised full coverage for all drivers, regardless of their driving records, and at prices that seemed reasonable. No mention was made of the fact that the insurers were not licensed by the state.

All licensed insurance companies in California are required to pay premium taxes that go into a state guaranty fund. When one of these insurers becomes insolvent, these funds are used to pay claims. However, nonadmitted insurers are not required to contribute to the fund and when they fail policyholders and are left with no funds from the state to pay their bills.

One of the unwitting victims of these offshore scams was Lorene Ferris, a resident of Los Angeles who, like Diane Collras whose plight was detailed in the Introduction, had the misfortune of purchasing an auto policy from Union

Pacific Fire and Marine, the nonadmitted insurer that was licensed in the British Virgin Islands. At first it seemed like a good deal; her yearly premiums went from $2,378 to $1,780. Then, in August 1991, she was involved in a serious accident while driving her Chevy Blazer. The vehicle was towed to an auto body shop where an adjuster estimated the damage at $3,000. The body shop did the repairs and, after receiving a check from the insurance company, released the car to Ms. Ferris. A week later, the shop called her back and said the check from Union Pacific had bounced, it had been written on a closed account. Ms. Ferris later explained her reaction at a legislative hearing:

> I got threatened by the auto body shop. I had to hide my car for three days because they were threatening to come take the car because I had a $3,000 bill. So I ran over to GMAC [where the car had been financed]. The car was one month from being paid off and . . . I refinanced my car. Was bailed out and I paid the auto body shop back.
>
> So let me be very clear that when you're a victim of this you spend a lot of time crying. These people do bank on you giving up. I suggest anybody who has insurance documents to check them thoroughly. When I got car insurance I looked at the front cover, I folded it back, I looked at the numbers, I put it back in the envelope and I filed it with my business files. Done deal, thought it was gold, thought it was fine. My big mistake for being that stupid.[16]

## The Alan Teale Legacy

Several of those individuals who showed up early on in the California insurance "gold rush" of the 1980s and 1990s had direct ties to Alan Teale. Having mastered insurance fraud techniques while working with Teale, they were eager to apply their skills to the wide open California market.

One of Teale's colleagues who made a big impact in the state was Robert Campbell, an insurance agent based in Kentucky. Campbell had been a central figure in several of the Teale scams described in Chapter 1. Campbell operated some fourteen insurance and reinsurance companies, chartered mostly in Caribbean countries, from his offices in Lexington, Kentucky. Two of those companies—Cie. Internationale Financiere de Reassurance, of Belgium, and Northern Commercial Fire and General Insurance, of the Turks and Caicos islands—were used in the World Re scheme to reinsure risks, even though the companies had few assets. In addition, Northern Commercial was one of the three offshore companies that Teale used to provide reinsurance to the International Forum of Florida.

Campbell also owned Apex Placement Insurance Co., licensed in the Turks and Caicos islands. Apex's primary business was selling auto policies in California. In 1990 and 1991, the company wrote tens of millions of dollars in insurance policies in the state.[17] The company and its assets were so flimsy that, according to a newspaper account, when Campbell was in the Turks and Caicos registering the company he ripped out two pages of a phone book. He then lined up the first names on one page to the last names on the other and thereby generated a list of phony names for his board of directors.[18]

One of those victimized by Apex was Eduardo Ramirez. On a summer day in 1990, he was in a friend's car en route to the Western Union office in Santa Ana, California, where he was going to wire money earned from his job as a dishwasher back to his wife and children in El Salvador, when a tractor trailer crashed into the car, throwing him into the windshield and fracturing his wrist. Unfortunately, the truck was insured by Apex. Eventually, Apex agreed to pay $25,000 to Ramirez and the other occupants of the car and even sent them a check for that amount. The check bounced and Ramirez, who later complained about having trouble picking up boxes at work, never did get his wrist treated.[19]

In 1991, Apex was hit with a cease and desist order by the state Department of Insurance. In its order, state officials were skeptical of the value of the assets claimed by the company. First, the accountant who submitted a financial statement claiming the firm held $16.3 million in assets was neither licensed nor certified. Further, $11.9 million of those assets consisted of a note issued by a bankrupt Japanese company. Another $4.4 million was claimed to exist in the form of common stock issued by an obscure Sable Palm Airways. After the company was placed into conservatorship, its assets were revalued at $1.2 million.[20] State officials would later estimate that Apex defrauded Californians out of $80 million to $100 million.[21]

In 1994, Campbell pleaded guilty to federal charges in Philadelphia for his role in the World Re scam and was sentenced to twelve months in prison to be served concurrently with a seventy-one-month sentence he was serving for a Florida conviction and a sixty-month sentence resulting from a case in New Jersey.

Another colleague of Alan Teale who prospered in the California market was an Australian, James E. Charge. On August 8, 1998, Charge stepped off a Kuwait Airlines flight from London to New York's JFK and proceeded to customs where immigration officials, having been tipped off by the FBI, recognized him as the subject of an arrest warrant from Florida. Charge was promptly arrested and eventually transported back to Miami where federal prosecutors had filed a sealed indictment against him in 1997. This was the same James Charge who was listed as the president on the application made by Victoria Insurance (see Chapter 1) for an insurance license to the state of Delaware. Charge did not become the president but did stay involved with the company after it was licensed in Georgia.

In June 1991, Charge incorporated West Point Insurance in Antigua, a small, former British colony, located in the Caribbean, east of Puerto Rico. Charge operated West Point out of offices in Miami, but, importantly, the company sold no policies in Florida, thus allowing him to escape the scrutiny of Florida regulators. Instead, the firm concentrated on selling auto insurance in California's overheated market. Over a two-year period, West Point would collect over $22 million in premiums from Californians. After the company closed its doors, prosecutors would claim that the company failed to pay $6.9 million in claims.[22]

Charge's scam was similar to the others described thus far. He would submit financial statements to regulators showing false, rented, or overvalued assets; then, when regulators would question those assets, he would simply substitute new, equally valueless assets in their place, until regulators would reject those assets. The scheme was made much easier by California's "file and write" system, which allowed nonadmitted insurers to begin selling insurance immediately after filing financial statements with the California Surplus Lines Association (CSLA), but before those statements had undergone any review process. Thus, all Charge had to do was submit documents showing an appropriate level of assets and he could begin taking in premium dollars immediately.

Over the course of the next two years, Charge submitted no less than five financial statements to the CSLA, each showing that his company had assets in excess of $15 million. Many of these assets consisted of stock in foreign, particularly African, companies, and ventures whose value and even existence were difficult to trace. Moreover, West Point did not actually own these assets, but instead rented them from a London firm, Buckingham Gardner. Among the companies West Point claimed to have an interest in was Sierra Leone Resources, P.L.C., a joint venture primarily owned by the government of the African country Sierra Leone. The firm purportedly owned the rights to an undeveloped bauxite deposit at Port Loko, Sierra Leone, but in order for the project to get off the ground it needed at least $100 million in start-up capital. Another asset claimed by West Point was shares in Maritime Protective Services of Sierra Leone, a firm whose mission was to enforce fishing laws in Sierra Leone and sell fishing licenses. In its eighteen-month existence, the company failed to pay any dividends to its investors.[23] In exchange for the use of these essentially worthless assets, West Point paid Buckingham Gardner approximately $1.4 million.

West Point was hit with a cease and desist order from California regulators in 1993. Despite this, West Point continued selling policies in the state for at least six months.

In 1996, after his California operation was shut down, Charge chartered a reinsurance company, Colonnade Insurance Co. A.V.V. in the tiny Caribbean island of Aruba. Colonnade provided reinsurance for a health insurance plan named The ERISA Advantage, operated by two California men with long histories of involvement with shady health care plans.[24] In August 1998, The ERISA Advantage was shut down by the U.S. Department of Labor, which claimed that the operators had illegally diverted to themselves nearly half of the $2 million the health care plan took in during an eight-month period in late 1997 and early 1998.[25] A little over 5 percent of the premiums went to Colonnade for reinsurance. Less than 4 percent of the premium dollars was set aside to pay medical claims.[26]

In late 1999, Charge was convicted on federal charges in Miami. The following June he was sentenced to serve only forty months in prison—less time than was required by sentencing guidelines—even though he admitted that losses from his crimes totaled $10 million to $20 million.

## Big Rigs and Bogus Insurance

California's insurance crisis of the late 1980s hit not only individual motorists but commercial truckers as well. Particularly desperate for coverage were both small trucking companies and Mexican truckers who hauled loads across the border into the United States, neither of whom could obtain insurance at the rates available to large companies with fleets of trucks. As in the private auto insurance market, offshore, unlicensed carriers moved in to fill the gap. Campbell's Apex Placement was one carrier, and a small firm called Serpico Insurance Trust Association was another.

Serpico was allegedly chartered in the British Virgin Islands and sold policies to truckers in California, Texas, and Florida. In 1988, company officials claimed that 3,000 truckers were participating in their insurance plan.[27] According to its Arizona-based operator, Donald L. Lamb, the firm was technically not an insurance company but, rather, a "self insured group of truckers," and therefore not subject to state regulations.[28] Regulators had a different view of the operation. To them, Serpico was simply an unlicensed insurance company that was taking in premiums but not paying claims. In the fall of 1988, California and Florida ordered the company to stop doing business in their states. Serpico officials protested the California decision claiming they had paid over one hundred claims in the state.[29]

One of those one hundred was not Jan Walker's. In 1988, Ms. Walker was crossing a downtown Sacramento street on her lunch hour, returning to her office with a plate of food, when she was hit by a truck and suffered severe injuries. The truck's owner had purchased insurance from Serpico. Eventually, Walker took the trucking firm to court and was awarded $850,000, but the firm declared bankruptcy. Serpico refused to pay all but a minimal amount on her claim, leaving her with $25,000 in unpaid medical bills. As a result of her injuries Walker was forced to quit her job and live on $712 a month in disability payments. Looking back at her situation she told a reporter, "It doesn't seem fair. I didn't do anything wrong. All I did was come back early from lunch hour."[30]

As Serpico's legal battle with Walker dragged on, the company was also under investigation by a Los Angeles grand jury. Rather than face the jury's decision, Donald L. Lamb fled to Panama. However, this would not be the last time he would appear in connection with an offshore insurance scam.

On February 25, 1999, Donald Lamb's nephew, J. Brian Lamb, was arrested and led away in handcuffs just outside his office, which happened to be the courthouse in Chandler, Arizona, where he was a justice of the peace. Lamb came from a prominent Mormon family in the Chandler area, where he was connected to many politicians and business leaders. But he was also leading a double life, calling himself Bob Mathias and Jim Wright when he was conducting insurance business. Federal prosecutors charged Lamb with running an insurance scam that had many similarities to the one run by his uncle. Specifically, they charged that J. Brian Lamb and his partners sold insurance policies at cut-rate prices to truckers claiming that the insurance was provided either by several legitimate insurance companies (that had no connection with the scheme) or by fictitious insurance companies, not licensed to do business in any state. Among the latter, was Comagre Insurance Company, a Panamian firm run by Lamb's uncle, Donald L. Lamb.

According to prosecutors, J. Brian Lamb and his colleagues set up an elaborate, but crude, money-laundering strategy for putting premium dollars in their own pockets. Truckers who agreed to purchase policies from Lamb's companies sent their checks to locations in Arizona and Florida, where they were then transferred to an address in St. Johns, Antigua, and then back to Lamb et al. in the United States. Some of the checks were then cashed at a convenience store in Arizona. Over a sixteen-month period in 1997/1998, the small market cashed over $196,000 in premium checks. In total, the scam netted J. Brian Lamb and his associates over $1.5 million.[31]

While his nephew awaited trial in Arizona, Donald L. Lamb, speaking from his home in Panama City, told reporters that the missing $1.5 million was being held by Comagre Insurance in Panama and that the case against his nephew was really an effort by federal authorities to silence him, the elder Mr. Lamb, in retaliation for an unrelated legal action he had taken against the U.S. government. Beginning in 1994, Donald L. Lamb filed a series of lawsuits in which he claimed that in the early part of the twentieth century the U.S. government illegally seized the property that would become the Canal Zone without compensating the families that held the titles to the property. Lamb claimed that his family owned much of that property. U.S. officials denied the claim but did admit that there was no proof that the American government ever actually legally owned the property.[32] Donald L. Lamb also claimed that the U.S. government's case against his nephew was without merit because the government had no legal grounds for requiring foreign truckers to have insurance when they entered the country. "The United States government doesn't have any business trying to enforce anything on the Pan American Highway system because they surrendered that jurisdiction to the Organization of American States."[33]

Despite his uncle's remonstrations, in August 2000, J. Brian Lamb was sentenced to serve two-and-a-half years in prison (the minimum allowable under federal sentencing guidelines) having pleaded guilty to three counts of mail and wire fraud.[34] Those concerned about the well-being of the former justice of the peace were undoubtedly relieved to hear that despite his conviction Lamb was still eligible to collect a pension for his five years as a magistrate that would potentially provide him with up to $331,000 over a thirty-year period.[35]

## Riots and Redlining

Small business owners in inner-city neighborhoods of Los Angeles had long suspected that they had a more difficult time obtaining insurance for their businesses than did their counterparts in the suburbs. These suspicions were confirmed after the riots of 1965. A 1966 report on the availability of insurance in the areas of Los Angeles affected by the riots admitted that insurance was "not readily available" in these areas and that after the riots many of the businesses in the area would be paying two-and-a-half times the normal rate for fire and riot coverage.[36]

It took another riot, twenty-seven years later, to show that little had changed since the civil disturbances of the 1960s. On April 29, 1992, Los Angeles erupted in flames after the announcement of a jury's decision to acquit four white police officers who were charged with beating Rodney King, a black motorist, despite a widely broadcast video tape of what appeared to be a brutal assault by the officers on an unarmed civilian. For three days, rioters roamed the streets of south central Los Angeles, hurling bricks at innocent bystanders and looting stores, hauling away televisions, groceries, diapers, and anything else that could be carried out.

Among the changes that had occurred in this urban area since the 1960s was an influx of Korean Americans, many of whom bought and operated small businesses. One of the lasting images of the riots, one that was broadcast worldwide, was of Korean American merchants, laden with ammunition belts, holding automatic weapons while they stood guard over their businesses. These images came to symbolize the changed nature of urban racial strife in the 1990s: conflicts not simply between blacks and whites, but that pitted Latinos and African-Americans against whites and Asians. To many observers it appeared that the rioters were targeting Asian businesses.[37]

After the riots, many of these immigrants returned to their gas stations, convenience stores, and Laundromats to find them in ruins—heavily damaged, or even burned to the ground. And many of them would soon find that they had been victimized twice: first, by the rioters, and second, by unscrupulous insurance agents who had sold them worthless policies from unlicensed off-shore insurance companies. When they filed claims to begin rebuilding their businesses they were met with either no response from the companies or explanations of delays in the adjusting process. After several months, many policy-holders realized that they were never going to be paid; they had been defrauded by the same bogus insurers who had been stealing from California motorists.

More than simply suffering monetary losses, many of the victims found that their whole lives had changed. A significant number were unable to reopen their businesses and ended up unemployed or underemployed. The victims also suffered disproportionate rates of mental illness, divorce, and several even attempted suicide. Others were forced to return to Korea having lost all faith in the American dream.[38]

An analysis by the California Department of Insurance proved that these were not isolated incidents but reflected a widespread problem. Based on interviews with riot victims the Department reported that over half of the victims had no insurance to cover their losses. The Department also surveyed surplus lines brokers and found that fifty-one nonadmitted companies had a total of 520 claims from the riots totaling $64.1 million in losses. By the time the report was released, four months after the riots, less than one-third of those claims had been paid.[39] Hardest hit were Asian American business owners in the area. A survey conducted by the Korean-American Grocers Association after the riot found that half of its more than 3,000 members had no insurance.[40]

## First Assurance

In April 1993, 110 small business owners from the south central area of Los Angeles, most of them Korean Americans, banded together to file a class action lawsuit against more than one hundred insurance companies, brokers, and agents who had sold them polices that turned out, after the riots, to be virtually worthless. The merchants claimed in their suit that because of the defendants' misconduct they had "lost their sole means of survival . . . their life savings [, and] have given up any hope of obtaining the monies due to them after having diligently paid insurance premiums for years," and that they "have been unable to put the events of the Los Angeles Civil Disturbance behind them and move forward with their lives."[41]

One of the more prominent defendants named in the case was a company called First Assurance & Casualty Company, Ltd., an offshore insurer licensed in the Turks and Caicos islands, which the plaintiffs asserted left $6.7 million in unpaid claims following the riots.[42] First Assurance was just one of more than a dozen offshore insurers that were exposed as frauds by the Los Angeles riots. But the company and its activities warrant a closer, more detailed examination, because, in many ways, First Assurance symbolized everything that was wrong with the surplus lines industry in California in the early 1990s, and, in its later reincarnations, many of the problems that continue to plague the global insurance industry. In the First Assurance story we will see many of the same features that were found in other offshore insurance scams—phony assets, bogus policies, manipulation of loopholes in the law—but we will also see how the easy flow of capital to countries with deregulated insurance markets allowed these global criminals to continue perpetrating their frauds even after being shut down in the United States.

In July 1988, First Assurance & Casualty Company, Ltd. was incorporated in the Turks and Caicos islands. A year later, the company was purchased by Jesse Maynard, an accountant who operated the company from his hometown, Enid, Oklahoma.[43] To help run the company and its affiliated entities, Maynard assembled a group of individuals who had considerable experience in the shadier side of the insurance business.

One of those was Marvin Lewis, who processed claims for First Assurance at a Texas company. Lewis was a former attorney who had earlier helped to set up Cheyenne, Wyoming–based Commercial General Insurance Co. After Commercial General failed in 1989, regulators discovered that the insurance company held several million dollars in worthless Ginnie Mae securities leased by David Lloyd (see Chapter 1). Commercial General's owner was prosecuted and sentenced to prison for his part in the scheme, which included bribing the

Wyoming insurance commissioner (just as Wining and Schonacher had).[44] Lewis was never charged. In 1993, he was indicted in St. Louis along with notorious insurance swindler Arthur Blumeyer on charges that, in the late 1980s, he helped Blumeyer in a land deal that falsely inflated the assets of Blumeyer's Bel-Aire Insurance Co.[45] Blumeyer was eventually convicted and sentenced to prison for twenty-two years, while Lewis was acquitted.[46]

Another key player on the First Assurance team was Vikash Jain. In 1989, Jain was fired by an American insurance company for allegedly taking bribes, including a Jaguar automobile for his wife, from companies with whom he placed reinsurance.[47] Samuel B. Love, also a principal in the firm, operated Frontier Administrators, an Arizona company that provided administrative services for First Assurance. Love had previously worked for Herman Beebee, the "godfather" of the Texas savings and loan crisis, who also appeared to have played a behind-the-scenes role in the phony Ginnie Mae securities scandal.[48]

In June 1990, First Assurance began selling insurance to truckers, first in California, where it became the insurer for the National Association of Truck Owners, and then in Texas where it sold policies to Mexican truck drivers who traveled to the United States. The company sold those policies despite the fact that its license would not be granted by the Turks and Caicos authorities until a year later. The fact that the company was not licensed to sell insurance did not hinder its financial success, which was phenomenal. By January 1991, First Assurance was taking in $600,000 a month in premiums in California alone. In the first four months of 1991, First Assurance took in $2.3 million in premiums, while paying out only $4,933 in claims.[49] Not a bad profit margin.

While the company's "profits" piled up, California regulators became increasingly concerned about its financial stability, as well as the solvency of other offshore companies that were selling large volumes of insurance in the state. To safeguard consumers, in June 1991, the Department of Insurance implemented an emergency regulation (§2174) that required nonadmitted carriers to have $15 million in capital and surplus and a $5.4 million trust account.[50] Nonadmitted insurers were required to comply with the regulations by September 1, 1991.

With the new financial requirements hanging over their heads, First Assurance's principals undertook a series of moves designed to create the illusion of financial solvency. Using techniques that had worked well for Teale and his colleagues, they placed rented and highly overvalued stocks on the company's books. And, like other insurance con artists, they enlisted the help of insiders within a large, well-known institution, in this case PaineWebber, to lend an aura of legitimacy to their illusions. They did not need to go very high up the corporate ladder at PaineWebber in order to achieve their goals. An account executive in the San Diego office named Craig Aalseth would suffice.

In July 1991, First Assurance contacted Aalseth and discussed opening a claims reserve account at PaineWebber into which the rented and highly inflated stocks would be placed. These stocks would be presented by First Assurance to state regulators as evidence of the company's financial solvency and therefore compliance with regulation §2174.[51]

To accomplish this financial alchemy, Aalseth—like Teale and Forum Rothmore—used micro-cap ("penny") stocks that were sold in the over the counter (OTC) market. As such, their value was established by a "market maker," which turned out to be Aalseth. One of these was 1,400 shares in the Independent Business Alliance (IBA), valued at $8 a share. This was the same stock that Teale had placed in an escrow account to create the illusion of solvency at World Re. They continued to place these stocks on First Assurance's books despite the fact that, in November 1991, an article appeared in the *Dallas Business Journal* that described an investigation by the SEC into rented assets, which included IBA stock; the SEC said there was "no active market" for the stock, meaning that it was virtually worthless.[52] In total, the value of the stocks in the reserve account was purported by Aalseth to exceed the $5.4 million minimum required by the new state regulation.[53]

With these bogus assets listed on the books, Aalseth and First Assurance's owners held sales meetings with both the surplus lines brokers who represented the company and the retail agents who sold the policies directly to consumers; at which, they declared the firm to be on solid financial grounds and to be in compliance with all state regulations for nonadmitted insurers. The scheme worked well. In one month, August 1992, First Assurance took in $1.8 million in premiums.[54] Things were going so well for the company that, in early 1992, the company's principals decided to expand its business beyond auto and commercial trucking and began writing policies for rental cars, contractors, and small businesses in redlined areas, such as south central Los Angeles.

After several states questioned the value of the stocks listed on First Assurance's books, Maynard et al. instructed Aalseth to replace them with other, equally bogus, assets. In August 1992, he placed 1.4 million shares of a company called Bora Capital Corp., with a claimed value of $4.3 million, on the company's books. Bora's real assets would later be estimated at $243,000, with holdings that included a bankrupt hospital and a company whose chief asset was the license to market a program for writing on and reading finished laser cards.[55] Also, included on the books were 300,000 shares of Logos International, at a value of $10 a share. Logos's business appeared to include operating a car-towing and used-auto-parts business. First Assurance's shares in the business were estimated, by its own accountant, to be worth $3 million, despite the fact that an independent auditor had raised questions about whether the firm could remain in business.[56] First Assurance claimed that the Logos stock had been obtained in an exchange for a $3 million bond issued by the New St. Paul Baptist Church in Texas. However, when the California Department of Insurance began looking into First Assurance's assets it could not find any such bond registered with the SEC, nor could they find the New St. Paul Baptist Church.

First Assurance's house of cards began its inevitable collapse in May 1992, when the Los Angeles riots occurred and policyholders began complaining to the state Department of Insurance that their claims were not being paid. Despite these complaints, the company continued selling policies in the state until April 1993, when the California Department of Insurance issued a cease and desist order prohibiting the insurer from doing business in the state. The next month, the state of Texas ordered First Assurance to stop selling policies to Mexican truckers who drove into the state. In that same month, the Turks and Caicos islands suspended First Assurance's insurance license. In May 1993, Aalseth was terminated by PaineWebber after he was caught fabricating the value of leased securities in an FBI sting.[57] He would eventually be convicted on federal charges related to those crimes. Finally, in October 1993, Maynard put First Assurance into bankruptcy in Oklahoma City.

## First Assurance's Scams

In its short life, First Assurance was involved in an amazingly diverse set of insurance scams, defrauding truckers, small business owners, municipal governments, and health insurance policyholders.

### Truckers

Early on, First Assurance focused on selling policies to commercial truckers in California. Hard hit by Proposition 103, many were desperate for insurance and failed to look closely at the fine print describing where the company was located, and their brokers did not bother to tell them. Among First Assurance's victims were Guy and Anita Burke, the owners of Burke and Son Trucking, a small California company that paid the company $52,000 a year for a $1 million liability policy to cover their trucks. In May 1993, as First Assurance teetered on the brink of bankruptcy, one of those trucks crashed into a car driven and occupied by two sisters. The accident left the girls with horrible injuries— head trauma, brain damage, and a broken jaw. When First Assurance failed to pay on the claims, the Burkes were forced to sell the business they had owned for twenty-three years to help pay the sisters' medical bills. Meanwhile, the agent who sold him and other trucking firms policies from First Assurance slipped out of the state and set up shop in Montana.[58]

### Small Business Owners

In early 1991, First Assurance expanded its business beyond private auto and commercial trucking and began selling policies to inner-city merchants in places like south central Los Angeles. The offshore insurer became one of the largest insurers of small businesses in the area, selling its policies through local agents who either did not care about the company's financial status or relied on the word of the surplus lines brokers they went through to obtain the coverage for their clients.

The list of those who ended up with worthless First Assurance policies included John Ham and his wife, Chung. Immigrants from Korea, the Hams owned and ran a small convenience store in south central Los Angeles. On the day that the Rodney King verdict was announced, Mr. Ham returned to his store after looters set off the fire alarms. By the time he arrived the damage was done, the store had been burned to the ground. Ham tried to contact the First Assurance offices but no one answered the phone. He contacted the head of the insurance agency who had, a few years earlier, sold him his policy, and was told there was nothing he could do for the Hams. Yet, John Ham and his wife were luckier than most. They eventually qualified for a small business loan and were able to rebuild their grocery store. But, the pain of their loss lingered: "I still have such bad memories from that, so much pain," Mrs. Ham told the *San Francisco Chronicle*.[59]

Another Korean American merchant who was victimized by First Assurance was Young Ki Kim. Mr. Kim owned a liquor store that was burned to the ground during the riots, causing $400,000 in damages. Since he had purchased a policy from First Assurance that provided coverage of up to $500,000, and had been diligently paying his premiums of $1,000 a year, Mr. Kim assumed that his losses would be covered. He was wrong. First Assurance never paid him a dime. Like Mr. Ham, however, he was fortunate enough to receive a loan from the Small Business Administration that enabled him to open a new business, a small gas station and convenience store.[60]

The initial response of First Assurance to many of the riot victims who filed claims was to deny them on the ground that their policies contained "Riot Exclusion" clauses that excluded any claims based on damages resulting from riots, civil commotions, or mob actions. However, in their class action suit, riot victims pointed out that where these clauses actually existed in the policies they were described in extremely fine print in the middle of the policies and that their agents never informed them of the clause until after they filed their claims.[61]

In other cases, First Assurance simply refused to pay claims on the ground that they were fraudulent. Jesse Maynard, First Assurance's president, told the bankruptcy court in Oklahoma City that 80 percent of the 114 claims they had received from riot victims were fraudulent. He went on to complain that the company had referred some of the "grossly fraudulent claims" to the Los Angeles district attorney, but had gotten no reply.[62]

### Municipal Governments

Another of the areas that First Assurance expanded into was the writing of surety bonds for contractors. Many publicly financed construction projects require contractors to purchase surety or performance bonds that guarantee that the contractor will complete the job within a specified period of time and will meet certain standards. If the contractor fails to finish the job, the company writing the bond becomes responsible for fulfilling the contract. At least two local governments were defrauded after they hired contractors who had purchased bonds from First Assurance. One of them was Orange County, California.

In 1992, a contractor who had originally agreed to build a new firehouse for the county filed bankruptcy. The contractor had purchased a surety bond, but unfortunately that bond was written by the fraud-ridden Winston-Hill Assurance Co., which itself declared bankruptcy five months later.[63] The county went from bad to worse when it agreed to let First Assurance take over work on the project, without first checking out the company with state regulators. The county paid First Assurance $322,678 before they discovered that First Assurance was not paying subcontractors.[64] All of the money was lost after First Assurance declared bankruptcy.

Officials at the Denver Museum of Natural History might have also been well advised to check into First Assurance's history before they did business with the company. A local construction contractor had been hired in 1992 to build a Prehistoric Journey exhibition at the museum. In the course of the project it was discovered that the contractor was not paying its subcontractor and the museum turned to First Assurance, the writer of a surety bond on the project, to complete the work. The museum took First Assurance to court and was eventually awarded damages, but by that time First Assurance had declared bankruptcy and the museum was forced to pay out some $300,000.[65]

## Health Insurance Policyholders

For the first eight months of 1993, First Assurance provided coverage for a bogus health insurance plan sponsored by a group known as the Western Businessmen's Association (WBA).[66] WBA was but one incarnation of a fraudulent health insurance provider that bilked thousands of small business employees and self-employed individuals out of millions of dollars in premiums in the late 1980s and early 1990s.[67] First Assurance was the last of a series of infamous offshore insurers that were involved in the scam, including Winston-Hill Assurance and Teale's Old American Insurance.

Among the many victims of the health insurance scam was Cathy Green, a young paralegal from Van Nuys, California. In 1990, Green was forced to quit her job because of a serious, chronic kidney condition. After learning that the health insurance provided by her former employer would soon run out, she began searching for a new insurer, but found it to be nearly impossible to find a company willing to sell her a policy given her "pre-existing condition." The one company that did agree to sell her a policy at a reasonable rate turned out to be the predecessor to the Western Businessmen's Association, a phony labor union known as the Consolidated Welfare Fund. Over the next several years, her condition worsened, her treatments became more expensive, and her medical bills were not paid. In response to her many inquiries, Ms. Green received numerous letters reassuring her that her insurance had been switched from one Caribbean-based insurer to another, and that all her bills would be paid. Finally, facing $300,000 in unpaid medical bills, she became so desperate that she wrote a letter to Attorney General Janet Reno, referencing the fact that prison inmates routinely receive the kind of treatment she needed, and asked "Should I rob a bank so I, too, can be cured at taxpayers' expense?"[68]

Where did all the money go? In bankruptcy court, Maynard stated that the company's "cash flow" problems stemmed from a judgement by a California court that ordered First Assurance to pay the Fujitsu Corporation $1.1 million after it failed to pay on a surety bond.[69] Federal prosecutors had another explanation. In their indictment of Maynard et al., they alleged that much of the premium money taken in by First Assurance was siphoned off for their personal use; in a one-year period, the company's principals transferred $7.5 million out of First Assurance and into businesses they controlled.[70]

Part of the money drained from First Assurance's accounts was used to create a new insurance company. In September 1992, $450,000 was transferred from a PaineWebber account controlled by Maynard et al. to a bank in New Zealand.[71] Those funds were then used to capitalize International Casualty and Surety (IC&S), a company incorporated in New Zealand in the summer of 1992 by Maynard, Samuel Love, and other First Assurance principals.

In its 1992 financial statement filed with New Zealand regulators, IC&S claimed as assets many of the questionable stocks that appeared on the books of First Assurance, along with several other dubious assets. Part of these $5.7 million in claimed assets were: $2.4 million in Bora Capital stock; $1.4 million in notes issued by West Virginia Oil & Gas Co., assets that were determined by California regulators to have "questionable liquidity and value";[72] and $926,100 in preferred stock in a company owned by Love.[73] In other words, having looted First Assurance and placed it into bankruptcy, the company's principals then created a new company in New Zealand, and backed it with many of the same assets that U.S. regulators had declared to be of little or no value.

Over the next several years, IC&S played a shell game with its declared assets, replacing one bogus OTC stock or corporate note with another. For example, of the $6.9 million in assets declared on its 1994 financial statement, $2 million was in the form of stock in a New Zealand company, Lifeguard Financial Systems Ltd., a subsidiary of Lifeguard Reinsurance, Ltd., whose president was a colorful Houston businessman named Leon Excalibur Hooten III. Texas regulators shut down Lifeguard Re after they determined that the company's primary assets were bonds and certificates of deposit issued by a fictitious country, the Dominion of Melchizedek, of which Hooten claimed to be a past president (see Chapter 4).

Why New Zealand? Why would a group of businessmen who hailed from Oklahoma, Texas, and Arizona, and whose business experiences consisted primarily of insurance sales in the western United States, decide to set up their new company in a country in the south Pacific? The answer is, for many of the same reasons why they chartered First Assurance in the Turks and Caicos islands. Under New Zealand law, insurers were only required to post a $500,000 bond and have $100,000 in capital to receive a license. Moreover, the agency that oversaw insurance companies, the Registrar of Companies, did not have the power to investigate insurers who did not sell insurance within New Zealand.[74] As a result of this deregulated environment, IC&S, along with other "rogue" insurance companies, were drawn to the country that one business publication called the "Insurance Industry's Wild West."[75] The New Zealand Insurance Council, the regulatory agency responsible for overseeing the industry, explained the regulatory environment in the following way on their Web site:

> Compared to other countries, New Zealand has one of the least regulated insurance markets in the world. The relaxed regulatory environment that we enjoy in New Zealand works because the industry has

been pro-active in developing its own codes of practice, independent dispute resolution processes and solvency requirements. . . . The Insurance Council of New Zealand's member companies are committed to self-regulation . . .[76]

IC&S never became a major player in the international insurance industry; but it did pretty well, given that its principals were facing numerous civil suits and eventually a criminal indictment back in the United States. In 1998, the firm took in $9.5 million in premiums and earned $730,000 in profit.[77]

IC&S's name surfaced in a number of shady and questionable insurance deals around the world. In 1994, IC&S was mentioned as a potential reinsurer in a deal brokered by the infamous insurance rogue, F. T. Riley, in which Chase Manhattan would later claim to have been defrauded of $579,000.[78] In that same year, the company was also named as one of five reinsurers of "hull" insurance placed on the ship the *MV Nassia*, owned by a Greek company. In March 1994, the ship was enroute to Genoa with a cargo of crude oil when it collided with a motor bulk carrier and exploded, resulting in the death of thirty-one sailors. It appears that very little of the $7 million coverage on the hull, a portion of which IC&S was responsible for, was ever paid.[79]

IC&S was also implicated in a scheme in Utah. In 1996, Bill Patterson, a "smooth talking Texas in a ten-gallon hat," approached county officials in Ogden with a proposal to build a $5 million tire-recyling plant. All he had in the way of assets was a performance bond purportedly written by IC&S. After collecting $86,000 from the county, Mr. Patterson disappeared, leaving local officials with nothing more than a pile of used tires. When those officials tried to collect on the performance bond, Samuel Love, then the head of IC&S, denied having ever issued the bond.[80]

Despite the apparent success of the IC&S/First Assurance's owners and operators in eluding the law and their clients, by 1997 their past had begun to catch up with them. Early that year, First Assurance and PaineWebber settled a civil racketeering suit filed against them the previous year by First Assurance's trustee. PaineWebber agreed to pay $7 million and First Assurance was ordered to pay $150,000 to cover unpaid claims.[81]

But the biggest blow to the enterprise would come in October 1998, when a federal grand jury in Oklahoma City handed down an indictment charging Maynard, Love, Vikash Jain, and Clara Jones Faulk, the secretary/treasurer of First Assurance, with bankruptcy fraud. The indictment focused on the diversion of $450,000 out of First Assurance and into IC&S accounts, just two months before it was placed into bankruptcy. The indictment also alleged that, during the same period of time, Maynard had kept a $270,000 refund from a reinsurer that had canceled its agreement with First Assurance out of the bank-ruptcy estate by transferring the funds to an account in Panama and then mov-ing the money into an account he controlled in Kansas.[82]

At their trial the defendants repeated the argument that they had every intention of paying valid claims, but many of the L.A. riot–related claims were fraudulent, and the aggressive pursuit of their firm's assets by litigants in civil suits against them prevented them from paying legitimate claims.[83]

Apparently, the jury did not believe their argument and, in November 1999, convicted Maynard and Love. Three months later the judge sentenced the pair to seventy-eight and sixty-five months in prison, respectively, and ordered them to pay $7 million in restitution.[84]

One might think that with its principals behind bars and a "D" rating from A.M. Best (the lowest rating an insurer can receive), that IC&S would have quickly shut down. Not so. In February 2000, IC&S was sold to a firm based in St. Kitts, British West Indies. The company's new chairman was no stranger to the world of dubious offshore insurance deals, having previously been the head of another St. Kitt's–based insurance company that had gone out of business under a cloud of allegations that it had failed to pay on a surety bond.[85] In a remarkably sanguine statement, a spokesperson for the new com-pany stated, "It's had some problems, [but] we want an image of integrity."[86]

## Closing the Golden Gates

The gates that had been left wide open to insurance fraud in California in the late 1980s were closed suddenly in June 1993, when insurance commissioner John Garamendi banned 250 nonadmitted insurers who had failed to comply with the state's new regulations requiring they have at least $15 million in capi-tal and surplus, plus at least $5.4 million in a U.S.-based trust account.[87] The new regulations also changed the old "file and write" system that allowed crooks to file a financial statement and immediately begin writing policies. Under the new standards, the state creates a list of "acceptable" surplus lines carriers—those who have met the financial requirements listed above, and sur-plus lines brokers cannot place business with insurers not on the list.

While the state was successful in putting many of the insurance perpetra-tors of fraud out of business by tightening regulations, it was not so successful at changing the conditions that gave them their opportunities. In a 1997 analy-sis the state Department of Insurance concluded, "[T]he data still presents a picture of far too many communities in California that are disconnected from the insurance marketplace."[88] The problem was particularly evident in the area of auto insurance. The Department estimated that in 1997, the percentage of uninsured vehicles in the state was 22.6, only slightly lower than the estimates from the late 1980s and early 1990s.[89] In the inner city the rates were much worse. In south central Los Angeles, for example, the proportion of uninsured motorists exceeded 60 percent.[90] Thus, with unmet demand for insurance persistently high, the likelihood of a resurgence of illegal activity remains high.

California's offshore insurance crisis lasted only four or five years, but in that time massive damage was inflicted on unsuspecting consumers. According to the state's insurance department, in 1992, Californians lost $200 million to fraudulent, unlicensed insurers.[91] These monetary estimates do not capture the pain and suffering endured by the thousands of individuals who ultimately also lost their businesses or homes or, worse, their health, as a result of their involvement with offshore, unlicensed insurance companies.

While a number of the major players in these scams were prosecuted and sent to prison, many others, indeed the majority, remained free to set up new fraudulent schemes. Even among those who were eventually prosecuted, the lag time between their California crimes and their convictions gave them ample opportunity to defraud more consumers. Take James Charge, for example, whose West Point Insurance was shut down in California in January 1993, but who wasn't convicted until 1999. In the interim he set up an Aruba-based reinsurer that became part of a nationwide health insurance scam that caused not only financial but physical harm to many of its victims. Or, consider IC&S, the phoenix that rose from the ashes of First Assurance. Long after First Assurance was placed into bankruptcy, its principals were using its assets—specifically, cash stolen from policyholders—to operate a series of international insurance frauds. The public and policymakers remain seemingly unperturbed by these events. Imagine, by contrast, the outrage that would follow if an accused armed robber was released on bail and for the next several years wantonly committed many more crimes.

The word globalization was not part of the popular vocabulary in the late 1980s when segments of the California insurance market were transformed into criminogenic markets. Yet it was the globalization of the insurance industry that played the biggest role in transforming those markets. And, while the industry was changing rapidly, regulatory agencies were not. In California, the existing system of regulation may have worked fine in an environment in which most nonadmitted insurers were still U.S. based, and in which their share of the insurance market was minimal. But things had changed by the late 1980s, as the insurance industry became increasingly international in scope, and as many small countries in the Caribbean and elsewhere invited insurance companies—both legitimate and illegitimate—to obtain licenses in their jurisdictions (with the important proviso that they would not sell their products there). State regulators in California who had traditionally enjoyed a clubby relationship with those they regulated, found themselves ill equipped to deal with the "new world order" they confronted. Unlike the occasional errant broker they were accustomed to dealing with, who diverted premiums for his or her personal use, they now were faced with a "new breed of schemer," a sophisticated international white-collar criminal who set up elaborate networks of fraudulent companies, located in a variety of countries, and claiming to be backed by obscure assets whose value, let alone existence and ownership, were exceedingly difficult to establish.[92] In the face of these changes, they were simply outmanned and outgunned.

Other states experienced similar problems with unlicensed, offshore insurers, notably Louisiana, where a combination of political corruption and a tradition of cronyism in the business community helped open the door to criminals like Carlos Miro, who would later refer to the state as a "banana republic" because of the ease with which public officials could be bribed.[93] But it was in California where the confluence of two factors—a huge market that had been all but abandoned by legitimate insurers and a regulatory system that was full of gaps—created a situation that made many insurance company operators instant millionaires. The situation in the private auto, commercial trucking, and small-business commercial insurance markets was similar to the conditions in another segment of the insurance market that had become criminogenic in character: the small-business health insurance market. There, one saw the same pattern of abandonment by legitimate insurance companies and the existence of major loopholes in the law that allowed "noninsurance companies," such as MEWAs, to market health insurance outside of state regulation. Organized networks of white-collar criminals moved in to take advantage of this situation and sold millions of dollars in worthless health insurance policies to desperate consumers. Indeed, many of the same individuals—Teale, Campbell, and Charge, for example—were involved in fraudulent schemes in all of these markets.

# 3

# Promises, Promises

By the mid-1990s, state and federal regulators had begun to close some of the loopholes that had allowed con artists like Alan Teale and Jesse Maynard to steal millions of dollars from unsuspecting victims while hiding behind ambiguous regulations and the shields of foreign sovereignty. Financial requirements were tightened for surplus lines carriers and federal MEWA regulations were modified to allow more rigorous state scrutiny. Congress passed the Violent Crime Control and Law Enforcement Act of 1994, which made fraud committed by insurance company officers, directors, and employees a federal crime, punishable by up to fifteen years in prison.[1] At the same time, many of the individuals who had been involved in offshore insurance scams in the late 1980s and early 1990s were either in prison or under indictment. As a result, the savings and loan–style debacle that many had predicted for the insurance industry never happened.[2]

This did not mean, however, that the "financial knaves and buccaneers" who operated fraudulent offshore insurers simply packed up, went home, and sought legitimate employment. Some, as we saw in the last chapter, continued to promote their schemes under the auspices of new organizations. Others refocused their attention on new scams and new victims, following the financial trends toward those markets where big money could be had quickly. And, in the mid-1990s, the best place to find that big money was the stock market.

By the middle of the decade, the American economy was in the midst of the longest period of sustained growth in history, and this economic prosperity was evident in the stock market, which climbed ever upward in a seemingly unstoppable ascent. At the same time, the stock market was being democratized as the advent of the Internet and high-speed personal computers enabled millions of average Americans to have the same direct access to the markets that had traditionally been restricted to brokers and Wall Street traders. As a result, billions of new dollars were being pumped into the market daily by small investors eager for instant riches. Many of those investors were undoubtedly motivated by tales of overnight fortunes being made by those lucky enough to have invested early in companies like AOL and Netscape.

In this environment, con artists found easy marks in the thousands of people who, afraid of being left out in the rush to riches, were ready to invest their savings in highly speculative ventures without adequately checking into the offering's financial credentials. As one Florida investigator put it:

> You got people sitting in their houses in West Palm Beach listening to how everyone in the world is making money in the stock market. Somebody calls on the phone with a high-pressure pitch saying the train is leaving the station, and this is their last chance to get aboard.[3]

To exploit these gullible investors, innovative con artists with experience in insurance scams joined forces with individuals with backgrounds in securities fraud to put together sophisticated investment scams that preyed on elderly investors.

On October 14, 1998, the Florida state insurance commissioner announced that a statewide grand jury had charged five insurance agents, a stockbroker, and seven others with cheating 145 Florida residents, many of them elderly, out of $10.9 million in an investment scam. The scheme involved the sale of promissory notes issued by a company called Legend Sports that claimed to be in the business of developing golf courses. The scam was able to lure in so many victims because it involved several key components. First, the securities were marketed through insurance agents who often pitched the investment scheme to couples to whom they had previously sold life insurance policies; consequently, these customers trusted them. Second, the promissory notes were said to be risk free—guaranteed by bonds written by insurance companies. Third, the notes generally matured in nine months and paid 12 to 15 percent per annum, considerably more than the return on more conventional investments such as certificates of deposit. Those skeptical enough to check on the notes and discover that they were not registered with state authorities were told by the agents that, according to Florida law, promissory notes that matured in nine months or less were not required to be registered.

What prospective clients did not know was that the whole thing was a Ponzi scheme. The company had no intention of paying off most of the notes. Florida law did not exempt the notes from registration; they were simply unregistered securities that were being sold illegally.[4] And, the bonds that supposedly guaranteed the notes were worthless pieces of paper issued by unlicensed, offshore insurance companies that would ultimately renege on their obligations to guarantee payment on the notes.

As regulators began to investigate, it soon became clear that Legend Sports was not an isolated case but only one of a series of related promissory note scams that were being operated all over the country. In many ways, it was a template for all the other scams. Promoters would offer investors promissory notes issued by start-up companies, like Legends Sports, that had no track records and little in the way of financial statements that could be verified by potential investors. Potential investors heard sales pitches about the riches to be made from golf course developments in Florida, oil and gas wells in Texas, laser devices for treating eye diseases, new technologies for storing blood from umbilical cords for medical purposes, television programs for children, land purchases to build Indian-sponsored gambling casinos, Italian resorts, and many other pie-in-the-sky schemes. The notes offered to pay an annual interest rate of 9 to 18 percent and they matured in a short period of time, often nine months. And, finally, there was the feature that attracted so many otherwise cautious investors: The investments were said to be risk free, guaranteed by bonds written by insurance companies.

By the end of 1999, regulators had identified at least thirty of these promissory note offerings that were being sold by over 1,000 insurance agents that collectively had taken in an estimated $200 million.[5] The magnitude of the problem was indicated by the fact that in 1999 the North American Securities Administrators Association (NASAA), the organization that represents state securities regulators, ranked promissory note fraud among its "Top 10 Investment Scams."[6]

In this chapter we will examine several of these illegal schemes in detail. The case studies presented here are representative of this new form of white-collar crime that combines elements from different financial industries to give the illusion of solid foundations to what are in fact houses of cards.

## Legend Sports

Legend Sports got its start in 1991, when a businessman from Knoxville, Tennessee, James T. Staples, put together a group of investors that included several former professional football players to raise money to build a series of golf courses and driving ranges. Staples envisioned a company that operated a network of golf courses, like the highly successful Family Golf Centers of New York (which had no connection with Legend). However, by 1996, the company had built only one golf facility in Altamonte Springs, Florida, and the company was operating at a loss.[7] At some point, the principals behind Legend determined that there was more money to be made in investment scams than golf courses and concocted a plan that would make them rich. They began recruiting insurance agents and investment brokers in Florida and elsewhere around the country to market promissory notes issued by the company. The agents they recruited then contacted former clients, to let them know about a "promising investment opportunity," often encouraging them to take their money out of annuities, CDs, or life insurance policies, and putting it into the Legend notes.

A typical sales pitch worked like this: After being told about the tremendous growth potential for the twenty-five golf courses and entertainment centers the company planned to build across the southeastern United States, and shown artists' renderings of the Altamonte Springs facility, prospective investors were given the specifics: The promissory notes would mature in nine months and pay a 12 percent annual return—not so high as to be suspicious but substantially more than they were earning from their CDs or annuities. Investors were told that nearly all of their money would go directly into the development of future golf courses and "entertainment centers" and that there were no "front end" or "back end" loads or management fees.[8] They were also told that the notes did not need to be registered with state securities regulators because of a loophole in Florida law that gave exemptions to the registration requirement to notes that matured in nine months or less.

Perhaps the strongest part of the sales pitch was that the investments were risk free; even if the company was unable to make good on the promissory notes, an insurance company had written a surety bond guaranteeing payment. Investors received a signed copy of the bond when they purchased the promissory notes. These bonds were issued by several offshore insurers including Westwood Insurance and Tangent Insurance Co.

The scheme was extraordinarily successful. Between 1994 and 1996, Staples and his associates raised $16.8 million by selling promissory notes.[9]

Like most pyramid schemes, Legend Sports had a short life. On November 6, 1996, the Florida comptroller filed an emergency cease and desist order against Legend Sports and its parent company, LSI Holdings. In its complaint, the comptroller's office claimed that LSI's principals were operating a Ponzi scheme: While they had taken in $16.8 million from investors who bought its promissory notes, they had paid out only $993,000, or less than 6 percent.[10]

Then, in September 1998, the Securities and Exchange Commission (SEC) sued Legend Sports claiming that it had defrauded investors. Specifically, the SEC alleged that, in contrast to what investors were told, most of the money raised was not used to develop golf facilities, but instead was siphoned off in various ways by officers of the company, the salespersons who recruited investors, and the offshore insurance companies that issued the surety bonds guaranteeing the notes. In addition to the 6 to 8 percent in commissions paid to the salespersons and the 10 percent that went to the insurers, the principals behind Legend Sports took 20 percent in commissions. Thus, nearly 40 percent of the capital raised went to pay for commissions, instead of the projects the money was supposed to finance. Also, a good portion of what was left of the company's capital went to make payments to early investors in order (as in all Ponzi schemes) to keep the scheme going long enough to attract new investors. As a result, there was no way that the company could stay afloat very long and, in 1997, the scheme collapsed, leaving investors with $15 million in worthless notes.[11]

Given the central importance of the surety bonds that supposedly guaranteed the Legend Sports promissory notes, it's amazing that so few investors looked into the status of the companies that issued them or the backgrounds of the people associated with those companies. Had they done so they would have learned that not only were these firms unlicensed and located in foreign countries, but also that the people who ran them had histories of involvement in insurance swindles. Two of these companies, Westwood and Tangent, were chartered in Antigua and both had ties to the ubiquitous Alan Teale.

Westwood's history began in 1987, when the company's predecessor, Wirral Insurance Co. Ltd., was incorporated in Antigua. In documents submitted to a congressional subcommittee investigating the insurance industry, Wirral was listed as part of Alan Teale's International Underwriting Association.[12] In 1994, the company was sold to a firm known as Lock Investments, and the name was changed to Westwood.

Westwood's assets, like those of many other offshore insurers, were always a matter of controversy. A September 1994 financial statement showed $13.8 million in assets, including $10 million in "Certificates—U.S. Currency Notes," which, according to the statement, were "U.S. currency notes issued by the United States of America to the Phillipines and known as Series 66 Notes" during World War II.[13] According to Westwood's representatives, the notes were backed by the "full faith and credit of the U.S. government."[14] In fact, the notes had been issued by the Philippine government, not the U.S.

government, and were first used by General Douglas MacArthur's troops in 1944. By 1957 they were no longer accepted as legal tender. The notes were obtained by Westwood from the same broker who had supplied the Indonesian "National Defense Security Council" bonds to Palisades National Insurance, the company that was thrown out of California after regulators determined those bonds were worthless (see Chapter 2).

Not only were the company's assets cloaked in mystery, but so too were the owners and directors of the company. The company's managing director was Owen Guidry, a former insurance regulator who had previously worked for the Louisiana and Arizona insurance departments as an examiner. While he worked for the Louisiana Department of Insurance in the late 1980s, he became part of the biggest insurance failure in the state's history: the collapse of Champion Insurance Co. In 1989, he was hired by then Commissioner of Insurance, Douglas Green, to audit Champion. In his audit he found the company to be solvent, with $19 million in surplus. Four months later the company collapsed, leaving $180 million in unpaid claims that were eventually paid by Louisiana's guaranty fund. Green was eventually convicted and sentenced to prison for accepting bribes from Champion's owners.[15] In 1994, Guidry went to work for Westwood.

Although Guidry often served as a spokesperson for the company, the real force behind Westwood was a New Jersey real estate developer, Peter Stanley. Like Guidry, Stanley brought considerable experience in shady financial deals to the venture. Stanley had made a fortune in the 1980s, building mansions on speculation and then selling them to the wealthy. He was widely known in northern New Jersey for his flamboyant style that included driving a blue Rolls-Royce convertible and dressing "as if he had been outfitted by Ralph Lauren."[16] In 1987–1988, Stanley bribed a loan officer at a New Jersey thrift, that would eventually fail, in exchange for a $1.8 million loan, on which he later defaulted. Both Stanley and the loan officer were ultimately convicted in connection with the case.[17]

Westwood's primary business was in marine insurance, specifically, what is known as "hull insurance," in which policies are written to cover damage to cargo ships. One of the policies that the company issued was to Woodland Shipping Ltd., a firm that was in the business of shipping cargo between the United States and South America. The policy, issued in February 1995, provided coverage for any damages incurred by the *MV Woodlands*, the company's only cargo vessel, during its voyages to and from South America. On December 17, 1995, the ship ran aground in a storm just outside the Port of Houston. At the time, no serious damage was detected; but, later in the voyage, the ship began to take on water, indicating the need for extensive repairs. When the ship was eventually put into drydock in Tampa, Florida, adjusters determined that the accident had caused some $518,000 in damages.

After Westwood failed to cover the bill for the damages, the shipping company filed a civil racketeering suit against the insurer in federal court in New Jersey. In the suit, lawyers for the shipping company claimed that Westwood was financially incapable of paying their claim because Guidry and Stanley had looted the company by transferring several hundred thousand dollars out of the company's accounts and into accounts controlled by Stanley's wife. The suit further alleged that Westwood had repeatedly misrepresented its financial status to brokers and at one time suggested to a broker that he tell a client that the reason why his claim payment was delayed was because a hurricane in Antigua had destroyed the bank where Westwood kept its accounts, making it impossible for the company to access its funds.[18] The shipping company eventually won a judgement of several million dollars in the case, but their chances of ever seeing any of the money were slim.

Their insurance clients were not the only ones conned by Guidry and Stanley. In 1995, in order to impress brokers to whom they wanted to sell their policies, Guidry and Stanley invited a number of them to their new headquarters: a grand mansion in northern New Jersey, originally built by a railroad tycoon at the turn of the century, replete with busts of Roman Emperors and suits of armor. The mansion was owned by the Sisters of St. John the Baptist, an order of Catholic nuns, who had leased the estate to Westwood with the understanding that the insurance company would later purchase the property, and with the stipulation that its original character would be maintained.[19] In the end the Sisters were stiffed by Guidry and Stanley, who not only failed to make their lease payments, but also reneged on their promise to purchase the property. Worse still, the state of New Jersey later ruled that the mansion was no longer being used for religious purposes, pulled the property's tax-exempt status, and slapped the nuns with a tax bill of more than $100,000.[20]

In the summer of 1996, a business periodical published a report revealing the source of the notes that were used to capitalize Westwood, and by the fall the company was hit with several lawsuits over its failure to pay claims for the damaged cargo ship.[21] By the end of the year, Guidry had closed the company's offices and returned to his native Louisiana. But by then the damage had been done to Legend's investors, who were holding notes backed by surety bonds from the company and were anxiously awaiting payment.

Another guarantor of Legend promissory notes was Antigua-based Tangent Insurance Co. Like Westwood, Tangent's principals had established pedigrees in the world of international financial fraud.

Tangent was originally incorporated in Antigua in 1992, under the name,

World Wide Insurance. The name was changed to Tangent in 1995 when the company was placed under the management of Sussex Insurance Group of London and Barbados. The London office of Sussex was run by one Charles Gordon-Seymour, the same Charles Gordon-Seymour who had been the president of Victoria Insurance Co. in the late 1980s (see Chapter 1).

Since parting company with Alan Teale, Mr. Gordon-Seymour had been busy. Among other things, he was the director of an English company, Intervest Capital Plc., that ran a promotional scheme in which customers buying products from certain companies were given "checks" that were redeemable in five years for all or part of the value of the products they had purchased if they were unsatisfied with the products. Among the 300 companies that took part in the promotion were Apple Computers in Ireland and Honda's motorcycle division in the Netherlands. The scheme worked on the premise that only a small proportion of those holding the checks would be able to complete the complex procedures involved in filing a refund claim. For example, to be eligible for the refund, purchasers had to register within fourteen days of the sale and then apply for their cash back within a thirty-day period, five years later. The scheme came to an end after Intervest was shut down by British authorities after they determined that the company was financially incapable of paying claims.[22]

Other members of the Tangent team also had tainted résumés. Day-to-day management of the insurer was handled out of Sussex's Barbados office by Eamon Baird. Baird had been sued in 1994 by the Department of Labor for his involvement with a bogus California-based labor union that was fraudulently marketing a phony health insurance plan.[23] Tangent's U.S. claims representative was Francis O. Clarkson, a former North Carolina lawyer who had been disbarred in 1984 and sentenced to jail for embezzling clients' funds.[24] Tangent's auditor was Merle S. Finkel, who, not coincidentally, also audited the books of Intervest, Ltd., the American parent company of Intervest Capital. Finkel pleaded guilty to securities and bank fraud charges in a Nevada court in March 1997.[25]

None of these facts, of course, was disclosed to prospective buyers of Legend's notes. Instead, what they saw was an official-looking set of documents that stated that, in the event of a default by Legend Sports, Tangent would pay off the balance owed to the investors within sixty days.

Most of Legend's victims lived in Florida, but others were as far away as Maine. One of these was Anita Richardson, an eighty-two-year-old woman from Winthrop, Maine, who was persuaded by a man she met at her church to invest $110,000 in a Legend's promissory note. That man, Steven England, was a financial adviser and representative of the Hanover Financial Group operating out of Florida. State regulators would later contend that England sold more than $600,000 Legend notes to Maine investors, earning nearly $180,000 in commissions. A year later, Ms. Richardson's health began to fail; she learned that the notes were no good and that the insurance company that issued the surety bonds refused to pay. Soon thereafter, she died with her investment still not recovered.[26]

Another Maine victim was Herman Gatchell who, in July 1996, purchased a promissory note issued by Legend Sports in the amount of $100,000 from another one of Hanover's sales representatives, Lawrence Gowell. A former pitcher for the New York Yankees, Gowell persuaded Gatchell to move money out of an individual retirement account (IRA) to purchase the note and received a 6 percent commission (approximately $6,000) from the transaction. By July 1998, Gatchell had received neither the promised 12 percent interest from Legend Sports nor repayment of the loan from Tangent Insurance, and he filed a lawsuit in federal court in Maine.[27] Gatchell was awarded the amount of his principal, interest, and civil penalties by the court, but given that Legend Sports was in receivership and James Staples was on his way to jail the likelihood that he would ever see the money was slim.

## Goodfellas Meets Boiler Room

According to Florida regulators, part of Legend's master plan was to "erase some $15 million in debt" from the sale of promissory notes by convincing investors to exchange their notes for stock in Legend Sports, then manipulating the value of that stock.[28] The details of the stock manipulation scheme came to public light in 1999 when the federal law enforcement officials made a sweep of stock brokers who were illegally trading micro-cap stocks.

In the early morning hours of June 17, 1999, federal law enforcement officials arrested more than sixty stock brokers in New York, New Jersey, and Florida. Eventually eighty-five individuals were indicted in one of the biggest security fraud sweeps ever. Among those indicted were twenty-five individuals who worked for, or were associated with, five brokerage firms in New York, New Jersey, Maryland, and Vancouver, British Columbia, and who were charged in what is called a "pump and dump" scheme, in which they falsely inflated the value of several micro-cap stocks, including Legend's. In "pump and dump" scams, stockbrokers, or people claiming to be stockbrokers, contact potential investors urging them to buy a particular stock, often claiming to have some inside information, but without disclosing that their firm has large holdings in the stock. The goal is to inflate the value of the stock by creating a frenzy of buying, then, when the stock's price peaks, the operators sell their shares, reaping big profits, while unwitting investors lose big. This case was just one part of an SEC crackdown on micro-cap stock frauds across the country. One of the more interesting aspects of the case was that it involved not just the usual cast of white-collar brokers and traders, but also members of traditional organized crime groups and Russian mobsters.

At the center of the cases was the owner of a defunct brokerage firm, David Houge. According to federal prosecutors, in late 1996, Houge and his associates gained control of large blocks of Legend Sports stock that were listed on the Over-the-Counter Bulletin Board.[29] The "pump" part of the scheme was carried out by individuals at several brokerage firms who received cash payoffs from Houge. Those individuals, many of whom were not actually licensed brokers, made cold calls to prospective buyers and pitched the stock, reading from prepared scripts that contained misleading and simply false information about the company. When the price hit an inflated high, the "dump" part of the scheme kicked in; the shares owned by Houge and his confederates were sold through offshore accounts.[30] In total, prosecutors estimated that Houge and his associates defrauded unsuspecting Legend's stock investors of over $5 million.

Among the "cold callers" were several members of the Colombo mob organization and members of the Bor Russian crime family, who worked out of brokerage houses in New York.[31] According to federal prosecutors, Houge had been caught on tape telling confidential informants that he was committing stock fraud with organized crime families in New York, in which he provided "the brains" and they provided "the brawn."[32] When the defendants were hauled into a Brooklyn courthouse shortly after their arrest, the scene was like something out of the television show *The Sopranos*. One observer described it as "a bunch of young guys in muscle suits with very well put-together girlfriends."[33]

The Houge/Legend Sports case was one of a series of securities fraud schemes discovered by authorities that involved traditional organized crime groups. Having been forced out of their traditional economic strongholds, such as the construction industry and garbage hauling, by unrelenting pressure from law enforcement agencies, by the mid-1990s several organized crime groups had moved into financial industries. In March 2000, Brooklyn prosecutors charged nineteen organized crime members, including the brother-in-law of the notorious Sammy "the Bull" Gravano, with participating in a "pump and dump" scheme that defrauded investors out of $40 million and that was remarkably similar to the Houge scam. The combination of wiseguys and telemarketing hustlers led New York City Police Chief Howard Safir to dub the case "*Goodfellas* meets *Boiler Room*," a reference to two popular movies.[34]

## Oil and Lasers

Many of the promissory note scam operators claimed to have access to, or have found applications for, new technologies that would lead to instant riches. To many investors these claims were highly persuasive. At the time, the news media were full of stories about entrepreneurs who had made fortunes from the Internet or from advances in biotechnology. Promissory-note salespeople took advantage of the common response that many have to such stories, which is to think, *If only I had gotten in early on that, I'd be rich by now.*

But the people behind the companies being promoted were neither scientists nor computer experts, but, rather, old-fashioned con artists and the new technologies they were hawking either did not exist or were simply old ideas repackaged. One of these con artists was Peter J. Buffo, a real estate appraiser with a history in financial fraud that spanned three decades. Buffo operated a pair of Utah-based companies that would sell a total of $32 million in promissory notes, mostly to elderly retirees. To appreciate the evolution of these schemes requires a closer look at Mr. Buffo's résumé.

In 1979, Buffo was convicted in Alabama for his part in a scheme to deceive insurance regulators to permit an insolvent insurance company to stay in business. In that scheme, Buffo had appraised California property owned by the company at $4,000 an acre when the true value was closer to $55 an acre.[35] Buffo was ultimately sentenced to three years in state prison for his participation in that scheme.

While fighting his conviction in the appellate courts, Buffo did not let his swindling skills go to waste. In 1983 he obtained a loan from a Texas thrift, Irving Savings Association, for $3.5 million, allegedly to develop property in Washington state in partnership with a former president of Irving.[36] The pair later defaulted on the loan and Irving collapsed amidst allegations of insider dealing.[37]

In the late 1980s, Buffo resurfaced in connection with a Utah insurance company that would become the subject of a congressional inquiry into the use of fraudulent Ginnie Maes (see Chapter 1). According to its president, Buffo and another convicted felon provided the capital to start Commercial Surety & Insurance Corporation. After Buffo and his associate pulled their money out of the company, the president obtained replacement capital from two Beverly Hills lawyers in the form of phony Ginnie Maes.[38]

In 1995, Buffo and two associates were indicted on federal charges in Utah alleging that they organized scams involving surety bonds issued to government contractors. The schemes worked in the following way. Buffo and his associates would contact contractors doing construction work for federal agencies and other construction projects and offer to provide them with corporate surety bonds that guaranteed the completion of the project in the event that the contractors were unable to do so. This is perfectly legal, but only if the issuer of the bond actually possesses the assets required to indemnify the project. According to federal prosecutors, Buffo and his associates manufactured assets for their surety bond companies by forging signatures on deeds showing that ownership of parcels of property were transferred to those companies, inflating the value of those properties with phony appraisals, and then pledging those assets as collateral in the surety bonds they sold. Using these techniques, their surety bond companies showed assets of $279 million, which enabled Buffo et al. to pledge nearly $7 million in surety bonds. In a one-year period, these transactions netted Buffo and his colleagues at least $425,000 in profits.[39]

Once again demonstrating that he was not the type to let a few legal problems slow him down, soon after his indictment Buffo embarked on another scheme. He teamed up with fellow Utahans Wayne Notwell and Clealon Mann to set up a scheme to sell promissory notes via two companies controlled by Notwell: Capital Acquisitions and Laser Leasing. Capital Acquisitions was a Utah-based subsidiary of a Bahamian company that claimed to own more than 225 oil and gas wells in Kansas and California. Mann organized a sales force that offered investors promissory notes issued by Capital that would return 20 percent annually over a three-year period. Prospective investors were also told that the interest was 100 percent tax deductible because of certain tax advantages for coal and gas production. Laser Leasing claimed to have a plan for renting to clinics laser machines used in the treatment of eye disease. Investors were promised a 20 percent annual return on funds they were told would go to purchase the machines[40]

Both the Capital Acquisitions and the Laser Leasing notes were guaranteed by surety bonds issued by an offshore insurance company, New England International Surety (NEIS).[41] Unlike many of the offshore insurers examined here that pop up as part of a fraudulent scheme, operate for a year or two, and then are abandoned when the scheme has run its course, NEIS had remarkable longevity, particularly in light of the legal difficulties it encountered.

In 1986, NEIS received a charter in Panama with its president listed as a Canadian named Hendrik Reinstra. The company began operating out of offices in Brussels, Belgium. About the same time, NEIS opened a subsidiary, New England International Surety of America, and obtained an insurance license in Louisiana. (The Louisiana insurance commissioner at the time was Sherman Bernard who was later convicted on charges of extorting money from insurers in exchange for licenses.[42]) The primary business of the company was providing insurance to risk purchasing groups consisting of liquor dealers, asbestos removal contractors, and diet centers.

In 1988, NEIS was listed as part of Alan Teale's International Underwriters Association. The company provided insurance for several risk purchasing groups managed by Teale's wife, Charlotte Rentz.[43]

In April 1989, NEIS of America was shut down by the Louisiana insurance commission. After disallowing $6.7 million of the company's assets, including a $5 million certificate of deposit from a Panamanian bank, regulators declared the company to be insolvent by $1.8 million.[44] The day after the state's action, $1.1 million was wired from the company's offices in New Orleans to a Swiss bank account controlled by a subsidiary of NEIS.[45] Later that year, Reinstra dumped the company's records on the Louisiana Insurance Commission, along with a letter that stated, "[W]e have decided to turn the Louisiana company's business over to you."[46]

NEIS kept a low profile until the mid-1990s, when its name started to appear in connection with a number of promissory note scams. The companies that issued the notes were remarkably diverse, including a chain of drive-in espresso shops, an airline that was purportedly in the process of establishing a route between Los Angeles and New York, a company that produced children's television programs, an Italian resort, and Buffo's Capital Acquisitions and Laser Leasing.

The individuals who bought NEIS-backed notes were not, of course, told many things. In the Capital Acquisitions case, they were not told that 46 percent of the money they invested went to sales agents in commissions and that 20 percent went to NEIS to pay for the surety bonds. In other words, very little of the money they invested actually went into the ventures they thought they were funding. They were also unaware that the notes were not tax deductible and that NEIS would refuse to make good on the surety bonds.

Federal prosecutors would later claim that both offerings were simply Ponzi schemes. There was no way that the oil wells could produce the kind of output that would provide 20 percent annual interest to investors. Laser Leasing purchased only one laser machine and rented it for a limited amount of time. Any payments made to investors were not the result of profits from the ventures but were taken from the funds obtained from other investors. Both schemes were set up with the intent of defrauding the more than 1,000 investors who put a total of $32 million into them.

In the end, Buffo was sentenced to prison for five years, a term to be served concurrently with the prison sentence he received in the earlier surety bond case. NEIS ultimately agreed to pay investors $28 million over a four-year period. However, as of March 2001, it was unclear how much of this investors would actually see. By that time, NEIS was the subject of regulatory actions in at least half-a-dozen states and class action suits by investors in Florida and Ohio.

The Capital Acquisition scam represents the global nature of insurance fraud. Here we have a Canadian citizen operating an insurance company chartered in Panama from offices in Brussels, that was selling surety bonds in Utah through a company owned by a Bahamian corporation that guarantees payment on promissory notes issued by companies operating in Texas, Oklahoma, and Kansas.

## A Recidivist Securities Violator

One of the companies whose promissory notes were backed with NEIS bonds was Ameritech Petroleum. NEIS was one of several offshore insurance companies that issued bonds for Ameritech's note offering. In 1999, Ameritech was run by a forty-one-year-old Texas oilman named Brent A. Wagman, who controlled a half-dozen interlinked companies out of offices in the Dallas area. Wagman and his associates offered promissory notes issued by Ameritech and a related company, Redbank Petroleum, which were sold by investment brokers across the country. Between 1996 and 1999 they sold $30 million of the promissory notes, mostly to retirees.

The Ameritech notes were first put on the market in 1996. The company's operators claimed to be able to extract oil and gas from barren wells through the application of a new technology for producing subsurface maps of geological formations, developed by a related Wagman-controlled company. Investors were told that they would receive a 10 to 12 percent return on the nine-month promissory notes issued by the company. They were also told that no part of their investments would go to pay for fees and commissions. And, as in the other promissory notes scams, the notes were "fully guaranteed" by surety bonds written by what appeared to be a legitimate insurance company.

Of course, much of what investors were told was false. Sales agents received 9.5 percent commissions, none of the funds would be invested in the oil and gas projects, much of the money collected from investors would be siphoned off for the use of Wagman and the other principals, and the surety bonds backing the notes were worthless pieces of paper issued by bogus offshore insurance companies.

In 1998, Ameritech was hit with a cease and desist order by the state of Maryland, which ordered Wagman to repay investors in the state $2 million. In order to make those payments, Wagman and his confederates began selling promissory notes from another of his companies, Redbank Petroleum. The terms and conditions were the same as the Ameritech offering.

One of the people who invested in Redbank Petroleum was Frank Mc-Nerlin, a sixty-eight-year-old retired businessman from upstate New York. McNerlin was persuaded by an insurance agent, whom he trusted because he had helped him earlier with his retirement accounts, to buy $103,000 worth of Redbank promissory notes.[47] McNerlin was one of fifty-seven people to whom the insurance agent sold a total of $3.4 million in notes, for which he received $300,000 in commissions.[48] He later told the media, "You never expect this to happen to anyone, especially when you have dealt with the person before and he gives you a promissory note that says you can't lose anything. You . . . really feel embarrassed. Who wants to say that you lost $300,000 at the click of a finger?"[49]

The agent who sold Mr. McNerlin the promissory notes later told attorneys with the state Attorney General's Office that he, too, was a victim, having invested his own money in the Redbank notes. The insurance agent and securities broker explained that, despite his experience in selling securities, he was not suspicious about the unusually high (11 percent) yield being paid by the notes:

Q: Didn't the fact that a stranger called you and offered you an opportunity to invest in a company that was paying a higher interest rate than you were able to get anywhere else at that time, make you suspicious?

A: Well, it didn't necessarily make me suspicious. I get calls from brokers all the time.

Later in his testimony the broker went on to say:

A: The only reason I invested my money, the reason I recommended many of my clients to invest their money is, because the bonding company was protecting them.

Q: Did anyone, either Mr. Ontiveros or this Mr. Barria [the head of Threshold Insurance, the bonding company], whoever you spoke to at Threshold; did they discuss with you the risk of this venture?

A: They said it was a very low risk.

Q: Why?

A: Because of the fact that the insurance company was bonding them and the insurance company held securities from Red Bank Petroleum. In case Red Bank defaulted in the payment, the insurance company had securities from them.

Q: As a registered securities broker, you said, you took certain examinations and you have to have a certain familiarity with the insurance business. Had it ever been brought to your attention that when an investment carries a greater interest than is normal at the time, that generally reflects that there is a higher risk of that investment?

A: Yes, again the bonding company was protecting them. That's what I went by.[50]

In June 1999, after receiving numerous complaints from investors who received no payments on their notes, the SEC obtained a restraining order against Redbank and Ameritech that halted the sale of their notes. Referring to Wagman as a "recidivist securities violator," the Commission claimed that he was defrauding investors, using their money to fund his lavish lifestyle and to set up other stock frauds.[51]

In its complaint, the SEC charged that investors' money went to fund many things other than development of the oil and gas production. Wagman's wife was paid an annual salary of $84,000 for a job that required her to do no work. Warren Donohue, an officer in several of the companies and a longtime friend of Wagman, received a $500,000 loan with no demand for repayment. Another officer received, for no apparent reason, 100,000 shares in a Wagman-controlled company.[52]

The SEC also contended that much of the investors' money was used to commit stock fraud involving another Wagman company, Lyric International. Lyric, whose offices were next to Ameritech's and Redbank's in Texas, was also purportedly in the oil and gas business. In its stock offering, Lyric claimed to have acquired fifty-six oil and gas wells in Texas that produced during one month in 1998 4,800 barrels of oil. In fact, the SEC claimed, in their best month the wells produced only 1,400 barrels. Using this and other false claims, Wagman and associates were able to inflate the value of Lyric's stock. When it reached a peak, Wagman sold a substantial amount of stock in the company and profited $389,657.

The court order that the SEC obtained against Ameritech/Redbank also froze Wagman's personal assets and required that he turn over his passport to prevent him from leaving the country. Among those assets were his-and-hers Chevrolet Suburbans, an emerald collection valued at $900,000, houses in the Florida Keys and Texas, and a 27.5-foot Proline Sportsman boat that he kept in Florida.[53]

Three weeks after the order was handed down, Wagman violated the order by selling his Florida house and boat. A week later he and his wife fled the United States for Panama.[54]

Choosing Panama as their new home was not a random decision by the Wagmans. Brent Wagman had extensive ties there, particularly to an exiled financial guru, Marc Harris. Harris was part of a shady world of entrepreneurs who, for a price, helped people set up offshore tax havens and other enterprises that operate outside of the normal regulatory process. A former whiz kid who earned a Columbia MBA at age twenty, Harris worked as a CPA in Florida until state regulators put special limitations on his practice for violating auditing standards. Even before the final suspension order, Harris had renounced his U.S. citizenship and moved to Panama, declaring that he was disgusted by IRS "abuses" and "persecution."[55] In the late 1980s, Harris set up two banks in Montserrat, a British dependency located in the Caribbean, which were later shut down by British authorities.[56] In 1998, Harris filed a libel suit against David Marchant, a Miami journalist, who had published an article in which he claimed that, among other things, the Harris Organization was "one of the biggest offshore scams of all times," was "hopelessly insolvent" by $25 million, and that "the group may be laundering the proceeds of crime, including drug trafficking."[57] The judge hearing the case ruled against Harris, concluding that "Marchant had evidence which provided persuasive support for each of the allegations at issue."[58]

While Harris's headquarters were physically located in Panama City, most of his services were marketed on several Web sites, which advertised "One-Stop Shopping for All your Offshore Financial Needs," "How to Legally Obtain a Second Passport," and "How to Protect Your Ass and Assets."

Many of the notes issued by Ameritech and Redbank were guaranteed by bonds written by Threshold Insurance Services. Threshold was a "paper" international business corporation that was formed by the Harris Organization. The company was operated from Harris Organization offices in Panama and the titular president of the company was a Harris employee, Ilka Barria.[59]

Threshold also wrote surety bonds for another promissory note offering, Lifeblood Biomedical Inc., a Florida-based company that claimed to be a biotech firm whose main focus was on developing a procedure for storing and regenerating "cord blood" (blood from umbilical cords) that might have medical applications. Like other promissory note scams, Lifeblood sold its notes through insurance agents and offered investors a 12 percent "guaranteed" return.[60] Florida regulators halted sales of the notes in November 1999, after the company stopped making payments to investors and Threshold refused to cover the bonds. By that time, the company had already taken in $8 million from over 180 investors.[61]

Having fled to Panama, Brent Wagman and his wife did not lead the lives of typical gangsters on the lam, wearing disguises and furtively glancing over their shoulders at all times. Instead, they moved in high-society circles. They enrolled their two children at an exclusive school in Panama City and attended the annual Who's New formal Christmas dinner along with diplomats. Mrs. Wagman cochaired the American Society's Easter egg hunt held at the residence of the U.S. ambassador to Panama.[62] Meanwhile, Brent Wagman set up offices in the same complex as the Harris Organization.

The Wagman's good life in Panama came to an end on March 10, 2000, when FBI agents used a clever ruse to arrest Mr. Wagman. Just as he was arranging to leave Panama, Wagman received a phone call from a U.S. embassy official inviting him to lunch at a five-star hotel. Wagman couldn't resist the offer and rode to the hotel in a car registered to Marc Harris and driven by one of Harris's chauffeurs. When Wagman arrived he was quickly grabbed by Panamanian police who took him to the airport where he was turned over to the FBI and put on a flight to Miami.[63] Just before his apprehension, Wagman was apparently preparing to flee Panama; police discovered several fake passports on him when he was arrested.[64]

Back in Dallas, Wagman and two of his colleagues were indicted on federal charges. Two months later, Wagman pleaded guilty after prosecutors agreed not to prosecute his wife, who told reporters in Panama, "[W]e never stole anything."[65] In the meantime, Wagman was ordered to repay his victims nearly $24 million in an SEC lawsuit.[66]

## The Broader Context

Legend Sports, Capital Acquisitions, and Ameritech were just three of dozens of companies that were used to sell bogus promissory notes. On June 1, 2000, the SEC and state securities regulators announced a crackdown on promissory note scams. The SEC reported that it had taken actions against twenty-one issuers of promissory notes in cases involving a combined total of $300 million in investments.[67] In California, the problem had become so serious that when state securities regulators published their own list of "Top Ten Investment Scams" in the spring of 2000, promissory note frauds were at the top of the list.[68] Between July 1999 and May 2000, the state issued 435 orders against agents who sold the notes in the state.[69]

One of the implications that these promissory note scams hold for our understanding of white-collar crime is that they signal a trend toward the merger of frauds involving different financial industries. As we saw in Chapter 1, in the 1980s Alan Teale and his associates put together sophisticated insurance swindles that also involved securities frauds. However, until recently most white-collar criminals have limited their activities to a single industry. In promissory note scams, offshore insurance companies were but one component in schemes that combined insurance agents and brokerage firms selling securities that were backed by surety bonds written by offshore insurance companies and, in some cases, those bonds were supposedly backed by reinsurance contracts. White-collar criminals like Peter Buffo with backgrounds in surety bond scams have seen the value in collaborating with people with experience in securities fraud and offshore insurance companies, to perpetrate schemes that confound regulators long enough to take in millions of dollars.

This trend in financial crimes mirrors changes that are taking place in the financial industries themselves. When Congress passed the Gramm-Leach-Biley Act in 1999, which repealed important provisions of the Glass-Steagall Act, members of financial industries gained the ability to "cross-market," for example, for banks to sell insurance and securities. As one California investigator put it:

> These industries want the ability to cross-market, and the risk to investors is that the people selling the product don't understand it and don't want to know anything other than he is getting a commission. . . . Where we're going is to one-stop shopping. The guy in the mall may have an insurance license, he might have a securities license, he might have none of them. He's a guy in a mall wearing three hats.[70]

The "godfather of cross-marketing" may have been Charles Keating, who was ultimately convicted on federal charges for selling junk bonds (securities) in the lobby of his Lincoln Savings and Loan, mostly to retirees who were misled into believing that the bonds they bought were federally insured the way their deposits at the thrift were.

One of the keys to the success of the promissory note scams was the existence of relatively unsophisticated investors who were willing to believe in the possibility of high-yield, low-risk investments, despite the economic axiom that high yields are always accompanied by high risks. In another era, potential investors, particularly older retirees on fixed incomes, might have been more skeptical and the schemes would not have worked. The 1990s has been described as an era of "irrational exuberance" over the equities markets, in which stock prices rose higher and higher not on the intrinsic value of the companies whose stock was being traded but on the belief by investors in the infinite capacity of stocks to increase in value.[71] Economist Robert Shiller has argued that this climate of irrational exuberance was caused by a number of factors, including the emergence of the Internet, the growth of mutual funds, the decline of inflation, the popularity of day trading, and the rise in gambling opportunities. One of the consequences of the growth in casino gambling or in lotteries has been to create "an inflated estimate of one's own ultimate potential for good luck, a heightened interest in how one performs compared with others, and a new way to stimulate oneself out of a feeling of boredom or monotony."[72] The same could likely be said about many ordinary people who trade in stocks.

The 1920s was another era of irrational exuberance. It was an era in which, for example, Charlie Mitchell, the president of National City Bank, the predecessor to Citibank, was able to convince many average Americans to buy bonds supposedly issued by South American governments. In much the same way as contemporary promissory note scam artists have operated, Mitchell recruited an aggressive sales force of young men who scoured the country in search of investors who were willing to sink their savings into his eclectic variety of bonds, most of which would end up in default. Mitchell's exploits were described in great detail before an outraged congressional committee in 1933. Mitchell himself testified about the billions of dollars in bonds from a Brazilian state, the Republic of Peru, and elsewhere, whose value he and his colleagues essentially manufactured.[73] Congress responded by enacting the Glass-Steagall Act, which attempted to prevent these kinds of abuses by prohibiting banks from selling securities.[74] By the end of the century, it would appear that Congress had forgotten these earlier lessons and was attempting to reverse history by enacting legislation that would return us to the roaring twenties and an environment in which ordinary Americans are once again extremely vulnerable to sophisticated con artists.

# 4

# Fantasy Islands

Though he probably did not realize it at the time, back in the mid-1970s when Herbert Williams, a.k.a. Little Bird on the Shoulder, created the Sovereign Cherokee Nation Tejas out of a sandbar in the middle of the Rio Grande, he was ahead of his time in the evolution of white-collar crime. Not only did his newly formed country issue bonds and passports (with a seal that proclaimed the country had been "Created by an Act of God") but he also envisioned the Sovereign Cherokee Nation Tejas as an "offshore tax haven" for "insurance companies, banks and other businesses."[1] With this strategy, Williams and his successors had taken offshore scams to the next logical step. Rather than being dependent upon foreign countries to issue them licenses for their phony insurance companies, banks, and investment firms, why not create their own country and issue these licenses themselves? Moreover, once the country has been created, why not sell the licenses to others? In this chapter we will see that this is exactly what a number of imaginative cyber criminals have done.

The idea of creating one's own country is not altogether new. In 1873, an American named Albert B. Steinberger arrived in Samoa claiming that he was a "special agent" for the United States and immediately set about establishing himself as the country's leader. Within two years he had himself appointed as premier and chief judge, had written a constitution for the country, had established an arrangement in which he received a commission on all taxes collected, and had used government funds to purchase a yacht for his personal use. Steinberger's rule in paradise was cut short when British sailors, acting on a request from the Samoans, seized and deported him.[2] Today, the Internet has made it much easier to "discover" a new country. Essentially, it allows one to create countries that exist solely in cyberspace, thus freeing one from the cumbersome and time-consuming task of finding an actual piece of land to claim as one's own. Though, as we shall see, in addition to their presence in cyberspace, many modern-day Steinbergers prefer to lay claim to some physical space, defined either by a land mass or by a man-made structure.

## The Dominion of Melchizedek

The pioneers of many of the techniques for creating a cyber-based country were the founders of the Dominion of Melchizedek, a self-proclaimed "ecclesiastical and constitutional sovereignty." When Melchizedek was created in 1990, its founders claimed that the country was located on an island—actually, a pair of rocks that jut out of the ocean—called Malpelo Island that lies 400 miles off the coast of Columbia (which is claimed as a possession of Columbia and is underwater most of the year). They also asserted jurisdiction over a 14,000,000-square-mile section of Antarctica. The country's "leaders" would later maintain that the Dominion also covered several small pieces of land in the South Pacific including: Clipperton Island, a barrier reef, which France claims as a dependency; Taongi Islands, an atoll, which is claimed by the Marshall Islands; and Karitane, a shoal, purportedly located in the South Pacific, that even Melchizedek officials admit may not exist.

Whatever the political and geographical status of these land areas, the real heart of Melchizedek is on its Web site, www.melchizedek.com. Over the years the site has developed into an intricate series of political and religious statements that make up the Melchizedek ideology, and that presents the various business opportunities offered by the country. On the Web site one can find information about: Dominion University, where one can become a "Doctor of Law" or a "Doctor of Philosophy"; the Dominion of Melchizedek World Wide Stock Exchange; the Melchizedek bible; the Dominion Bar Association; how to become a citizen of Melchizedek; how to obtain a passport and drivers license issued by the country; and how to form a corporation under the laws of Melchizedek.

At first glance, all of this might seem like an elaborate joke or the fantasy games of people with too much time on their hands. However, as we shall see, these fantasies have had very real consequences in the noncyber world, illustrating what W. I. Thomas called "the definition of the situation." This concept is summed up in Thomas's well-known maxim, "If men define situations as real, they are real in their consequences." What Thomas meant was that, even though certain phenomena might not be "real" in any objective sense, if people believe them to be real, believe them to exist, and act on that belief, then the consequences of those acts can be very real. In the case of the Dominion of Melchizedek, the fact that its existence as a legitimate country has always been in dispute has not prevented its self-proclaimed representatives from using its purported existence to engage not only in a wide variety of criminal activities, but political activities as well, and these activities have had very real consequences for others. For this reason, Melchizedek, and other new cyber nations, are phenomena to be treated seriously.

### Jeff Reynolds, Zillionaire

One of the offshore companies selling cut-rate auto insurance policies in California in the early 1990s was California Pacific Bankers & Insurance Ltd., a firm started in 1990 by a twenty-eight-year-old entrepreneur from Texas, named Jeffrey Reynolds, who also claimed to be the secretary of commerce of the Dominion of Melchizedek. The company was offering policies at rates far below those offered by legitimate, licensed insurers. For example, for minimum liability coverage for a thirty-year-old driver with one accident and one speeding ticket, California Pacific was charging $463 a year. The same policy from a large, state-licensed company would have cost between $1,000 and $2,500.[3]

In the spring of 1993, California Pacific was shut down by California regulators who were concerned about a number of aspects of the company's operation.[4] One of these was the fact that the country that originally granted California Pacific a license, the Dominion of Melchizedek, was not recognized as a country by the U.S. State Department, and that "the country of Columbia is the true and recognized owner of the island that Melchizedek purports to occupy."[5]

In 1992, Reynolds changed California Pacific's home base to the Caribbean island of Aruba. However, California regulators discovered that the company was only registered with the Chamber of Commerce in Aruba and had not been issued a license there. Then, there was the matter of California Pacific's assets. The company's financial statements showed $450 million in assets, but California regulators concluded that the insurer "has failed to prove that it has a single dollar to its name, much less its claimed $450 million in assets."[6] The company's financial statement was audited by a Washington, D.C., firm whose headquarters were listed as "Sir Francis Drake Financial Center, Malpelo Island, Dominion of Melchizedek, Mid-Pacific."[7] The Washington address of the accounting firm was the same as the one listed for the Dominion of Melchizedek's U.S. "embassy," which turned out to be a mail drop.

The idea of using a fictitious country to charter and finance an insurance company may not have originated with Mr. Reynolds himself. One of his employees was none other than Dallas Bessant, a.k.a. Chief Wise Otter. California Pacific's marketing representative in London was another Teale associate, Matthew Bonar, the former president of World Re (Chapter 1).[8] Bessant would later tell a court in Philadelphia that he knew the company was bogus from the start and told Bonar that California Pacific was a "bullshit company."[9]

In 1996, Reynolds was charged in federal court in Dallas with having filed false financial statements and defrauding individuals to whom he had sold surety bonds.[10] In pretrial hearings, Reynolds argued that the court had no authority to determine the authenticity of Melchizedek and pointed out that the country had been officially recognized by the Central African Republic and had its own bible.[11] The judge didn't buy it. Reynolds was convicted and sentenced to fifty-four months in prison.[12]

Jeffrey Reynolds was not a major player in the world of offshore insurance scams, but his innovative use of bogus assets from a fictitious country put him at the forefront of an emerging form of white-collar crime. Reynolds learned his craft at the feet of a master, his father, George Reynolds a former insurance salesman and petroleum geologist. In the early 1980s the elder Reynolds defrauded investors who had placed money with him to drill for natural gas in northeastern Oklahoma. A few years later, accompanied by his young son, Jeffrey, who had recently dropped out of college, George Reynolds gained control of two companies in the Pacific Northwest and began issuing press releases announcing that the companies were developing mines that contained significant mineral deposits. The announcements caused the value of the companies' stock to soar, and the Reynolds profited immensely when they sold off their shares. They were among the few to profit, however, as the minerals never materialized and the companies' shares ceased trading in 1988.[13]

Jeffrey Reynolds's fifteen minutes of fame would come in 1990 when he announced his intentions to invest $197 million in Bond Corporation Holdings, a $7 billion conglomerate run by the well-known Australian entrepreneur, Alan Bond, who was facing serious financial problems.[14] Reynolds became the subject of intense media attention when he made his announcement in January 1990. Reporters wanted to know who the mysterious Texan was and where he got his money. Reynolds claimed to be the president of a firm called Weatherby Investments, which was based in Beverly Hills, and owned by a parent company called California Pacific International of Singapore. He also claimed to have done business with the royal family of Saudia Arabia and the Sultan of Brunei.[15]

For a week after the announcement, Reynolds was the biggest story in Australia. He was interviewed on radio and television programs and the Australian press compared him to J. R. Ewing, a character on the TV show *Dallas*.[16] Bond's representatives backed out of the deal after they learned that the supposedly wealthy Reynolds lived with his mother in Houston and that the address for Weatherby Investments was simply a rented mailbox in Beverly Hills. Bond may have also been concerned about the fact that California Pacific International "was capitalized for a grand total of $1.05 and its managing director was a former physician whose license had been suspended."[17]

One of California Pacific's victims was the hapless Orange County, California, which just couldn't seem to win in its ill-fated attempt to build a new firehouse (see Chapter 2). After First Assurance, which had taken over the job after Winston-Hill declared bankruptcy, was sued by several contractors on the project for nonpayment, the firm purchased a $73,000 surety bond from California Pacific to guarantee completion of a portion of the project. Soon thereafter, First Assurance declared bankruptcy and both First Assurance and California Pacific were banned from doing business in the state.[18] A little more than a year later, as if infected by an insolvency virus, the county itself declared bankruptcy after sustaining heavy losses in the complex and risky derivatives market.[19]

### President Hooten

Jeffrey Reynolds was not the only Texan to start an insurance company with the backing of the Dominion of Melchizedek. Another was a colorful former used-car dealer named Leon Excalibur Hooten III. Recall from Chapter 2 that, in 1994, International Casualty and Surety, the New Zealand–based successor to First Assurance, declared as assets on its financial statements $2 million in stock in Lifeguard Financial Systems Ltd., a subsidiary of Lifeguard Reinsurance, Ltd., whose president was Leon Hooten.

Three of Hooten's companies, including Lifeguard Re, were shut down by Texas insurance regulators in September 1996, after they received complaints that the companies were not paying claims made on performance bonds issued by the companies. When the regulators looked into Hooten's enterprises and his background they encountered a bizarre tangle of phony assets and bogus credentials. Lifeguard Re's financial statement listed as assets $15 million in certificates of deposit issued by Asia Pacific Bank and $20 million in bonds issued by St. Charles University of DeQuincy, Louisiana.[20] The Texas regulators discovered that St. Charles University's president was none other than Hooten himself and that the institution had no assets. They also learned that Hooten claimed to be the former president of the Dominion of Melchizedek, a country that, to their knowledge, did not exist.

Their investigation also turned up the fact that Asia Pacific Bank was chartered by the Dominion of Melchizedek, and was operated out of California by the wife of one of Melchizedek's founders, Pearlasia, a.k.a. Elvira Gamboa. In 1991, the Indiana Department of Corporations granted Asia Pacific Bank permission to do business in that state, apparently not realizing "that anyone using the word 'bank' needed to be licensed by the Indiana Department of Financial Services."[21] Hooten reportedly contacted Indiana officials to check on the status of Asia Pacific and was told it was authorized to do business in the state.[22] Several years later, Pearlasia declared "spiritual war" on a California deputy attorney general after his office sued to have one of her banks shut down. In a letter, she warned, "I will do metaphysical battle with you in your dream state."[23]

Hooten had a long history of trouble with regulators. In 1983, he appeared on *The 700 Club*, a religious TV show, to pitch a prepaid dental plan he ran out of Oklahoma City. He later resigned from the company after Oklahoma regulators raised questions about his "competence, experience and integrity."[24] In the late 1980s, he was the head of Member Services, a telecommunications company, in southern Texas. Hooten resigned in 1990, after the company sued him and his wife, alleging that they had illegally converted company securities to their names.[25] That same year, he told a reporter:

[I]n 1985, I underwent a personal conversion that removed alcohol, false pride and enmity from my life. It is only within the last two years that I've come to understand that my own personal failures were a result of these false doctrines of pride. I am, of course, referring to my conversion after reading and accepting the book of Mormon as gospel.[26]

In the early 1990s, Hooten opened an office in Houston that offered counseling services. In 1995, his license to provide drug abuse counseling was revoked by state authorities who charged that his degrees were from unaccredited universities.[27]

A month after Texas regulators shut his operations down, the forty-three-year-old Hooten died of a heart attack in Scottsdale, Arizona. For some, even his death was questionable. A lawyer for his estranged wife said, " 'My understanding of Leon Hooten's background suggests to me that he is capable of faking his own death."[28]

## Two Versions of History

By the late 1990s, the Dominion of Melchizedek was showing up regularly in the media. An article in the *Wall Street Journal* referred to it as "a nation in cyberspace."[29] A *Washington Post* article described the country as the "ruse that roared."[30] A segment on the television program *60 Minutes* referred to it as a "fantasy island."[31] The media provide one history of the Dominion of Melchizedek. It is a history that generally focuses on the criminal activities and various scams run by its founders and representatives. Another history can be found on Melchizedek's elaborate Web site. The two histories overlap at many points, covering many of the same events, but with very different interpretations of those events.

Both versions of the Dominion of Melchizedek's (DOM) history agree that it was created in 1990 by a bearded, thirty-seven-year-old man named Branch Vinedresser, whose legal name was Mark Logan Pedley. At the time, Pedley had just been paroled from Walla Walla State Prison in Washington. According to the DOM version, Melchizedek was actually the brainchild of Pedley's father, David Pedley, who had died in 1987, and who is described on the Dominion's Web site as "a financial genius able to resurrect public companies from their financial death, find endless loopholes in the legal system, and purchase large corporations without paying any cash up front."[32] According to law enforcement officials, the elder Pedley was a career con man with a long history of involvement in financial frauds. In the early 1970s, he had been sentenced to prison after, according to DOM's version, "receiving four false convictions as a result of various trials from coast to coast."[33]

According to a published account, "Vinedresser was convicted in 1983 in Federal court in San Francisco . . . in connection with a bogus land deal near Sacramento" and was sentenced to three years in prison.[34] In the Melchizedekian version, "with foreknowledge of an imminent indictment, during the summer of 1982, David and Mark moved to Mexico in order to negotiate with the USA as free men. . . . Mark was arrested by Mexican officials for not renewing his visa permit, and deported to the U.S."[35]

In the DOM version of events, "during their sojourn to Mexico . . . David and Mark founded a Saipan 'Class A' Bank that helped Mexicans convert fast devaluating pesos into more than $8,800,000 in U.S. dollars."[36] A *Wall Street Journal* article, published in 1986, reported that a grand jury in Boston had indicted the Pedleys for "using a bank they had established in the Mariana

Islands to defraud holders of Mexican pesos of about $6 million."[37] The article
went on to state that David and Mark Pedley, "formed Merchant Bank without any assets in September 1982," and, "in advertisements in several newspapers including the *Wall Street Journal,* the bank offered to convert Mexican
pesos to certificates of deposit and other instruments issued by the bank . . ."[38]

After serving a prison term that resulted from his conviction in the Boston
case, Mark Pedley was paroled in 1990 and, according to the DOM Web site,
"on the bus ride home from Walla Walla, Washington, to California, Mark
received a revelation, that he was to go by the 'new name,' Branch Vinedresser,
which translates from his Hebrew name, 'Tzemach Korem,' which is a portion
of his full legal and Hebrew name: Tzemach 'Ben' David Netzer Korem."[39]
Soon thereafter, the Dominion of Melchizedek was born. Pedley/Vinedresser/
Korem began chartering a number of companies, including California Pacific,
International Auditors, and scores of banks, including several in the Washington, D.C., area whose addresses were the same as the Dominion of Melchizedek's "embassy," which turned out to be nothing more than a telecommunications device that forwarded calls to Vinedressser in California.

Vinedresser also created the Dominion's own currency, which he called
"Equicurrency," and set about establishing its reputation around the world as
legal tender. For a monthly fee of $855, he had Equicurrency listed in the
financial tables of the widely read, Paris-based newspaper, the *International
Herald Tribune,* with a total value of $10 billion. He also listed "$2 billion
of redeemable convertible debentures supposedly issued by two Panamanian-
chartered institutions . . ."[40] And he also rented a terminal from Bloomberg
Financial Market Systems, the well-known financial database, and had Equicurrency listed there.[41] Thus, with the wave of his financial wand, Vinedresser
had created billions of dollars in assets for his mythical country.

The Dominion of Melchizedek, however, might not have become so successful had it not been for the emergence of the Internet in the early 1990s. On
the Net, Melchizedek found not only a home but also a base from which it
could reach potentially millions of investors and others who wanted to become
part of this "wealthy," new nation. It was on the World Wide Web that the
full political, economic, and legal infrastructure for the Dominion could be
created. It was on its Web site, for example, where people could read the nine
pages of provisions of the Dominion Insurance Act of 1991, which had been
approved by the Dominion's legislative body, the House of Elders. They could
also read about the various ministers who served the country including the
Minister of Education, former television talk-show host, Morton Downey Jr.
(it is not clear if Downey was aware of his exalted position).

The Web site also provided a handy breakdown of the Dominion's "Organizational Structure," which, as of 1999, listed "Mz. Pearlasia" (*sic*) as the President and Tzemach "Ben" David Netzer Korem as Vice President, Head of the House of Elders, and Chief Justice of the Supreme Court. According to the Web site, "during the Spring of 1994 'Ben' David and Pearlasia experienced a cosmic wedding uniting their common interests in magnifying the Dominion for the benefit of Mankind."[42]

The Web site also declares the Dominion of Melchizedek to be an "ecclesiastical sovereignty" based on the principles found in the Melchizedek bible, a document that purports to be a new translation of the Christian bible completed by David and (the former) Mark Pedley. The original scriptures have been reinterpreted so as to define "the heavenly region of the Dominion of Melchizedek," which is "not only to be found in the foregoing identified South Pacific [islands, it] is also found in each of the human earthly body 'temples' of clay which constitute each citizen who answers the call of the Most High God . . ."[43] Doubts about the country's legitimacy based on the fact that it has no clear-cut geographical ties are refuted with analogies to the Vatican City, which "had absolutely no land area over which it had sovereign rights until 11 February 1929 (when independence was achieved from Italy) . . ." and the "State of Israel, which achieved the acquisition of its own land on 14 May 1948."[44]

The Dominion's leaders, thus, see their country as a legitimate political entity, in their words, a "postmodern state."[45] As such it has all the rights of any nation, including the right to sign formal treaties, the right to establish embassies and exchange ambassadors with other countries, the right to issue passports, and even the right to declare war. In 1994, the Dominion announced that it was in a state of war with France after the European country detonated nuclear devices near the island of Karitane in the south Pacific, which Melchizedek claimed as its territory.[46] Despite France's refusal to take the declaration of war seriously, a posting on DOM's Web site later claimed victory: "DOM won the war, since nuclear testing stopped two tests ahead of schedule shortly after the declaration of war was announced . . ."[47]

In March 1998, the president of the newly created Republic of Kosova, a self-proclaimed state that emerged out of the crisis in Kosovo, in an attempt to obtain international recognition and apparently unaware of Melchizedek's outlaw status, announced that the country had been officially recognized by the Dominion of Melchizedek and that "[w]e will soon exchange ambassadors with this country."[48] In response, DOM issued its own press release stating that it had "invited Kosovo to claim its status as an autonomous region of Melchizedek and thereby receive all of the advantages associated therewith . . ."[49]

The most serious involvement of Melchizedek representatives in the affairs of other countries occurred in early 2000 when David Korem entered the island of Rotuma, a remote speck of land inhabited by 3,000 people that is one of the islands that make up Fiji, on a "diplomatic passport," and began working with dissident groups who were seeking to secede from Fiji.[50] Korem, along with DOM "Minister of Environment" Taraivina Rae Costello, reportedly drafted a constitution for Rotuma, which contained the statement, "Rotuma and its sovereign owners may only grant sovereign status within Rotuma to the Dominion of Melchizedek."[51] Korem and Costello were later banned from the island by the ruling Rotuma Council of Chiefs who rejected Korem's efforts to incite a secessionist movement.[52]

### Global Scams

In an address to an international convention in London in 1999, John Shockey, former special assistant to the U.S. Comptroller of Currency, described the Dominion of Melchizedek's illicit activities in the following way:

> Promoting a phony sovereign country provides diversified opportunities to engage in fraudulent activities. One's imagination of the various types of fraud possible has become a reality with DOM. A phony government consisting of fraudsters creates phony citizenships, ambassadorships, embassy and legation offices, issues diplomatic passports, registers financial aid, grants business licenses, creates a stock exchange, etc., etc.—all phony. However, each facet of this operation is a source which generates substantial illegal income.[53]

One of DOM's specialties has been the sale of bank licenses, which, according to the Melchizedek Banking Act of 1991, can be purchased for $10,000. By the end of the 1990s, Pedley claimed, some 300 such licenses had been issued. Many of the entities operating with these charters appeared in scandals around the globe.

In the early 1990s, several Melchizedek-licensed "banks" set up offices in Washington, D.C., where, not coincidentally, the law allowed any company to use the word "bank" in its name even though it was not a bona-fide lending institution.[54] One of these, Banco de Asia, also received permission from the state of Nevada to conduct business there, despite the fact that it had no real assets.[55]

In 1995, an organization calling itself Swiss Investment Bankers, operating with a DOM license, appeared in England as part of a scheme operated by a group called the Inner Sanctum that was issuing checks from the alleged bank as part of an investment scam.[56] Several years later, the "bank" was also a component in a lottery scheme, Big International, run by one of the principals of Inner Sanctum.[57] In 1998, the Dominion of Melchizedek issued, via its Web site, a "warning that individuals should avoid doing business" with Big International and Swiss Investment Bankers.[58]

In the late 1990s, several Melchizedek-chartered "banks," operating out of the Caribbean, were involved in a string of frauds. One of these organizations was Credit Bank International (CBI). On August 26, 1998, the U.S. Office of the Comptroller of Currency issued an "alert," warning people about CBI and two other unauthorized banks operating with Melchizedek licenses.[59] CBI was run by a French citizen Roger Rosemont, who claimed to be Melchizedek's "ambassador at large to the Caribbean." The primary activity of CBI was an investment scheme based originally in the tiny Caribbean island-nation of Dominica, but later expanded to the United States. The scheme offered fantastic returns of more than 300 percent to potential investors. Rosemont, who had been thrown off the island of St. Lucia in 1996 for running the same scheme, and his U.S.-based agents were able to convince at least 1,400 people, primarily in Dominica and Brooklyn, New York, to invest over $4 million in his plan, which was nothing more than a Ponzi scheme.[60] The Securities and Exchange Commission was blunt in its assessment of the operation: "Credit Bank is not a bank, Melchizedek is not a country and Rosemont is not an ambassador."[61]

Another Melchizedek-affiliated Caribbean bank with even more grand ambitions was the First International Bank of Grenada (FIBG), run by an enigmatic ex-con from Oregon named Gilbert Allen Ziegler, a.k.a. Van A. Brink. Gilbert was listed on the Melchizedek Web page as the country's ambassador at large to Hawaii. FIBG was granted a license by Grenada in 1998, with assets that included a ruby valued at $15 million, and claimed to have a gross income in 1999 of $26 billion, which, if true, would have made it equivalent in size to the fifth-largest U.S. bank.[62] The bank lured potential investors to the tiny island to hear presentations about how they could receive a return of 250 percent per year on their investments.[63] The bank assured investors that their deposits were insured by an organization called the International Deposit Insurance Corporation (IDIC), which claimed to be one of the largest insurance companies in the world, even though it did not hold a license from any country.[64] FIBG and IDIC were part of a shadowy web of offshore banks, insurance companies, and other financial services companies that were constantly changing their names, physical locations, and Web sites.[65]

In late 1999, Ziegler/Brink showed up in the unlikely locale of the Democratic Republic of the Congo, where he signed a contract with a Congolese rebel group to establish a privately owned central bank and a monetary system tied to the value of Congolese gold and minerals in exchange for a 35 percent commission.[66] As part of the deal he was supposed to advance the rebel group $1 billion to get the local economy going once they gained power. Ziegler/Brink described his motives in Africa as humanitarian and claimed he would funnel more than $40 million from FIBG to build roads and hospitals in the Congo.[67]

The CBI and FIBG swindles were not the only investment scams in which DOM-affiliated entities have been involved. When David Korem visited the island of Rotuma to sponsor a secessionist movement he mixed politics and business. Two of the DOM representatives who accompanied him were later charged with selling fake stocks issued by Melchizedek to islanders.[68] In Australia, securities regulators charged George Andrew Balos, a former bookbinder, with conning investors out of $10 million (Australian) by convincing them to invest money in two companies that were purportedly licensed by the Dominion of Melchizedek.[69] Instead of investing their money, Balos spent it on a luxurious lifestyle that included $1 million (Australian) at a casino in Melbourne, where he lived, and $250,000 (Australian) on two Rolls-Royces, a Bentley, and a Mercedes Benz.[70]

In a global economy where many citizens of poorer nations feel economic pressure to migrate in search of work, a commodity of increasing value is a passport. Representatives of the Dominion of Melchizedek have exploited demand for this commodity by selling DOM passports to individuals around the world. In 1998, three individuals claiming to be officials of the Melchizedek government were arrested by the police in Manila for selling Melchizedekian passports for $3,500 each to Filipinos, Chinese, and Bangladeshis who were told they could use them to obtain U.S. visas. Some of the victims also paid as much as $32,500 for "government jobs" on one of Melchizedek's "territories." The scam netted the three "officials" over $1 million.[71]

The Dominion of Melchizedek broke new ground, figuratively if not literally, for white-collar criminals around the world, by pioneering a new strategy for fraud. During the U.S. savings and loan crisis of the 1980s, an oft-repeated quote was "The best way to rob a bank is to own one."[72] The Melchizedek strategy would modify this statement to: "The best way to rob a bank is to license one." The success of the strategy is evidenced by the numerous imitations that surfaced in Melchizedek's wake.

## The Kingdom of EnenKio

In 1997, the Domion of Melchizedek reported that it had opened "official and formal diplomatic relations" with the Kingdom of EnenKio, a "country" that consisted of three small, largely uninhabited islands with a total land area of 6.6 square miles, located halfway between Hawaii and Guam. The Kingdom is a virtual community that purports to represent a diaspora of persons displaced from their native land. In place of a religion (as Melchizedek claims to possess), the founders of EnenKio substituted an ideology that asserted that the true citizens of the islands had been historically forced off the islands by the imperialistic actions of the United States. Like Melchizedek, the Kingdom of EnenKio exists, in large part, on its elaborate Web site.

According to the U.S. government, the islands claimed as the Kingdom of EnenKio are actually part of the atoll known as Wake Island. The uninhabited atoll was claimed by the United States in 1899 for use as a cable station. It is currently an unincorporated territory of the United States, administered by the Department of Interior. The legitimacy of these claims is disputed by Robert Moore, who, in 1994, acting as the "Minister Plenipotentiary" for a government-in-exile in Hawaii, declared the Kingdom of EnenKio to be a sovereign country. When the U.S. government failed to respond to his claim, he took his proclamation to EnenKio's "Royal Court of Justice," a virtual court that announces its decisions on the Kingdom's Web site. In his "law suit," he asserted that King Hermios, a.k.a. Iroijlaplap (Paramount Chief) Murjel Hermios, was the "undisputed owner of record" of the EnenKio atoll. King Hermios, the "suit" claimed, was the rightful heir to the throne, having descended from a 2,000-year-old lineage of Polynesians who inhabited what is now the Marshall Islands. The atoll, Moore explained in the suit, was uninhabited when the United States claimed it in 1899 because, "in accordance to native Marshallese customs and practices, the atoll was kept uninhabited as a game preserve (or 'pantry' atoll) and was ruled over exclusively by the prevailing Iro-ijlaplap ancestor in the matriarchal lineage of King Hermios."[73]

The U.S. annexation of the atoll was, according to Moore, illegal, constituting no less than a "crime of piracy on the high seas," and his "suit" demanded, and the "court" later ordered, that the U.S. government pay the Kingdom of EnenKio a total of $170,202,474.22 for its "illegal occupation" of the atoll.[74] After the United States failed to pay, or even pay Moore any attention, the Minister Plenipotentiary declared that a state of war existed between the two countries.[75]

These pseudo-political maneuvers are reminiscent of the Peter Sellers movie, *The Mouse that Roared*, in which the leaders of a tiny nation on the brink of bankruptcy declare war on the United States intending to immediately surrender and then collect foreign aid. However, the real business of EnenKio can be found on its Web site. There, one learns that an offshore banking license can be obtained for $5,000. One also learns about opportunities to buy bonds issued by the government of EnenKio that are "backed by gold reserves, guarantees, real property or other significant assets." According to the Web site, the bonds were to be used to build: a 200-room floating hotel ("Embassy Suites quality") that "will be moored in the lagoon of the atoll where the King resides" and that was to include "restaurants, casinos, ballrooms, shopping and craft shops"; a fishing fleet of one hundred boats; twenty-five semiportable mills to process coconut lumber; and a satellite telecommunications system.[76] From the Web site one also learns about the opportunities to purchase Enen-Kio commemorative gold stamps, which have no practical value:

> Since the islands are occupied by foreign forces, the EnenKio Postal Authority also functions in exile and no means of utilizing stamps for actually posting mail is possible. . . . EnenKio's situation is similar to other states that issued stamps prior to being released from subjugation by their colonial masters or administrators.[77]

One of these commemorative stamps features a picture of the mushroom cloud from a nuclear explosion (one of EnenKio's complaints against the United States involves its testing of nuclear weapons in the area), with the caption, "EnenKio, A Virtual 'State of War' is Declared March 21, 1997."

Of more practical interest to many, however, is EnenKio's offer to extend "economic citizenship" to nonnatives of the country. For fees ranging from $500 to $10,000, one can obtain an EnenKio passport. The reasons cited for obtaining a second passport include: "Your assets are vulnerable to loss, attachment or litigation, You and your business are overburdened by taxation, You are not allowed to work or settle in another country."[78] The potential value of these passports was illustrated in early 2000, when EnenKio's "foreign minister" announced that the country had signed a deal with the Arab nation of Kuwait to provide passports to the roughly 112,000 stateless Arabs who live in Kuwait, which would allow them to continue living and working there. Within days the Kuwaiti government publicly stated that it had refused to sign the agreement after learning that the Kingdom of EnenKio was an imaginary country.[79] Nonetheless, the demand for passports from foreign countries, imaginary or real, was clearly demonstrated.

## New Utopia

Both EnenKio and Melchizedek laid claims to natural land masses as their sovereign countries, which led them into disputes with legitimate nations. The creators of subsequent cyber states realized that such conflicts could be avoided by simply constructing or appropriating man-made physical space that would constitute their countries. One of the more innovative of these schemes was the Principality of New Utopia, the brainchild of a Tulsa, Oklahoma, resident, in his sixties, who used the title Prince Lazarus Long, but whose given name was Howard Turney.

From his Web site, Prince Lazarus announced his intention to build his sovereign domain on a series of platforms to be constructed in the Caribbean upon several reefs that, at their shallowest point, lie just one foot below sea level. According to the plan, the platforms would be supported by concrete piles poured at thirty-foot intervals on the Caribbean reef. The platforms themselves would be constructed in Miami and barged to the site. The total above-water area would be large enough to support, "1,200 apartments, a 350,00 [square foot] shopping mall, five hotels, a bank, a 150,000 [square foot] medical centre, a casino, a convention centre and a university offering scholarships to students from every country in the world."[80]

More than just a physical infrastructure, however, Long envisioned New Utopia as a new kind of society, one based on a philosophy that combined the radical individualism of Ayn Rand and the futuristic ideas of science fiction writer Robert Heinlein. (Prince Lazarus took his name from a character in Heinlein's novel, *Time Enough for Love*.) Long explained his vision of the new society in the following way:

> New Utopia is envisioned as a banking and insurance centre. . . . A tax haven designed to 'out Cayman' the Cayman Islands. With no taxes of any kind, its citizens will be able to live anywhere in the world, tax free, so long as their assets are located or titled in New Utopia. We will have the most modern and effective offshore and asset protection legislation in the world, a 'safe haven' where everyone from private individuals to international institutions can rest assured in the knowledge that their capital and income is safe from the predators of the world.[81]

Prince Lazarus saw himself as a free-thinking pioneer and entrepreneuer who wasn't afraid to defy convention and the authorities to strike out in new directions. In the mid-1990s, when he was still known as Howard Turney, the

future prince ran a company in Texas that claimed to be developing a process
to remove the fetuses from women who had undergone abortions, freeze them,
and store them, to be later reimplanted and the pregnancy continued. Medical
experts were highly skeptical of the procedure.[82] At the same time, he operated
a clinic in Cancún, Mexico, that dispensed growth hormones that he claimed
retarded the aging process and increased virility.[83]

In order to fund his new venture, Long offered $350 million in bonds,
that claimed to return 9.5 percent interest annually, issued by New Utopia and
advertised on the "country"'s Web site. He also sold citizenships from the
country, which included passports, for "contributions" ranging from $100 to
$500. In April 1999, the Securities and Exchange Commission (SEC) filed a
suit against Long in federal court seeking to prohibit him from selling his
bonds. The numerous misrepresentations cited by the SEC included a claim
on Utopia's Web site that one of the country's officials was the nephew of Alan
Greenspan, the chairman of the Federal Reserve (Long later admitted that he
had no idea if the two were related).[84] The court agreed with the SEC and
ordered him to stop selling the bonds and return the money he had already
collected from investors.

Despite this financial setback the ever-resilient Long pushed on with his
plans, announcing on his Web site that "there will be a registration of the New
Utopia Investment Fund on the Cayman Island Stock Exchange by independent developers when construction begins."[85] He also continued to offer "charter citizenships" for a "contribution" of $1,500, which would give purchasers
"preferential treatment for housing and space for businesses" on the new
"island."[86]

One of the problems with Prince Lazarus Long's scheme to sell passports,
bonds, and bank and insurance licenses from a giant platform in the Caribbean
was that in order to maintain credibility he actually needed at some point to
complete the enormously difficult task of constructing the platform. A much
more efficient strategy would have been to gain possession of an existing offshore platform upon which one's country could be founded. The problem
there is the simple fact that such structures are not that common, but they can
be found.

## Sealand

Less than forty-eight hours after he allegedly shot and killed fashion
designer Gianni Versace on a sidewalk in Miami, serial killer Andrew Cunanan
made a phone call to an associate on the West Coast asking where he could
obtain a phony passport to flee the country. Days later, Cunanan was found

dead, apparently from a self-inflicted gunshot wound, on a houseboat owned by an exiled German businessman. Torsten Franz Jacomb Reinceck reportedly drove around Miami in a Mercedes Benz with diplomatic plates and frequently flashed a passport from a country called the Principality of Sealand, which he claimed gave him diplomatic immunity.[87]

Little more was heard about the mysterious Sealand, until nearly three years later when police in Spain broke up a ring of sixty people who were selling passports over the Internet issued by the Principality of Sealand. The group claimed to have sold 160,000 of the passports for about $6,000 apiece.[88] The passports were sold, along with university titles, drivers licenses, and other documents, on the country's Web site. The country itself was said to be located on a platform, seven miles off the northeast shore of England. The country's head, or "regent," was a Spaniard, Francisco Trujillo, who admitted that the country had actually been founded by an Englishman, Paddy Roy Bates.

All of this came as a surprise to Mr. Bates who had founded the country in 1967, at first as a joke. A World War II hero, Bates had learned about the existence of seven gun platforms, each 130 yards by 40 yards and supported by two massive concrete pillars, that had been built by the British government in 1940 to guard against German aircraft invasions. Two were destroyed, but five remained intact after the war. He also learned that English territorial right extended only three miles off the coast, four miles closer to land than one of the platforms, which, in 1966, he commandeered to operate a pirate radio station. The next year, he declared the platform to be a sovereign country, the Principality of Sealand. By the late 1990s, Mr. Bates and his wife, now referring to themselves as Prince Roy and Princess Joan, operated a Web site for the Principality that presented the country's official coat of arms, a series of Sealand stamps, images of Sealand dollar coins, and a copy of a marriage certificate issued by Sealand in 1979.[89] The Web site also announced that Sealand was a "Free Trade zone and no Customs duties or Gaming restrictions will be imposed."[90]

At the same time, a very similar Web site promoting Sealand was being operated by the Spanish group out of Madrid. When Spanish police raided the group's offices they found equipment for making Sealand license plates and evidence indicating that the group had sold diplomatic passports to Moroccan hashish smugglers. They also learned that the group was brokering "a $50 million deal to send 50 tanks, 10 MIG-23 fighter jets and other combat aircraft, artillery and armored vehicles from Russia to Sudan . . ."[91]

By late spring 2000, with their Spanish rivals out of business, Bates and his associates were moving ahead at full speed back on their platform on the North Sea. Bates had hooked up with a group of American "computer rebels" to set up a "data haven" in Sealand that would operate outside of government regulatory intrusions. According to the company's founder, the firm "will offer an environment where you can put your business, where the regulatory environment won't change on you."[92] Guided by a libertarian philosophy (as are most of the cyber nations) the founders of the new company envisioned a cyberspace in which one could, for example, operate Internet gambling that could be accessed from any country in the world, regardless of the regulations that govern gambling within the country. The venture's philosophy was summed up succinctly in a computer magazine article: "Sealand won't just be offshore. It will be *off-government*"[93] (italics in original).

## Virtual Nations

The preceding discussion of cyber nations like Sealand and Melchizedek may seem like a detour from an examination of fraud in the offshore insurance industry. The discussion, however, was intended to show how, in the evolution of white-collar crime, we have moved from fictitious capital to fictitious countries, and that the latter is the logical extension of the former. Once it became accepted in the world community that countries could create offshore financial centers (OFCs) and international business corporations (IBCs) as legal spaces in which companies could operate outside of normal regulatory oversight, it was not a huge step for individuals to usurp the exclusive authority of recognized countries to create those spaces by creating their own countries and their own legal spaces. And, as we have seen, these new spaces are prime environments for many forms of economic crime. In its 1999 report, the U.S. State Department's Bureau for International Narcotics and Law Enforcement Affairs warned of the criminal possibilities in these trends:

> Thus, it is now possible for an enterprising jurisdiction anywhere in the world to establish itself as an emerging OFC. The newest OFCs, e.g., Niue and the Marshall Islands, are now sprouting in remote areas of the world, such as the Pacific. Even more "remote" are mere figments of fertile imaginations such as the Dominion of Melchizedek or The Kingdom of Enenkio Atol, both entirely fraudulent in intent and practice.[94]

To many people the idea that a country could exist on an uninhabited atoll in the middle of the Pacific Ocean with a government-in-exile in Hawaii run by someone who calls himself a Minister Plenipotentiary might seen ludicrous. Yet, in an era of rapid social change in which countries come and go and national boundaries are constantly being redrawn, the idea that a legitimate country could exist on an atoll or even on a platform in the Caribbean may not seem that implausible. Indeed, in the contemporary environment, the whole notion of the nation-state as something that is tied to a fixed geographical space has been challenged. Marc Harris, the exiled financial guru who gave refuge to Brent Wagman in Panama (Chapter 3), articulated this challenge clearly:

> In the same way that the virtual corporation has become the new model for global commercial enterprises, the virtual nation will become the model for emerging nations like Panama. Less developed countries that focus on production derived from land (e.g., Iraq) may still desire territory; however, in the new global economic order, economic inputs have become mobile. The new virtual nation would rather conquer the world market than acquire territory. The virtual state that has downsized its territorially based production capability is the logical consequence of this freedom.
>
> The economic equivalent of the virtual state, the virtual corporation, has discovered the advantages of locating its production facilities where it is most profitable. Increasingly, this is not in the same location as corporate headquarters. Parts of a virtual corporation are dispersed globally according to their specialties. The virtual state is the political counterpart of the virtual corporation.[95]

One of the important points to be made about "virtual nations" is that many of their programs are already in place in recognized countries. By 1999, for example, economic citizenships were not only offered by the Kingdom of EnenKio, but were sold by the Caribbean countries of Belize, Dominica, Grenada, St. Kitts and Nevis, and St. Vincent and the Grenadines, and, in the Pacific, Nauru.[96] Dominica, for example, sells economic citizenships via its Web site. For $15,000, one can purchase economic citizenship in the country, which includes a Dominican passport that allows one to travel in British Commonwealth countries.[97] Despite the fact that one of the requirements for the Dominican passport is that applicants "must be of outstanding character," the State Department warns that "when combined with 'special benefits' such as an instant change of name and the ability to travel to many countries without a visa on a new passport, economic citizenship can be misused by criminals."[98] Thus, one should take seriously Harris's prediction that "the new virtual nations will become the model for emerging nations like Panama," because many of them are already there.

# CONCLUSIONS

By the end of 1999, Alan Teale was long dead, Jesse Maynard was on his way to prison, and regulators had largely declared victory over the "white-collar crime wave" that had plagued the insurance industry just a few years earlier.[1] There were, however, troubling signs that all was not well in the global insurance industry and that offshore and onshore criminals were still out there pulling off big money swindles. Beginning in the spring of 1999, a dozen or more lawsuits were filed in the United States and overseas, alleging fraud by reinsurance companies and reinsurance brokers located both in the United States and abroad. In one of these suits, a London reinsurer, Odyssey Re, accused a Bermuda-based brokerage firm, Stirling Cooke Brown, of civil racketeering after it had placed workers' compensation reinsurance with Odyssey that was "grossly underpriced," allegedly resulting in $35 million in losses to the reinsurer.[2] Just a few years earlier, Stirling Cooke Brown had been the darling of the well-known investment firm Goldman Sachs, which had invested $19 million of its clients' money in the firm. At best, Goldman had not done its homework. The company's predecessor was owned by Ghaith Pharaon, a Saudi businessman who was deeply involved in the BCCI scandal, and one of its principals, Mark Cooke, had formerly been employed as a broker for Carlos Miro. In his testimony before Congress, Miro had stated that Cooke was intimately familiar with his scams.[3]

The Stirling Cooke case was related to a much larger fiasco that involved billions of dollars in losses to some of the largest insurance companies in North America. That case revolved around a relatively small managing general agency (MGA) based in New Jersey, Unicover Managers, that was able to handle $2.6 billion in reinsurance on $8 billion worth of workers' compensation policies, earning $250 million in fees and commissions in just fourteen months.[4] Several large insurers and reinsurers who took on portions of the risk later claimed that they were deceived by Unicover about the true nature of the risk they were assuming. One of these firms, Sun Life of Canada, claimed to have lost $500 million in Unicover's schemes and accused the MGA of engaging in "white collar fraud."[5]

These events suggest that reports of global insurance fraud's death may have been greatly exaggerated. While policymakers had moved to fill some of the regulatory voids that invited insurance scams in the early 1990s, others remained, and new ones were emerging. As we saw in Chapters 3 and 4, white-collar criminals and their schemes are constantly adapting to the changing financial environment. The persistent recurrence of these events also suggests that they were not historical anomalies but were the consequences of larger social and economic changes.

The case studies presented in the preceding chapters provide a narrative of events that unfolded initially in the insurance market, and more specifically the segment of that market serviced by companies located offshore, but later expanded to include other markets, including securities and banking. One of the things that case studies help to accomplish, particularly in previously unexplored areas, is what Robert Merton has called "establishing the phenomenon"—ensuring that "the phenomena . . . be shown to exist or to occur before one explains why they exist or how they come to be."[6] At the same time, the cases were chosen because they illustrate larger theoretical concerns. As John Walton succinctly put it, "Cases are always hypotheses."[7] That is, the process of choosing cases is always guided by theoretical questions.

For this study, cases were chosen that illustrated new forms of insurance fraud that took advantage of the increasingly global nature of the insurance industry. The cases also point to both theoretical and practical questions. First, what is it about the globalization process and, specifically, the globalization of financial industries, that makes these new forms of white-collar crime possible? A tentative answer was suggested in the Introduction: an answer that linked the process of globalization to deregulatory policies, which in turn create new opportunities for financial fraud. A related theoretical issue has to do with the changing nature of white-collar crime in an era of globalization. The suggestion was made in previous chapters that operators of fraudulent offshore insurance companies represented white-collar criminals of the future. The question remains as to the role that globalization has played in creating these and similar groups. Finally, there is the more practical question: What is to be done? What types of policies should be implemented to prevent the recurrence of these egregious frauds? It is to these questions that this chapter turns.

## Globalization, Deregulation, and Financial Crime

An important source of the crimes described in this book lies in changing markets. While individuals' motivations are important, it is the marketplace that provides the opportunities and inducements for white-collar criminal behavior.[8] Offshore insurance criminals take advantage of changes in markets in two places: first, in deregulated and under-regulated markets within the

United States, and, second, in the host countries where they obtain their licenses. To fully understand offshore insurance fraud, then, we need to know more about the origins of these deregulated environments.

As argued in the Introduction, the deregulation or liberalization of financial markets is part of the general process of globalization and has transformed financial markets around the world as countries seek to position themselves in the emerging global economy. As economic geographer Ron Martin has observed:

> During the course of the 1980s and 1990s, a tidal wave of deregulation (and re-regulation) swept across the globe. . . . Financial markets were dramatically redrawn as nations became locked in a process of "competitive deregulation," in a "race to the bottom" to free money and finance from the regulatory structures built up during the post-war decades.[9]

Players within these newly deregulated markets are exposed to increasing pressures and increasing opportunities to commit large-scale frauds. This has been evident, not only in the U.S. savings and loan industry of the 1980s, but in a variety of other markets around the world. In England, the deregulation of financial markets was begun in 1986 in an effort to keep up with foreign investment banks and securities firms that held a competitive edge in international securities markets.[10] One of the unintended consequences of these changes was new opportunities for "rogue activities." Two of these rogues were Robert Maxwell, the corporate magnate who used his employees' pension plans to fund his takeover maneuvers, and Nick Leeson, whose illegal trades in the Asian securities markets made while he worked for Barings Bank led to the ultimate collapse of that institution. Despite the tendency of the media and government officials to place responsibility for the scandals solely on the shoulders of these two individuals, their behavior was part and parcel of a new "culture of finance" that had emerged in the wake of deregulation.[11]

In the preceding chapters we saw how people like Alan Teale and his colleagues took advantage of certain niche markets in the United States that had largely been abandoned by legitimate insurers. Many of those markets had been effectively deregulated by federal and state policies that recognized such entities as MEWAs, risk retention groups, and surplus lines carriers that could operate outside of the regulatory restrictions traditionally placed on licensed insurance companies. In California in the late 1980s, for example, white-collar criminals took advantage of: (1) the fact that legitimate insurance companies had all but abandoned certain segments of the auto insurance market as well as the liability insurance market for small businesses located in the inner city; (2) loopholes in the law regarding surplus lines carriers; and (3) a laissez-faire attitude by regulators toward offshore companies. John Garamendi, the California insurance commissioner who inherited the problems created by the convergence of these factors from his predecessor, described the consequences of deregulation to a congressional committee:

> The 1980s were the great era of deregulation. The mantra that was sung every morning in the Nation's capital and in the capital's [sic] of the various States was deregulate. Get out of the way of business, let the businessman and woman have their day. After all, they will build a great economy for us all. In fact they all but destroyed the American economy and the deregulation mentality was a large part of the downfall and the problems that we see today.[12]

The operators of offshore insurance companies also took advantage of their ability to easily obtain insurance licenses from foreign countries that would cloak their businesses' finances in veils of secrecy. In the 1980s, as the insurance industry became increasingly global, U.S. regulators came to accept foreign insurance as a legitimate, indeed an essential, component of the American insurance market. At the same time, a number of generally small countries began to discover the benefits of allowing offshore insurers to operate from their soil. In its final report on problems in the insurance industry published in 1994, Representative John Dingell's committee observed this trend:

> The concept of government-sponsored havens to serve the needs of companies instead of consumers has become quite fashionable. Insurance-related enterprises have developed a cachet as non-polluting, white-collar businesses that protect natural resources and add to community wealth and prestige. Countries selling themselves as insurance domiciles typically offer tax relief and relaxed supervision in exchange for the outside economic stimulus given to resident businesses. They make no pretenses about attracting insurers to serve local customers, since their domestic markets are limited in size and usually controlled by native companies. . . . Through . . . selective licensing, problems of mismanagement and insolvency arising from lax regulation are carefully exported to other countries, particularly the United States. The sole purpose of export licensing laws, which exempt offshore operations from strict regulation, is to promote local community development and commerce at the peril of policyholders elsewhere.[13]

Governments in the Caribbean openly advertised the "ease and benefits of island life" to Americans interested in starting up insurance companies. A brochure prepared by the Association of Insurance Managers in the Turks and Caicos islands reads:

> Plan a visit to the Turks and Caicos Islands to meet with the Superintendent of Insurance and with your trusty but so far faceless manager. In normal circumstances all business with the Superintendent, the Manager, the Lawyer and the Accountant can be completed within 2 days with time left over to visit the bank and open your accounts. . . . Do not work on too tight a schedule as you may find it essential that you have at least 2 more days in which to sample the unspoiled beaches, virgin reefs and relaxing atmosphere. . . . Upon the approval of the license the prescribed capital of the company must be placed in the form undertaken within the application. One very attractive feature of the insurance legislation in the Turks and Caicos Islands is that there is no specific requirement that the approved capital be held in the Islands . . .[14]

Jesse Maynard was apparently convinced. His First Assurance, whose illegal activities were detailed in Chapter 2, was licensed in the Turks and Caicos as a "non-domestic" insurance company under that country's Insurance Ordinance of 1989, which meant that it could not sell insurance in the islands, but could do business in the United States.

To understand why offshore insurance fraud has become such a problem in the United States we have to better understand the motivations for foreign governments to sanction the companies that served as vehicles for these crimes. By the early 1980s, many of these countries were facing economic hardships as their traditional sources of employment and revenue were drying up. In some cases, agricultural production was undercut by subsidized farming in larger, wealthier countries. With few natural resources and generally unskilled labor forces, many of these countries saw financial services as a low-cost, high-revenue alternative to industries in which they were poorly suited to compete.[15]

A common technique for setting up offshore insurance companies is to charter them as international business corporations (IBCs). As an organizational form and legal entity, the IBC is an ideal vehicle for perpetrating insurance scams. In a report to the United Nations on "financial havens," Jack Blum and his colleagues make this point:

> In most jurisdictions the IBC operates without any government requirements. On the condition that it do no business in its home

jurisdiction, the IBC may hide its ownership and need not pay taxes. In many jurisdictions it is not required to keep books and records. The purpose of the IBC's corporate form is to enable its owners to act with complete anonymity, but the concept of limited liability has been extended to a concept of no legal responsibility for any action.[16]

One of the countries that has chartered many IBCs is the British Virgin Islands (BVI), home to many of the offshore insurance companies whose illegal activities were detailed in the preceding chapters. In 1984, as BVI saw tourism on the islands decline, its Legislative Council enacted the International Business Companies Ordinance, which allowed foreign investors to incorporate banks, insurance companies, and other businesses for a small incorporation fee and annual licensing fees. Significantly, the law exempted IBCs from income taxes. The law was intended to generate significant revenues for the country, and in that respect it was very successful. By 1995, when the country's entire population was only 18,000, more than 60,000 IBCs had been incorporated. In 1992, IBCs contributed $21 million directly to the government's revenue.[17] Beyond the economic importance of the law, BVI natives hailed it as a source of national pride, as "their" law, not one written and imposed on them by outsiders.[18] This theme of offshore financial centers and international business corporations as a source of national pride, one that gives countries a sense of independence from colonial powers, is in evidence elsewhere in the Caribbean.

From the perspective of governments of countries like the United States, offshore insurance fraud is a crime that is tacitly supported or at least tolerated by the host countries that grant them licenses and protect them from intrusive surveillance. It is a situation, in other words, in which sovereign states are intimately connected with the offenders and their offenses. Thus, efforts to remedy the situation involve the social control of what might be called "deviant states." In using the term "deviant states," no similarity is intended with what are sometimes called "rogue states," or "predatory states," governmental regimes that generally defy international conventions by supporting terrorists or by exploiting their citizens to enrich their leaders.[19] Nor, should these instances of deviance be confused with what is referred to as "state-organized crime."[20] Rather, the term is meant to refer to states that violate some widely held, but not necessarily universally agreed upon, norm of conduct. The term does not imply that a country has a "spoiled identity," or is fundamentally corrupt or dangerous, but rather that, while most of the time the state conforms to international standards of conduct, in this specific area it has been accused of violating those standards.[21] And, as in the case of individual deviants who have organized politically, those definitions of deviance can and have been challenged by the states that have been labeled as offenders.

In recent years a number of international organizations have attempted to exert social control over these deviant states, in part by publicizing their support of policies that facilitate financial crime. In the spring of 2000, the Organization for Economic Cooperation and Development (OECD), an organization comprised of twenty-nine countries with generally advanced economies, issued a report on "Harmful Tax Competition" that identified thirty-five jurisdictions as "tax havens." These tax havens are defined as jurisdictions that allow foreign-owned companies to pay no taxes, to evade effective supervision, and to be established "without the need for a local substantive presence," exactly the kinds of environments that would attract a fraudulent offshore insurance company.[22] Many of these putative tax havens were located in the Caribbean, including: Antigua and Barbuda, Aruba, the Bahamas, Barbados, the British Virgin Islands, and Dominica. That summer, OECD issued another list of jurisdictions defined as "uncooperative" in the organization's efforts to crack down on money laundering. The offenders were given one year to demonstrate their commitment to changing their ways or face international sanctions.[23]

The response from Caribbean states that found themselves on the OECD's lists tended toward indignation. Officials from many of the jurisdictions argued that the lists were an attempt by larger countries to push their economic interests at the expense of smaller nations, a first-world/third-world conflict. A Bahamian official stated that "rich nations" could not face the competition from Caribbean competitors, while the head of the Caribbean Development Bank called the reports "economic blackmail" and a "patently unfair attempt by the rich and powerful industrialized nations to recoup business they have lost to small developing states."[24] The Chief Minister of Montserrat, one of the British dependencies on the list of tax havens, stated that he would not cooperate with the OECD: "The territory will not be relegated to the position of informer . . ."[25] Dominica's Prime Minster declared: "They are out to defend their interests. We will not give up our sovereign rights."[26]

Ultimately, the responses of the "offending" states challenged the legal and political authority of those groups that have defined them as deviants. As critical criminologists remind us, behind definitions of crime lie political processes and behind those political processes lie the interests of powerful groups. This connection between power and the application of criminal definitions was made clearly by Richard Quinney in his influential book, *The Social Reality of Crime*, where he posited:

Crime is a definition of human conduct that is created by authorized agents in a political organized society. . . . Criminal definitions describe behaviors that conflict with the interests of the segments of society that have the power to shape public policy. . . . Criminal definitions are applied by the segments of society that have the power to shape the enforcement and administration of criminal law.[27]

In this formulation, Quinney had in mind criminal laws created by individual sovereign states and applied to their domestic populations. But the ideas could also be applied to definitions of deviance and criminality created by international organizations and applied to individual states.

In their responses to the OECD reports, many Caribbean leaders made similar connections, noting that designations of "tax havens" and "uncooperative" were made primarily on political grounds. As one Caribbean leader put it, "We do not place much faith in a report in which the categories in which you find yourself turns, not on technical criteria, but on whether you have signed a letter of political commitment or not."[28] In his response to the OECD's 1998 "tax haven" list on which his country appeared, the Senior Ambassador to the United Kingdom from Antigua and Barbuda wrote:

Antigua and Barbuda is not Switzerland or Luxembourg. It does not have the economic clout to stand up against coercion and pressure. For the coercion and pressure will take many forms. Amongst them will be a portrayal of the country as a rogue state, of the government and opposition as irresponsible, of the financial services sector as riddled with criminals and crime.[29]

In its response, the Caribbean Community Secretariat, an organization that represents fifteen Caribbean states, charged that the "adjustments to the system [required by OECD] are clearly to ensure that it serves the OECD's interest." The organization also objected to the report's narrow focus on financial harm while excluding other social harms and proposed that it widen its view to include

[i]n the social field, the impacts on Caribbean and other developing countries . . . issues like "harmful drug consumption practices," "harmful violent cinematic practices," "harmful gun control practices," and "harmful criminal deportation practices." All these emanate from their jurisdiction.[30]

Yet, the major obstacle to a U.S.-led crackdown on financial havens will likely not be resistance by the leaders of small states, but large U.S. corporations that reap significant benefits from offshore opportunities. In the area of insurance, U.S. corporations have profited greatly from the ability of insurers to operate from low-tax, low-regulation offshore locales. This has been particularly beneficial for corporations that have set up "captive insurers," insurers that are wholly or partly owned by noninsurance companies who are their sole clients. Captives allow large companies to self-insure, without having to rely on outside private insurance companies. In addition to the obvious benefit of not having to pay for the profits of an outside insurer, corporations that self-insure can deduct the premiums from their taxable income.

By the end of 1999, Bermuda was home to over 1,000 captives, and the Cayman Islands was home to nearly 500.[31] Significantly, both had been listed in OECD's 1998 "tax haven" list, but were removed in the 2000 report, after they agreed to eliminate "harmful tax practices."[32] In the case of the Cayman Islands, its new status as a "cooperative" country was granted despite substantial evidence that the country's policies were facilitating money laundering. Just two months after the OECD report was released, the U.S. Department of the Treasury's Financial Crimes Enforcement Network issued an advisory warning banks and other financial institutions of "serious deficiencies in the counter–money laundering systems of the Cayman Islands."[33]

But it's not just corporations with captive insurers that have profited from the ability to conduct business from offshore locations. Large U.S. banks and investment firms have long benefited from offshore financial havens.[34] A good example is provided by Frank Portnoy, a former derivatives trader at Morgan Stanley, in his kiss-and-tell book about the Wall Street investment firm. In 1994, Morgan Stanley wanted to sell Mexican bonds to large American institutional investors. The problem was that the bonds were denominated in pesos but the buyers were required to purchase only bonds denominated in dollars. To magically transform the bonds, Morgan Stanley set up a shell company in Bermuda, with tax advantages obtained by putting Bermudians on the board and selling the company's stock to a local charitable organization, which then issued its own dollar-denominated bonds, backed by the original Mexican bonds. Eventually, Morgan sold more than $1 billion worth of the bonds to a diverse group of investors that included the state of Wisconsin. According to Portnoy, "Morgan Stanley's actions were barely distinguishable from those of a drug kingpin seeking an appropriate tax haven to launder money."[35]

There is, thus, more than a kernel of truth in the statements of officials from putative "tax havens" when they argue that wealthy countries want "free markets" and deregulation, but only on their terms. On the one hand, organizations like OECD demand that smaller countries step up regulatory supervision and increase taxes on financial services companies to eliminate "unfair tax competition." On the other hand, influential figures like Alan Greenspan call on nations around the world to reduce regulation, arguing, as he did in a speech in August 2000, that "it has become generally understood that governmental actions often hinder incentives to investment by increasing uncertainties, boosting risk premiums, and raising costs."[36] It would appear then, that the wealthy nations of the world do indeed want markets free of "governmental actions," but only when it benefits them. This contradiction will ultimately impede any efforts to "crack down" on financial havens and the criminal enterprises they spawn.[37]

## The End of Geography?

One of the key features of global society, according to several theorists, is the declining significance of "place." Communities, provinces, nations—the traditional, geographically defined building blocks of society—are being surpassed in their sociological importance by "networks," the fundamental conduits through which information flows and that link individuals to one another.[38] In these networks, physical space has become less significant than what Manuel Castells refers to as the "space of flows," defined as

> the technological and organizational possibility of organizing the simultaneity of social practices without geographical contiguity. Most dominant functions in our societies (financial markets, transnational production networks, media systems, etc.) are organized around the space of flows.[39]

Like the "space of places," the "space of flows does have a territorial dimension," but the meaning of the content of these flows is generated independently from locality.[40] For example, as we saw in Chapter 4, in some countries like Dominica, physical residence is no longer required for citizenship. In a word, global society tends to become "deterritorialized"—a condition in which legally and politically defined territories begin to lose their significance in people's everyday lives."[41]

In an early analysis of the impact of globalization on finance, Richard O'Brien argued that the emergence of electronically linked, twenty-four-hour, global financial markets signaled "the end of geography."

> The end of geography, as a concept applied to international financial relationships, refers to a state of economic development where geo-

graphical location no longer matters, or matters less than hitherto. In this state, *financial market regulators* no longer hold sway over their regulatory territory; that is rules no longer apply to specific geographical frameworks, such as the nation-state or other typical regulatory/jurisdictional territories[42] [italics in original].

Later analyses by economic geographers took issue with O'Brien's assertion that geography was losing its relevance in the international flow of money. Ron Martin argued that

financial globalisation is inherently geographically constituted, the product of organisational, technological, regulatory and corporate strategies by individual firms, institutions and authorities in *specific locations*. Globalisation may have well annihilated *space*, but it has by no means undermined the significance of location, of *place*[43] [italics in original].

As Martin's comments suggest, location has become less a fixed parameter for financial industries and more a strategic decision made by actors in those industries. This is consistent with what we have observed in the preceding chapters. The operators of offshore insurance companies did not ignore geography; rather, they made strategic use of it. They purposely located their companies in countries that offered the best prospects for easy entry and low visibility and relocated them whenever that environment changed. In this context, geography did not so much disappear as it became much more fluid. It is important to understand that, in this new view, it is not the physical aspects of geography that are important, but rather its legal and political dimensions. Alan Teale and his colleagues were not interested in the beautiful beaches of the Turks and Caicos islands or the green, rolling hills of Ireland when they located their insurance companies there. Instead, they were interested in the shields to regulatory scrutiny offered by those countries' laws.

The diminished or changed role of geography in financial frauds is probably best exemplified by the fictitious countries described in Chapter 4. Their contested claims to physical geographical space were only a means for making claims to sovereign statehood, which, in turn, gave a veneer of legitimacy, albeit temporarily, to the various financial ventures they sponsored. In many ways what these "countries" were doing was but a short step from what legitimate countries have done to become players in the global economy. From consumers' perspectives, how much difference does it make if the worthless auto insurance policies they purchased were issued by a company with a license from Aruba or the Dominion of Melchizedek? What does it matter if the passports they bought over the Internet show them to be "economic citizens" of Dominica or the Kindom of EnenKio? In these instances, geography really is irrelevant.

## Offshore Insurance Fraud as Organized Transnational Crime

Responding to the opportunities for fraud presented by transformed domestic and overseas markets, over the last couple of decades new global crime groups have emerged. While this book has focused on white-collar criminals operating in the offshore insurance industry, their activities provide a window on the murky world of a network of international criminals who are part of what the United Nations has called "organized transnational crime." In the same way that globalization has transformed world markets, making them more vulnerable to financial crime, so has it created the conditions that have spawned this new form of organized crime.

In a 1996 report, the United Nation's Commission on Crime Prevention and Criminal Justice argued that organized transnational crime has become a "new form of geopolitics, with its own character, logic, structure and support systems."[44] The report identifies a number of factors linked to the process of globalization that have facilitated the emergence of this "new form of geopolitics," including: (1) location in countries with weak states; (2) the irrelevance of borders; (3) a global financial infrastructure; (4) the rise of global cities; and (5) strategic alliances among criminal groups and the prevalence of network structures. Each of these factors was also important in the offshore insurance schemes that were described in this book.

The decline of the authority of the state to both regulate commerce and to control illegal activities is directly related to the emergence of new forms of organized crime. As the authors of the U.N. report note,

> [i]t is not coincidental that what some observers have termed the era of the failed nation-State is also the era of organized transnational crime. Acting from a "sanctuary" or a safe haven criminal organizations are able to extend their criminal activities into other countries, often developing important regional networks and sometimes extending their operations globally.[45]

Many developing countries lack both the technical resources—computers and electronic surveillance equipment, for example—and the legal structures, such as stiff banking regulations, to control criminal operations. The individuals behind many offshore insurance schemes found safe havens in small Caribbean countries that lacked the means for monitoring their activities. The regulatory agency responsible for monitoring the 200 insurance companies domiciled in the British Virgin Islands in the early 1990s, for example, had two full-time employees and an annual budget of $120,000.[46]

Two of the hallmark features of globalization are advanced telecommunication systems that link the world and accessible transportation systems through which individuals can easily traverse that world. The U.N. report notes that these same features have also facilitated international criminal activities in a "borderless world."

> Transnational criminal organizations are able to exploit the vast increase in global trade, the increase in personal mobility and the development of instantaneous communication systems . . . The result is that many States become unwilling hosts for criminal organizations that meet the demand for illicit products.[47]

In the case of offshore companies selling insurance in the United States, it was not that their products were inherently illicit, as are drugs or certain weapons, but that they were sold under the false premise that the companies would pay claims as required by their contracts. Nonetheless, just as international drug cartels take advantage of unmet demand for their products, so do offshore insurance crooks.

The growth of organized transnational crime groups has been greatly facilitated by the emergence of a global financial infrastructure, "a system [that] has many points of access and makes it possible to trade anonymously, to move money rapidly and easily and to obscure both the origin and ownership of capital."[48] That system is, in other words, a money-launderer's dream. While money-laundering is essential for international drug dealers and smugglers, it is also a significant component of many financial frauds, including many of the offshore insurance schemes described in the previous chapters. Stephen Coker, for example, the Alabama-based Teale ally (Chapter 1), set up an elaborate scheme for laundering the proceeds from an offshore insurance company (British and American Casualty) that involved first setting up a bogus reinsurance agreement with a company he owned, then moving premiums out of that company and into a bank account in the Cayman Islands, then moving those funds into a bank account in the Bahamas (which, like the Cayman Islands, had strict bank-secrecy laws). Finally, Coker and his associates would fly to the Bahamas and bring the money back into the United States in the form of cash, either by hiding it on their person, or bringing in amounts less than $10,000, the threshold that would have required them to declare the money to U.S. Customs and pay federal taxes.[49] In a similar, albeit cruder, fashion, J. Brian Lamb, the Arizona magistrate (Chapter 2), had policyholders send their premium checks to addresses in Miami and Arizona, which were then forwarded to bank accounts in Antigua. Checks were written on those accounts and sent back to Lamb and his associates in Arizona where they cashed them at a local convenience store.[50] The goal in these schemes was the same as it is in all money-laundering schemes: to conceal the origins and whereabouts of illegally obtained funds.

Borrowing a concept from economic sociology, the authors of the U.N. report state that this new form of geopolitics has benefited from the rise of "global cities," places that are "characterized by the concentration of financial power and the availability of highly developed banking and financial systems."[51] But more than making available technical resources to criminals, global cities create a certain "criminal synergism, as different national groups pool their talent and expertise."[52] Miami, where Teale and his colleagues operated the Insurance Exchange of the Americas (IEA), was clearly one of these global cities, and IEA was purposely designed to take advantage of its position as a gateway to Latin America. Moreover, Miami was a cosmopolitan place that attracted a diverse group of internationals with backgrounds in global insurance whose talents and skills were combined in the elaborate schemes that emanated from IEA. Yet, in many of the schemes that were discussed in earlier chapters, it wasn't the nature of the places where they were organized that was important so much as the kinds of people who were involved: individuals who were equally comfortable living abroad as in their native land and who were at ease working with persons from different countries and cultures.

Traditional organized crime groups have been characterized by extreme insularity and exclusivity based on common ethnic or national ties. By contrast, the new geopolitics of organized transnational crime is characterized by "strategic alliances" among various criminal groups that "resemble not traditional military alliances so much as strategic alliances among transnational corporations."[53] As in the corporate world, these alliances vary in their duration. While some are "based on some kind of formal or tacit agreement and . . . are underpinned by mutual expectations of continued cooperation," others are "ad hoc arrangements or one-time deals, in which criminal organizations come together for a specific transaction without any notion that the relationship will become more enduring."[54] In addition to reducing the amount of risk incurred by any single group, "strategic alliances can also be an important means of entering new markets that would otherwise be unavailable to one of the parties."[55] This was clearly the case in the Legend Sports case described in Chapter 3.

There, an alliance between Russian-American and Italian-American crime groups, securities scam artists, and offshore insurers served to advance the interests of all parties. The organized crime groups obtained access to the securities industry, the securities brokers gained access to both the "muscle" they needed as well as new products (promissory notes) to market, and the offshore insurers were able to move into a new, relatively risk-free (since they never intended to pay claims) area: surety bonds written on the promissory notes.

In addition to these interorganizational features, the authors of the U.N. report note that these new criminal organizations are characterized not by the rigid, hierarchical structure of older crime groups, but by a "network structure" that is difficult for law enforcement to penetrate, in large part because the components of the network are "loosely coupled"; each organization in the network operates with a high degree of autonomy, there is a low level of coordination among the organizations, and little or no centralized control.[56] Unlike "tightly coupled" systems where a disturbance to one component will likely damage other components, in "loosely coupled" networks, the impact of disturbances can be contained as linkages among the components can be severed and new ones made without damaging the core of the operation.

The model of "loosely coupled" networks accurately describes the relationships among the various actors in many of the offshore insurance schemes. One of the strengths of these schemes, and one that vexed regulators, was that they consisted of continually shifting networks of insurers, reinsurers, and the providers of bogus assets. When regulators determined that the securities pledged as assets by insurers were worthless, they were replaced with new ones, usually equally worthless. When regulators ordered a primary insurer to cease and desist operating, their policies were often simply rolled over to another company whose real owners were the same as the initial company's. After California regulators, for example, shut down First Assurance, its owners transferred funds out of the company's accounts to New Zealand where they started International Casualty Surety, placing on its books many of the same assets that the California authorities had determined to be of questionable value when they appeared on First Assurance's financial statements.

In sum, the groups involved in offshore insurance fraud share many, though not all, of the characteristics of organized transnational crime groups. Moreover, in terms of their organizational form, both groups have much in common with successful global business organizations. They are diverse, flexible, and highly mobile, giving them the ability to respond quickly and adapt to rapidly changing environments. These strengths help to explain why so many of the individuals involved in fraudulent offshore insurance schemes appear to have such longevity, surfacing and resurfacing in schemes that combine the old with the new, mixing elements from different financial industries in seemingly endless variations on the classic Ponzi scheme.

## Bringing the State Back In[57]

To a certain extent, then, offshore insurance fraud is the inevitable out-growth of globalization and its attendant social and economic trends. The same forces that have given rise to global business enterprises have also created global financial frauds. This does not mean, however, that we should simply accept it as part of the new global economy and sit by passively as thousands of individuals and companies are defrauded. Policy changes have already been made that have made it much more difficult for the Alan Teales of the world to perpetrate white-collar crimes using offshore insurance companies. Before making any specific policy recommendations, however, the larger question of the role of the state in these changes needs to be addressed.

Globalization advocates often make the argument that the withdrawal of the state from the governance of financial industries is a normal and ineluctable part of the globalization process. In this view, the liberalization of economies and markets is, like globalization itself, an unstoppable and irreversible process. As Thomas Friedman has bluntly put it: "Globalization isn't a choice. It's a reality. . . . And the most basic truth about globalization is this: *No one is in charge*"[58] (italics in original).

By contrast, a strong counterargument can be made that, far from a natural and inevitable process, deregulatory policies are the consequences of specific decisions made by specific political figures in specific countries operating within specific environments.[59] The decision to open up the California surplus lines market in the 1980s was not an inevitability but a decision made by a particular insurance commissioner who was responding to the interests of the insurance industry, and who was operating in a broader political environment in which deregulation was viewed as the way of the future. Similarly, legislation creating MEWAs and risk retention groups was sponsored by certain politicians who were trying to open up specific insurance markets to alternative, largely unregulated insurance providers, after large insurance companies had largely abandoned those markets. Therefore, just as deregulation is the result of intentional efforts by policy makers, so are movements to re-regulate markets and industries.

The ability of governments to successfully reduce fraud in the insurance industry by reasserting their roles as regulators was clearly demonstrated by initiatives undertaken in the early 1990s. The U.S. Department of Labor, along with state regulators, closed many of the loopholes in federal law (e.g., ERISA) that had allowed white-collar criminals to use MEWAs to orchestrate massive health insurance scams.[60] The California Department of Insurance, as discussed in Chapter 3, was able to dramatically reduce the incidence of offshore insurance fraud by tightening asset requirements and requiring precertification of those assets before surplus lines carriers could sell policies in the state. Yet, soon after these policies were implemented, critics called for a return to looser regulatory standards that, in their view, would expand consumer choices and promote "free market solutions" to insurance capacity problems.[61]

If there is one lesson to be learned from the insurance scandals of the 1980s and 1990s, it is that we need more, not less, supervision over the insurance industry, particularly the fraud-vulnerable offshore sector of that industry. And, the best way to accomplish this goal is through a system of federal regulation. This was the conclusion reached by Representative Dingell's committee. The committee was particularly critical of the ability of state regulators to control offshore insurance fraud:

> [T]he Subcommittee found that, overall, [state regulators] are woefully under-funded and ill-equipped to combat the sophisticated international insurance con artist who frequently changes not only his modus operandi, but also his corporate identity and location to avoid detection and prosecution.[62]

The committee stopped short of calling for full federal regulation of the entire insurance industry, but recommended that, at minimum, "all insurers and reinsurers not licensed in the United States must be supervised by a Federal Agency."[63]

Dingell's recommendations were seen as a direct challenge to the traditional state-based regulation of the insurance favored by state regulators and the insurance industry itself. Both of these groups waged vigorous fights to resist any form of federal regulation. Their efforts received an enormous boost in 1994 when Republicans took control over Congress and Representative Dingell, a Democrat, was removed as chairman of the House Commerce Committee and "with deregulation a rallying cry of the Gingrich Congress, the threat of a federal takeover for the moment disappeared."[64]

The need for federal regulation was and remains today most acute in the reinsurance industry. In its 1992 report, Dingell's committee concluded that "the offshore reinsurance industry is grossly unregulated by the current U.S. regulatory system."[65] One of the main problems is that state regulators lack both the authority and resources to pursue reinsurers and their brokers offshore. The recent debacles involving Stirling Cooke Brown and Unicover

Managers in the workers' compensation reinsurance market cited at the beginning of the chapter demonstrate that the need for regulatory oversight in this
area is critical. With the enactment of the Gramm-Leach-Biley Act (GLB) in
1999, which allowed banks to engage in the business of insurance, the possibility of taxpayers being forced to pick up the tab for reinsurance fiascoes such as
Unicover has increased.[66] If, instead of life insurance companies, banks had
been the participants in the Unicover reinsurance deals, it is conceivable that
their depositors and thus federal deposit insurance funds would have been
responsible for the more than $1.3 billion dollars in losses sustained in that
case.[67] Thus, as the banking, securities, and insurance industries converge, the
need for multistate regulation of insurance intensifies.

Moreover, the movement of white-collar criminals from one industry to
another necessitates more direct linkages among different regulatory and law
enforcement agencies. The weaknesses of the current system, in which state
insurance regulators and federal securities regulators work largely independently of one another, was revealed in a high-profile case involving a former
securities broker, Martin Frankel. In the early 1990s, while he was under investigation by the SEC for misconduct in the securities industry, Frankel gained
control of several insurance companies, which he then used to perpetrate
investment frauds that netted him and his associates over $200 million. In a
review of the Frankel case, the General Accounting Office concluded that had
state insurance regulators accessed information on Frankel's history in the
securities industry, his acquisition of the insurance companies could have been
blocked and his scheme thwarted before it got started.[68] More generally, the
case revealed the existence of a larger problem: "The migration of undesirable
persons, or rogues, from one industry to another is one of the many issues of
concern for financial services regulators that are attempting to implement the
GLB Act . . ."[69] This is the same phenomenon described in Chapter 3 where
offshore insurance criminals teamed up with securities con artists. At minimum, this suggests the need for heightened coordination among regulators,
including the creation of joint data bases to track the criminal and regulatory
histories of financial "rogues."[70]

Whether or not these policy changes are actually implemented depends,
ultimately, on the prevailing view in Washington on the appropriate role of
the state in managing the economy. It is quite possible that this view will lean
towards the laissez-faire perspective espoused by globalization advocates. In
this view the appropriate role of government is to make sure that citizens/con-
sumers have access to enough reliable information about the sellers of goods
and services to make sound choices but to otherwise stay out of the picture.[71]
Individuals, in this perspective, are often reduced to market actors, processing

information about markets and products and rationally calculating the costs and benefits of prospective transactions.

But what about people like Diane Collras (Introduction) who was simply trying to obtain affordable car insurance, or Anita Richardson (Chapter 3) who wanted to make a modest investment? Is it reasonable to expect them, and the vast majority of Americans, to understand the arcane intricacies of complex financial industries in order to make informed and prudent decisions about their personal finances? In the past, these people looked to governments to help them make those decisions and to guarantee that the people to whom they gave their money were honest and that they would get what they had paid for. In the brave new world of the globalization, however, governments are backing away from this responsibility, declining to monitor industries that are now said to be self-regulating. Yet, from Teale's Insurance Exchange of the Americas to the surplus lines industry of California these self-regulated enterprises have often failed, with disastrous consequences for consumers. This brings us to the hard conclusion that, despite utopian visions of new societies populated by rational consumers processing pure information about global products, it is only the state that has the power and authority to provide protection to ordinary men and women who are otherwise cast adrift in the stormy seas of the global economy where they are easy prey for financial knaves and buccaneers.

# NOTES

## INTRODUCTION

1. California Legislature, Senate Committee on Insurance, Claims and Corporations, Subcommittee on Nonadmitted Insurance, *Hearing on State Regulation of Nonadmitted Insurers and Surplus Lines Brokers* (Sacramento, June 15, 1992), 19.

2. Ibid., 17.

3. Ibid., 18.

4. Michael Wagner, "Phony Insurers," *Sacramento Bee*, February 21, 1994, A1.

5. House Committee on Energy and Commerce, Subcommittee on Oversight and Investigation, *Insurance Company Failures, Part 2*, 101st Cong., 2d sess., March 12 and March 19, 1990, 3.

6. House Committee on Energy and Commerce, Subcommittee on Oversight and Investigations, *Failed Promises: Insurance Company Insolvencies*, H. Rprt. 101st Cong., 2d sess., February 1990, 3.

7. A. M. Best, *Solvency Study of the Excess and Surplus Lines Industry*, 1996, 20.

8. Insurance insolvencies are generally covered by guaranty funds, managed by individual states, but contributed to by licensed insurance companies. Immediately, then, insolvencies are paid for by other members of the industry. However, since payments to the fund are tax deductible, the taxpayers ultimately pick up the check.

9. House, *Failed Promises*, 6.

10. House Committee on Energy and Commerce, Subcommittee on Oversight and Investigations, *Insurance Company Failures*, 103d Cong., 1st sess., May 19 and June 9, 1993, 14. Manual Roig-Franzia, "Edwards Guilty," *Times-Picayune* (New Orleans), May 10, 2000, A1.

11. House, *Failed Promises*, 46–47.

12. Ibid.

13. Senate Committee on Governmental Affairs, Permanent Subcommittee on Investigations, *Efforts to Combat Fraud and Abuse in the Insurance Industry, Part 1*, 102d Cong., 2d sess., April 24, 1991, 3.

14. Robert Tillman, *Broken Promises: Fraud by Small Business Health Insurers* (Boston: Northeastern University Press, 1998), 5.

15. Insurance Information Institute, "Financial Services Facts," www.financialservicefacts.org/agg_fr.html (accessed August 28, 2000).

16. Scott Paltrow, "How Insurance Firms Beat Back an Effort for Stricter Controls," *Wall Street Journal*, February 5, 1998, A1.

17. John Emshwiller, "Unscrupulous Promoters of MEWAs Cause Problems for Small Businesses," *Wall Street Journal*, May 15, 1990, B2.

18. General Accounting Office, *Employee Benefits: States Need Labor's Help Regulating Multiple Employer Welfare Arrangements*, GAO/HRD-92-40, March 1992, 2.

19. Karen Cutts, "Learning From RRG Failures," *Best's Review*, July 1, 1993, 46.

20. Douglas McLeod, "Charges Filed Against Officials," *Business Insurance*, March 21, 1994, 2. Jeffrey Meitrodt, "A Tale of Missing Cash," *Times-Picayune* (New Orleans), January 29, 1994, C1.

21. Thomas Mulligan, "Insurance Without Guarantees," *Los Angeles Times*, January 19, 1993, 1.

22. Ruth Gastel, ed., *Reinsurance: Fundamentals and New Challenges*, 3d ed. (New York: Insurance Institute Press, 1995), 1.

23. Senate Committee on Governmental Affairs, Permanent Subcommittee on Investigations, *Second Interim Report on U.S. Government Efforts to Combat Fraud and Abuse in the Insurance Industry*, S. Rprt. 102–310, 102d Cong., 2d sess., July 1, 1992, 26.

24. Gastel, *Reinsurance*, 61.

25. Ibid., 142.

26. David Johnston and Joseph Treaster, "Bermuda Move Allows Insurers to Avoid Taxes," *New York Times*, March 6, 2000, A1.

27. Sam Howe Verhovek and Steven Greenhouse, "National Guard Is Called to Quell Trade-Talk Protests," *New York Times*, December 1, 1999, A1.

28. Immanuel Wallerstein, *The Modern World System* (New York: Academic Press, 1974).

29. Manuel Castells, *The Rise of the Network Society* (Oxford, U.K.: Blackwell, 1996), 92–93. The concept, "global economy," does not encompass all of the cultural, social, and political impacts of "globalization." Held et al. define globalization as "a process (or set of processes) which embodies a transformation in the spatial organization of social relations and transactions—assessed in terms of their extensity, intensity, velocity, and impact—generating transcontinental or interregional flows and networks of activity, interaction, and the exercise of power." David Held, Anthony G. McGrew, David Goldblatt, and Jonathan Perraton, *Global Transformations* (Stanford, Cal.: Stanford University Press, 1999), 16.

30. Thomas Friedman, *The Lexus and the Olive Tree* (New York: Farrar, Straus and Giroux, 1999). Daniel Yergin and Joseph Stanislaw, *The Commanding Heights* (New York: Simon and Schuster, 1998). John Micklethwait and Adrian Wooldridge, *A Future Perfect: The Challenge and Hidden Promise of Globalization* (New York: Crown, 2000). See also, the articles in a special issue of *Le Monde Diplomatique*, June 1997, recording a debate on globalization involving staff from *Le Monde Diplomatique* and the *Financial Times* of London.

31. Micklethwait and Wooldridge, *A Future Perfect*, 341–342.

32. Ibid., xxii–xxiii.

33. Ibid., xxiii.

34. William Grieder, *One World, Ready or Not* (New York: Simon and Schuster, 1997). Richard Barnet and John Cavanagh, *Global Dreams* (New York: Simon and Schuster, 1994). Jerry Mander and Edward Goldsmith, eds., *The Case Against the Global Economy* (New York: Random House, 1996). John Gray, *False Dawn* (New York: The New Press, 1998).

35. R. Thomas Naylor, *Hot Money and the Politics of Debt* (New York: Simon and Schuster, 1987).

36. R. Martin, "Stateless Monies, Global Financial Integration and National Economy Autonomy," in *Money, Power, and Space*, R. Martin and N. Thrift, eds. (Oxford, U.K., and Cambridge, Mass.: Blackwell, 1994), 253–278.

37. Barnet and Cavanagh, *Global Dreams*, 385–402.

38. As William Grieder has written, "Big money hides in the global economy. Respectable capital mingles alongside dirty money from illegal enterprises (drugs, gambling, arm sales)." Grieder, *One World*, 33.

39. Tillman, *Broken Promises*, 199.

40. Ibid.

41. Not all globalization scholars agree. Vogel, for example, argues that what many people see as governmental deregulation is actually "reregulation." Steven Vogel, *Freer Markets, More Rules* (Ithaca, N.Y.: Cornell University Press, 1996), 3.

42. Susan Strange, *The Retreat of the State* (Cambridge, U.K.: Cambridge University Press, 1996).

43. Manuel Castells, *The Power of Identity* (Oxford, U.K.: Blackwell, 1997), 243–308.

44. Saskia Sassen, *Globalization and Its Discontents* (New York: The New Press, 1998), 20.

45. Vogel, *Freer Markets*, 2.

46. For dissenting views see: Vogel, ibid., 9–24; and Paul Hirst and Grahame Thompson, *Globalization in Question*, 2d ed. (Cambridge, U.K.: Polity Press, 1999), 1–18.

47. Sassen, *Globalization*, xxvii.

48. Brian Johnson, "Manager's Journal: Financial Accord Will Benefit a Superbreed of Firms," *Wall Street Journal*, December 15, 1997, A22.

49. Remarks by Chairman Alan Greenspan at the Charlotte Chamber of Commerce, Charlotte, North Carolina, July 10, 1998.

50. Grieder, *One World*, 34.

51. Barnet and Cavanagh, *Global Dreams*, 397.

52. Manuel Castells, *End of Millennium* (Oxford, U.K.: Blackwell, 1998), 52.

53. Claire Sterling, *Thieves' World: The Threat of the New Global Network of Organized Crime* (New York: Simon and Schuster, 1994), 13–20.

54. John Kerry, *The New War* (New York: Simon and Schuster, 1997), 21.

55. Louise Shelley, "Crime and Corruption in the Digital Age," *Journal of International Affairs* 51 (1998): 605.

56. Jack Blum, a well-known investigator, who helped break the BCCI case, testified before a congressional committee looking into international organized crime: "The really large problem that's coming in international organized crime is in the area of financial fraud. That has been overlooked because it is not as dramatic, it is not as glamorous, but I would argue it's probably, in terms of social implications, the most dangerous of all." Testimony of Jack Blum before the House International Relations Committee, *The Threat from International Organized Crime and Global Terrorism*, 105th Cong., 2d sess., October 1, 1997, 39.

57. Martin Needleman and Carolyn Needleman, "Organizational Crime: Two Models of Criminogenesis," *Sociological Quarterly* 20 (1979): 517–539.

58. Sassen, *Globalization*, 199.

59. Ibid., 198.

60. Henry Pontell and Kitty Calavita, "The Savings and Loan Industry," in *Above the Law: Crime in Complex Organizations*, Michael Tonry and Albert Reiss, eds. (Chicago: University of Chicago Press, 1993), 203–246.

61. Tillman, *Broken Promises*.

62. John McArthur, "Anti-Trust in the New [De]Regulated Natural Gas Industry," *Energy Law Journal* 18 (1997): 18.

63. Susan Robertson, "Small Place, Big Money," *Economic Geography* 71 (1995): 253.

64. Testimony of Jack Blum before the House Committee on Banking and Financial Services, *Money Laundering Deterrence Act of 1998*, 105th Cong., 2d sess., June 11, 1998, 116.

65. Douglas McLeod, "Regulators in Turks and Caicos Beef Up Their Scrutiny," *Business Insurance*, April 18, 1994, 1.

66. Robertson, "Small Place," 246.

67. "Offshore Business in Antigua and Barbuda," www.antigua-barbuda.com (accessed January 12, 2001).

68. "1997 Exempt Insurance Act," www.ibuoffshoredominica.dm/einsact.htm (accessed January 12, 2001).

69. Blum, Testimony, 1997, 37.

70. Raymond Michaelowski and Ronald Kramer, "The Space Between Laws," *Social Problems* 34 (1987): 34–53.

71. John Walton, "Making the Theoretical Case," in *What Is a Case?, Exploring the Foundations of Social Inquiry*, Charles Ragin and Howard Becker, eds., (New York: Cambridge University Press, 1992), 122.

### CHAPTER 1

1. Robin Greg, "City: British Insurer Arrested in US," *Sunday Telegraph* (London), January 17, 1993, 35.

2. Peter Gartland, "Scalped by a Pin-Striped Cherokee," *The Times of London*, September 26, 1993.

3. Janis Johnson, "Miami Plans International Insurance Exchange," *Washington Post*, March 29, 1991, H1.

4. Kitty Calavita, Henry Pontell, and Robert Tillman, *Big Money Crime* (Berkeley: University of California Press, 1997), 11–15.

5. Frederic Dannen, "Miami Vice," *Institutional Investor*, February 1986, 170.

6. Johnson, "Miami Plans," H1.

7. Donald Maggin, *Bankers, Builders, Knaves, and Thieves* (Chicago: Contemporary Books, 1989).

8. Cornelius Foote, "State Sues Universal Casualty Owners," *Miami Herald*, November 15, 1985, 18. D. Dannen, "Miami Vice," 8.

9. Steve Lohr, "Record Fine by Lloyd's in Final Scandal Inquiry," *New York Times*, November 13, 1985, 1. James Schut, "On the Trail of a Fugitive from Lloyd's," *Institutional Investor*, December 1, 1996, 39. Cameron-Webb was forced out of IEA in December of 1985 by the board of governors who were concerned about bad publicity arising out of public allegations about his misconduct at Lloyd's.

10. William Griffin, Harry Knight, Donald Brown, and Michael Berry, *Insurance Exchange of the Americas, Inc.: Task Force Interim Report* (Tallahassee: State of Florida, 1989), Appendix 4b.

11. Ibid.

12. Senate Committee on Govenmental Affairs, Permanent Subcommittee on Investigations, *Efforts to Combat Fraud and Abuse in the Insurance Industry, Part II*, 102d Cong., 2d sess., June 26, 1991, 33.

13. Griffin et al., *Insurance Exchange*, 6.

14. Ibid., 19.

15. Dannen, "Miami Vice," 172.

16. "No Bull, Angus' Hide Covered by $1 Million Insurance Policy," *Chicago Tribune*, September 13, 1985, 3.

17. Steve Liesman and Lucy Morgan, "Insurance Project Under Investigation," *St. Petersburg Times*, September 6, 1991, 1E.

18. House Committee on Energy and Commerce, Subcommittee on Oversight and Investigations, *Failed Promises: Insurance Company Insolvencies*, H. Rprt. 101st Cong., 2d sess., February 1990, 10.

19. Ibid., 52.

20. Brent Schondelmeyer, "Feds Launch New Investigation into Insurance Company," *Kansas City Business Journal*, January 4, 1991, 1.

21. Brent Schondelmeyer, "Federal Complaint Links KC Area Firm to Alleged Bribery," *Kansas City Business Journal*, April 16, 1990, 1.

22. John Dauner, "Care for Disabled Son Is Factor in Probation," *Kansas City Star*, January 23, 1993, B1.

23. Editorial, "Judge's Lenient Sentences Don't Fit Massive Swindle," *Omaha World-Herald*, February 2, 1993, 6.

24. Odalys Mesa, "Intercontinental Bank Names New Officer from Westchester," *Miami Herald*, June 14, 1984, 27.

25. Senate Committee on Governmental Affairs, Permanent Subcommittee on Investigations, *Efforts to Combat Fraud and Abuse in the Insurance Industry, Part 1*, 102d Cong., 2d sess., April 24, 1991, 92–95.

26. *United States v. Alan Teale and Charlotte Rentz*, No. Cr-93–00002 (S.D. Ala. 1993) ("Complaint"), 2–3.

27. Ibid., 5.

28. Ibid., 6.

29. Ibid.

30. Ibid., 6–7.

31. Ibid., 5.

32. Ibid., 5–6.

33. Peter De Vos, "Insurance Fraud: Belgium," *Insurance & Reinsurance Solvency Report*, November 4, 1993, 562.

34. Douglas McLeod, "Another Player Rounded Up in Fraud Scheme," *Business Insurance*, January 24, 1994, 2.

35. *United States v. Stephen Coker*, No. Cr-94–00128 (S.D. Ala. 1994) ("Superseding Indictment"), 10.

36. Joanne Wjojcik, "Regulators Win in California," *Business Insurance*, December 23, 1991, 2.

37. Thomas Mulligan, "Insurance Without Guarantees," *Los Angeles Times*, January 19, 1993, A1.

38. Senate Committee, *Efforts to Combat, Part I*, 10.

39. Ibid., 9.

40. Ibid., 787.

41. Ibid., 31.

42. Ibid.

43. Ibid., 32.

44. Ibid.

45. Ibid., 802.

46. Ibid., 804.

47. Ibid., 793–794.

48. Ibid., 799–801.

49. Ibid., 53.

50. Ibid., 564.

51. The exploits of James Charge and Charles Gordon-Seymour are described in Chapters 2 and 3. Mr. Yorke-Wade had an equally colorful career. As a *Business Week* article put it: "trouble does seem to follow wherever Yorke-Wade goes." In the early 1990s, he was affiliated with a Uruguay-based insurance company that sold policies to motel owners and cab drivers in the United States and had a history of not paying claims (Amy Barrett, "Bending the Rules—Or Breaking Them?" *Business Week*, November 13, 1995, 122). In 1995, California regulators shut down another of his Uruguayan clients, Azteca Insurances, S.A., which Yorke-Wade claimed was exempt from state regulation under the North American Free Trade Agreement (NAFTA) (California Department of Insurance, *In the Matter of Azteca Insurances, S.A. Order to Cease and Desist*, File No. SF15168-AP, 1995). In 1997, Mr. Yorke-Wade was arrested in the United Kingdom in connection to his activities at Dai Ichi Kyoto, the Belgium reinsurer that was at the center of a scandal that resulted in losses of £100 million to Lloyd's of London and other insurers (Douglas McLeod, "Former Teale Associate Arrested," *Business Insurance*, July 14, 1997, 23. Robert Tyerman, "City: London Insurers Hit by £100m 'Fraud,' " *Sunday Telegraph* (London), December 24, 1995, 1). In an even more bizarre incident, later that year Yorke-Wade's name appeared in connection with Equisure Inc., a U.S. reinsurance holding company with subsidiaries in Belgium that was forced to withdraw from the American Stock Exchange after allegations surfaced regarding stock manipulation by company insiders. A suit filed against the company claimed that its recently hired CEO, a purported South African national named David Suchman, was in fact Paul Yorke-Wade who had assumed a false identity (Douglas McLeod, "Equisure Won't Fight Ouster," *Business Insurance*, August 25, 1997, 2).

52. *The National Federation of State High School Associations v. Douglas Ruedlinger*, No. 93-2344 (Kan. 1993) ("Complaint"), 10.

53. Stephen Wermiel, "Injured Athletes Face Dilemma: Cash or Court?" *Wall Street Journal*, March 22, 1985, 27.

54. Clare Ansberry and Erle Norton, "Catastrophic Loss: High-School Athletes with Severe Injuries Face Huge Bills Alone," *Wall Street Journal*, June 21, 1993, A1.

55. *National Federation v. Ruedlinger* ("Complaint"), 4–5.

56. Senate Committee, *Efforts to Combat, Part III*, 204–205.

57. Bill Lodge, "Financial Injuries: Students Lose Benefits After Reinsurers Fail," *Dallas Morning News*, July 19, 1993, 1A.

58. Ansberry and Norton, "Catastrophic Loss." Gregory Smith, "Fund Drive Starts for Victims of UI Collapse," *Providence Journal-Bulletin*, January 29, 1994, 1.

59. Bill Lodge, "Indictment Alleges Businessman Siphoned from Funds for Students," *Dallas Morning News*, June 18, 1996, 15A.

60. Ansberry and Norton, "Catastrophic Loss," A1.

61. CBS news, Transcript, *Eye to Eye with Connie Chung*, Broadcast August 12, 1993.

62. Ibid.

63. Ansberry and Norton, "Catastrophic Loss," A1.

64. *United States v. Douglas Ruedlinger and Edwin Carpenter*, No. Cr-97–40012 (Kan. 1997) ("Second Superseding Indictment"), 9.

65. Justin Blum, "Defaulting Broker Back in Business," *Washington Post*, July 6, 1993, D3.

66. *United States. v. Ruedlinger and Carpenter* ("Sentencing Memorandum"), 2.

67. *United States v. Ruedlinger*, ("Douglas Ruedlinger's Consolidated Memorandum in Aid of Sentencing").

68. Ibid.

69. Ibid.

70. Susan Headden, Gordon Witkin, and Mary Lord, "Preying on the Helpless," *U.S. News & World Report*, May 24, 1993, 48.

71. *Florida Department of Insurance v. Doherty, et al.*, No. 90-6321-CA-16-1. (18th Judicial Circuit, County of Seminole, Florida 1990) ("Complaint"), 24–25.

72. Ibid., 24.

73. Ibid., 22.

74. Ibid., 21.

75. Robert McCabe, "5-Year-Old Insurance Fraud Is Still Haunting Its Victims," *Sun-Sentinel* (Ft. Lauderdale), July 3, 1995, 4.

76. *Florida v. Doherty*, 28.

77. Senate Committee, *Efforts to Combat, Part V*, 80.

78. Ibid., 105.

79. Ibid., 78.

80. California Surplus Lines Association, "Bulletin 565, Re: Promed International Limited (British Virgin Islands)," www.sla-cal.org/bulletin/5xx/bulletin565.htm (accessed April 16, 2001).

81. Senate Committee, *Efforts to Combat, Part IV*, 82.

82. Ibid., 88.

83. Bill Lodge, "Insurer Faces 7 Wire, Mail Fraud Counts," *Dallas Morning News*, January 11, 1991, 32A.

84. Joanne Wojcik, "Brokers Liable for Claims Under Garamendi Plan," *Business Insurance*, October 14, 1991, 1.

85. Calavita et al., *Big Money Crime*, 25.

86. Darrell Preston, "Fraud Probe Ropes In S&L Kingpins," *Dallas Business Journal*, August 23, 1991, 1.

87. Robert McCabe, "Gallagher Continues Legal Pursuit of Man He Says Duped State," *Orlando Sentinel*, April 28, 1994, D11.

88. *Florida v. Doherty*, ("Complaint"), 46–47.

89. Charlie Whited, "Loss of Benefits a Shocking Stroke of Fate," *Miami Herald*, September 2, 1990, 1B.

90. Ibid.

91. McCabe, "5-Year-Old Insurance Probe," 4.

92. Senate Committee, *Efforts to Combat, Part II*, 71.

93. *United States v. Dallas Bernard Russell Bessant*, No. Cr-96–177–01 (E.D. Pa. 1996) ("Government's Sentencing Memorandum"), 5.

94. Senate Committee, *Efforts to Combat, Part II*, 80.

95. Constance B. Foster, Pennsylvania Insurance Commissioner, *Findings of Fact*, June 6, 1991, 7.

96. Ibid.

97. *United States v. Philip Rennert, et al.*, No. Cr-96–51 (E.D. Pa. 1996) ("Indictment"), 16.

98. Foster, *Findings*, 7.

99. Ibid., 17.

100. Darrell Preston, "Investigators Widen Probe of Bogus Asset," *Dallas Business Journal*, November 1, 1991, 1.

101. *United States v. Rennert, et al.* ("Indictment"), 9.

102. Foster, *Findings*, 7.

103. *United States. v. Rennert, et al.* ("Indictment"), 20, 27.

104. Ibid., 9–10.

105. Ibid., 10.

106. Michael Schroeder, "Shell Game: Stock Scam Dolled Up Public Corporations Only to 'Rent' Them," *Wall Street Journal*, June 11, 1997, A1.

107. Foster, *Findings*, 7.

108. Securities and Exchange Commission, "About Microcap Fraud," www.sec.gov/news/extra/microcap.htm (accessed May 17, 1999).

109. Senate Committee, *Efforts to Combat, Part II*, 84–91.

110. Senate Committee, *Efforts to Combat, Part III*, 53.

111. Ibid., 54.

112. *United States v. Dallas Bernard Russell Bessant* ("Memorandum of Interview"), 5.

113. Senate Committee, *Efforts to Combat, Part III*, 59.

114. Ibid., 65–67.

115. Ibid., 63.

116. Ibid., 69.

117. *United States v. Dallas Bernard Russell Bessant* ("Memorandum of Interview"), 2.

118. House Committee on Energy and Commerce, Subcommittee on Oversight and Investigations, *Insurance Company Failures*, 103d Cong., 1st sess., May 19 and June 9, 1993, 52.

119. Ibid.

120. Ibid.

121. Senate Committee, *Efforts to Combat, Part II*, 86.

122. Senate Committee, *Efforts to Combat, Part III*, 79.

123. Ibid., 81.

124. Ibid.

125. Ibid., 84.

126. Ibid., 104.

127. Ibid., 105.

128. Ibid., 106.

129. Senate Committee, *Efforts to Combat, Part II*, 93.

130. Ibid.

131. Barret, "Bending the Rules." Tyerman, "London Insurers Hit." William Goodwin, "SFO on Trail of £100m Insurance Fraudsters," *The Independent* (London), April 13, 1997, 1.

132. Senate Committee, *Efforts to Combat, Part II*, 84.

133. Senate Committee, *Efforts to Combat, Part III*, 5–6.

134. Ibid.

135. Ibid.

136. House Committee, *Insurance Company Failures*, 105.

137. Senate Committee, *Efforts to Combat, Part III*, 112.

## CHAPTER 2

1. California Legislature, Senate Committee on Insurance, Claims and Corporations, Subcommittee on Nonadmitted Insurance, *Hearing on State Regulation of Nonadmitted Insurers and Surplus Lines Brokers* (Sacramento, June 15, 1992), 4.

2. Alan Miller, "Inner-City Insurance Bias Cited," *Los Angeles Times*, June 10, 1992, D1. Robert Lopez, "Insurance Even Tougher to Find Since the Riots," *Los Angeles Times*, May 8, 1994, 7.

3. Leo Herzel and Daniel Harris, "Cal. Car Insurance Groups in a Spin," *Financial Times*, November 29, 1988, 33.

4. Scott Armstrong, "California Car Insurance Revolt," *Christian Science Monitor*, February 22, 1988, 3.

5. Ralph Nader, "Double Protection for Consumers in Prop. 103," *Los Angeles Times*, November 3, 1988, 7.

6. Albert Crenshaw, "Geico Curbs Operations in California," *Washington Post*, November 19, 1988, D11.

7. Thomas Mulligan, "Insurance Without Guarantees," *Los Angeles Times*, January 19, 1993, 1.

8. Ibid.

9. Ibid.

10. California Senate Committee, *Hearing*, 5.

11. Ibid.

12. *Bae, et al. v. Anchorage Fire & Casualty, et al.*, No. BC079891 (Super. Ct. of Los Angeles County 1992) ("Complaint"), 13.

13. Quoted by John Garamendi in testimony before the House Committee on Energy and Commerce Subcommittee on Oversight and Investigations, *Insurance Company Failures*, 102d Cong., 2d sess., April 9, 1992, 305.

14. Michael Wagner, "Millions in Premiums Vanished," *Sacramento Bee*, February 20, 1994, A1.

15. Ibid.

16. California Senate Committee, *Hearing*, 19–20.

17. Mulligan, "Insurance Without Guarantees," 1.

18. Michael Wagner, "Auto Insurance Scam Left $70 Million in Claims Unpaid," *Sacramento Bee*, February 20, 1994, A31.

19. Marc Lifsher, "Fly-by-Night Auto Insurer Thriving," *Orange County Register*, December 8, 1991, A1.

20. Kenneth Reich, "State to Go After 'Offshore' Insurers Auto Coverage," *Los Angeles Times*, October 5, 1991, 21.

21. "Calif. Sees Offshore Insurers Bilking Consumers," *National Underwriter: Property & Casualty/Risk & Benefits Management Edition*, November 2, 1992, 50.

22. *United States v. James E. Charge and John H. Nellmapius*, No. Cr-97–0168 (S.D. Fla. 1997) ("Indictment").

23. Ibid.

24. Prior to his involvement with ERISA Advantage, John B. Hyde had been associated with several health insurance scams, including a Texas organization known as the National Association of Preferred Providers (NAPP). After Texas regulators cracked down on NAPP, Hyde moved several hundred policyholders into a plan offered through a bogus New York labor union, that was later shut down by the U.S. Department of Labor (Douglas McLeod, "Plan Run by Operators of Failed Ventures Seized," *Business Insurance*, August 17, 1998, 1). Cordell Hull was a former Texas state legislator and insurance agent whose license was revoked after state officials determined he was selling insurance policies for a corrupt MEWA, Cabot-Day, that failed leaving $5.7 million in unpaid claims (Bill Lodge, "Three Accused in Health Care Scam," *San Diego Tribune*, September 6, 1998, A-25).

25. Douglas McLeod, "Plan Run by Operators of Failed Ventures Seized," *Business Insurance*, August 17, 1998, 1.

26. Ibid.

27. Josh Goldstein, "California Orders Serpico to Stop Business in State," *Journal of Commerce*, October 26, 1988, 11A.

28. Ibid.

29. Ibid.

30. Marc Lifscher, "Offshore Insurance," *Orange County Register*, December 9, 1991, A19. Mary Lynne Vellinga, "Hidden High Perils Truckers Insurance Often Not Legitimate," *Sacramento Bee*, April 20, 1992, A1.

31. *United States v. Jerry Brian Lamb, et al.*, No. Cr-99–127 (D. Ariz. 1999) ("Indictment").

32. Tod Robertson, "Title Fight in Panama," *Dallas Morning News*, November 12, 1999, 1A.

33. Jerry Kammer, "Lamb's Uncle: Cash in Panama," *Arizona Republic*, March 1, 1999, A1.

34. "Ex-JP Given 2½ Years for Insurance Scam," *Arizona Republic*, August 12, 2000, B1.

35. "Fraud Term Won't Halt Ex-JP's State Pension," *The Tucson Citizen*, June 26, 2000, 3C.

36. The Insurance Industry Committee for the Special Problems in the South Central Los Angeles Area, *The Insurance Business and the South Central Los Angeles Area*, 1966, 5.

37. These observations were confirmed by researchers at UCLA who found that three-fourths of the store owners reporting losses from the riots were Korean Americans. They estimated that losses to Korean American–owned businesses totaled $359 million (Paul Ong and Suzanne Hee, *Losses in the Los Angeles Civil Unrest, April 29–May 1, 1992*, Center for Pacific Rim Studies, University of California at Los Angeles, 1993), 12.

38. Testimony of Julie Paik, Asian Pacific American Legal Center before the California Senate Committee on Insurance, Claims and Corporations, Sacramento, March 24, 1994.

39. "Department of Insurance Report Shows Hundreds of Millions of Dollars in Uninsured Losses from L.A. Civil Disturbances," *Business Wire*, September 17, 1992, 1.

40. Robert Lopez, "Insurance Even Tougher to Find Since the Riots," *Los Angeles Times*, May 8, 1994, 7.

41. *Bae v. Anchorage Fire & Casualty* ("Complaint"), 183–184.

42. Ibid.

43. *Janice D. Loyd v. PaineWebber, et al.*, No. 95-cv-1194 (S.D. Calif. 1995) ("Exhibit 4: First Assurance Timeline").

44. Darrell Preston, "State Cancels Insurance Policies Backed by Worthless Assets," *Dallas Business Journal*, March 13, 1992, 28.

45. Tim Bryant, "Blumeyer Confident of Future After Trial," *St. Louis Post-Dispatch*, January 31, 1994, 1B.

46. Tim Bryant, "Ex-Insurance Executive Gets Nearly 22 Years for Fraud," *St. Louis Post-Dispatch*, July 20, 1996, 1B.

47. Fiona Rotherman, "Los Angeles Riot Victims Sue Kiwi Insurance Company," *Independent Business Weekly*, August 18, 1995, 1.

48. Bill Lodge, "Insurance Empire's Fall Leaves Questions," *Dallas Morning News*, October 2, 1991, 1A. Darrell Preston, " 'Godfather' of Thrift Failures Pulled into Ginnie Mae Probe," *Dallas Business Journal*, September 11, 1991, 1.

49. *Loyd v. PaineWebber* ("Exhibit 4").

50. California Code of Regulations, Title 10, §2174.

51. Ibid.

52. Darrell Preston, "Investigators Widen Probe of Bogus Asset: SEC Joins State Investigations of Penny Stock Manipulation," *Dallas Business Journal*, November 1, 1991, 1.

53. Ibid.

54. Ibid.

55. California Surplus Lines Association, "Bulletin 576, Re: First Assurance and Casualty Co., Ltd. (Turks and Caicos)," www.sla-cal.org/bulletin/5xx/bulletin576.htm (accessed April 16, 2001).

56. Ibid.

57. Ibid.

58. David Dietz and April Lynch, "State Lax On Insurance Abuses," *San Francisco Chronicle*, September 29, 1998, A1.

59. April Lynch and David Dietz, "Insurance Nightmares," *San Francisco Chronicle*, September 30, 1998, A1.

60. Lopez, "Insurance Even Tougher to Find," 7.

61. *Bae v. Anchorage, et al.* ("Complaint"), 170–173.

62. *In re First Assurance and Casualty Co., Ltd.*, No. 93–16187-TS (W.D. Okla. 1993) ("Proceedings Held Before Charles Snyder, Attorney at Law, Meeting of Creditors Taken on December 4, 1993, in Oklahoma City, Oklahoma"), 11–12.

63. Winston-Hill was a notorious offshore insurer that had a long history of involvement in corrupt schemes. The company was founded in the Bahamas in 1986 by a former Bahamian politician and an accountant. In 1999, the pair was charged by a federal grand jury in Houston with creating phony financial statements and perpetrating frauds that resulted in $15 million in unpaid claims (Douglas McLeod, "Two Indicted in Fraud," *Business Insurance*, January 18, 1999, 1).

64. Marc Lifsher, "O.C. Failed to Check Out Insurer of Contractor," *Orange County Register*, July 19, 1993, A1.

65. Dan Luzadder, "Phony Bond Stings Museum," *Rocky Mountain News*, April 17, 1994, 5A.

66. *DeWayne Bailey v. Empire Blue Cross/Blue Shield*, No. 93-cv-6179 (MP) (S.D.N.Y. 1993) ("Declaration of Jim Harrington of the California Department of Insurance"), 3.

67. Robert Tillman, *Broken Promises: Fraud by Small Business Health Insurers* (Boston: Northeastern University Press, 1998), 114.

68. Alfred Haggerty, "Scam Victim Appeals to Garamendi," *National Underwriter*, November 15, 1993, 28.

69. *In re First Assurance and Casualty*, 12.

70. *United States. v. Havenar*, No. 98-cr-164 (W.D. Okla. 1998) ("Indictment"), 11.

71. *United States. v. Havenar* ("Amended Synopsis"), 4.

72. California Surplus Lines Association, "Bulletin 576, Re: First Assurance and Casualty Co., Ltd."

73. Douglas McLeod, "Execs with Ties to Failed Insurer Form New Venture," *Business Insurance*, March 7, 1994, 1.

74. "Chalkie and AM Best Find IC&S Not the Best Bet," *Independent Business Weekly*, August 4, 1999, 32.

75. Fiona Rotherham, "Is NZ Becoming the Insurance Industry's Wild West?" *Independent Business Weekly*, August 2, 1996, 8.

76. Insurance Council of New Zealand, www.icnz.org (accessed February 16, 2000).

77. "Chalkie and AM Best," 32.

78. Douglas McLeod, "Execs with Ties." 908 F. Supp. 459; 1995 U.S. Dist. LEXIS 18505.

79. "Et Dona Ferentes," *World Insurance Corporate Report*, May 6, 1994, 1.

80. "Texan Collects $86,000 Tire-Recycling Subsidy, Skips Town," *The Salt Lake Tribune*, August 28, 1996, B2.

81. Douglas McLeod, "Indictment Alleges Diversion of Funds," *Business Insurance*, November 16, 1998, 2.

82. *United States v. Havenar* ("Amended Synopsis"), 8.

83. *United States v. Havenar* ("Defendant Maynard Memorandum of Points and Authorities in Support of Motion to Quash"), 2.

84. Jones was acquitted and charges were earlier dropped against Jain because of health problems. Another defendant, Donald Havenar, remains, as of this writing, in jail in Mexico where he awaits extradition to the United States. Charges against Lewis were dropped.

85. Douglas McLeod, "IC&S to Rise from the Ashes," *Business Insurance*, March 20, 2000, 1.

86. Ibid.

87. Thomas Mulligan, "Garamendi Bars Nearly 250 of State's Insurers," *Los Angeles Times*, June 4, 1993, 1.

88. California Department of Insurance, *1997 Commissioner's Report on Underserved Communities: Executive Summary* (Sacramento 1997), 2.

89. California Department of Insurance, *California's Uninsured: Preliminary Report* (Sacramento 1998), 1.

90. Ibid., 9.

91. Mulligan, "Insurance Without Guarantees," 1.

92. John Jenning, " 'New Breed' of Schemer Seen on Insurance Fraud Scene," *National Underwriter Property & Casualty–Risk & Benefits Management*, September 25, 1995, 10.

93. House Committee, *Insurance Company Failures*, 85.

## CHAPTER 3

1. Public Law 103-22. "Violent Crime Control and Law Enforcement Act of 1994," §320603.

2. Testimony of Frederick Wolf, General Accounting Office, before the House Committee on Energy and Commerce, Subcommittee on Oversight, *Insurance Company Failures*, 101st Cong., 1st sess., April 5, 1989, 591. Andrew Tobias, "Not a Sure Thing." *Time*, October 22, 1990, 49.

3. Dan Moffet, "Mobsters May Be Riding Bull Market," *Palm Beach Post*, June 19, 1999, 1A.

4. Florida statutes do exempt from registration notes that mature in nine months or less, but the provision refers "only to prime quality negotiable commercial paper of a type not ordinarily purchased by the general public," Fla. Statutes, Title XXXIII, §517.051(8).

5. Helen Huntley, "Some Insurance Agents Selling Junk Investments," *St. Petersburg Times*, December 26, 1999.

6. North American Securities Administrators Association, "State Securities Cops Release New List of 'Top 10 Investment Scams,' " Press Release, May 24, 1999, 1.

7. Alan Byrd, "Legend Sports Finding Its Home on the Range," *Orlando Business Journal*, December 23, 1996, 1.

8. *Securities and Exchange Commission v. James Staples, et al.*, No. 98-1061-cv-22c (M.D. Fla. 1998) ("Complaint for Injunctive Relief"), 6–10.

9. *Florida Department of Banking and Finance v. LSI Holdings*, Administrative Proceeding No. 0062-I-7/96 ("Amended Emergency Cease and Desist Order with Notice of Rights"), Filed November 26, 1996, 4.

10. Ibid.

11. *Securities and Exchange Commission v. Staples*, 5.

12. Douglas McLeod, "Worthless Notes Back Insurer," *Business Insurance*, August 12, 1996, 1. Senate Committee on Governmental Affairs, Permanent Subcommittee on Investigations, *Efforts to Combat Fraud and Abuse in the Insurance Industry, Part I*, 102d Cong., 1st sess., April 24, 1991, 92.

13. McLeod, "Worthless Notes," 1.

14. Ibid.

15. Janet Plume, "Trial of La. Commissioner Begins," *Journal of Commerce*, February 21, 1991, 9A.

16. William T. Quinn and Bev McCarron, "Intrigue Gathers on a Hilltop," *The Star-Ledger* (Newark), July 27, 1997, 19.

17. Ibid. Tom Demoretcky, "Bank Officer Gets 2 Years over Loan," *Newsday*, December 6, 1996, A52.

18. *International Capital Equipment v. Peter G. Stanley, et al.*, No. 97-cv-1423 (D. N.J. 1997) ("Complaint"), 14.

19. Quinn and McCarron, "Intrigue," 10.

20. Robert Rudolph, "Failed Insurer Admits Fraud," *Star-Ledger* (Newark), December 9, 1998, 17.

21. McLeod, "Worthless Notes," 1.

22. Sean MacCarthaigh, "Thousands May Lose Out on 'Cash Back' Guarantee," *Irish Times*, August 27, 1997, 14. Robert Wright, "Anger Expected over Closed Company's Dud 'Cheques,' " *Financial Times*, August 22, 1997, 6.

23. Douglas McLeod, "Regulators Bar Offshore Insurers from Colorado," *Business Insurance*, May 26, 1997, 1.

24. Douglas McLeod, "Reinsurers Refute Claim of Corporate Debt Guarantees," *Business Insurance*, February 24, 1997, 1.

25. Securities and Exchange Commission, *Litigation Release No. 15286*, March 12, 1997, 1.

26. *Philip Richardson v. Legend Sports, Inc.* No. Cv-98–201 (Super. Ct., County of Kennebec, Maine 1998) ("Complaint"), 1–8. *State of Maine and Securities Administrator v. Steven M. England*, No. Cv-98–55 (1998) (Super. Ct., County of Kennebec, Maine 1998) ("Complaint"), 1–9. Betty Adams, "Lawsuit Attempts to Recoup Investment," *Kennebec Journal* (Augusta, Maine), August 13, 1998, B1.

27. *Herman Gatchell v. Legend Sports, Inc.*, No. 98-cv-272 (D. Me. 1998) ("Complaint"), 2–5.

28. Florida Department of Insurance, "Statewide Grand Jury Indicts 13 in Scheme Targeting Elderly," Press Release, October 14, 1998, 1.

29. The Over-the-Counter Bulletin Board is an electronic quotation system maintained by NASDAQ, quoting prices and sales volumes for stocks not listed on NASDAQ or any other stock exchange.

30. *United States v. David Houge*, No. 98-cr-544 (E.D.N.Y. 1998) ("Indictment").

31. *United States v. Dominick Dionisio, et al.*, No. 99-cr-589 (E.D.N.Y. 1999) ("Superseding Indictment").

32. *United States v. Houge.*

33. Sharon Walsh, "Mob Ties Seen on Wall St.," *Washington Post*, June 17, 1999, E1.

34. Mike Claffey, "40M Stock Scam," *Daily News*, March 3, 2000, 38.

35. U.P.I. (no title), March 12, 1982.

36. "Texas Thrift Put Under Supervisory Control," *National Thrift News*, February 4, 1985, 5.

37. "Seattle Grand Jury Indicts 9 in Scheme to Defraud 3 Thrifts of $18 Million," *The American Banker*, July 30, 1986, 50.

38. Senate Committee, *Efforts to Combat, Part IV*, 470–477.

39. *United States v. Thompson, et al.*, No. 95-cr-2088 (D. Utah 1995) ("Indictment").

40. *United States v. Pete Buffo*, No. 99-cr-63W (D. Utah 1999) ("Felony Information").

41. *Securities and Exchange Commission v. Capital Acquisitions*, No. 97cv-0977s (D. Utah 1997) ("Complaint").

42. Steve Cannizaro, "Ex-Insurance Chiefs to Share Same Jail Time," *Times-Picayune* (New Orleans), September 1, 1993, A1.

43. Douglas McLeod, "A History of Controversy for Teale," *Business Insurance*, January 25, 1993, 69.

44. "Louisiana Closes Insurer," *Business Insurance*, April 10, 1989, 149.

45. "Belgian Court Helps La. Investigation," *Baton Rouge Morning Advocate*, October 20, 1989, 15A.

46. Douglas McLeod, "SEC Accuses Three of Fraud," *Business Insurance*, September 14, 1998, 1.

47. Jayson Blair, "U.S. and 28 States Plan Attack Against Promissory-Note Fraud," *New York Times*, June 2, 2000, C1.

48. New York Attorney General's Office, "Spitzer Charges Pair in $3.8 Million Promissory Note Fraud," Press Release, June 1, 2000, 1.

49. Blair, "U.S. and 28 States Plan Attack," C1.

50. *State of New York v. Frank Fucilo et al.*, Index No. 402214/00 (Supreme Court, County of New York, New York 2000) ("Exhibit F"), 31, 36–37.

51. Securities and Exchange Commission, *Recidivist Securities Violator's New Oil and Gas and Microcap Schemes Shut Down by SEC*, Litigation Release No. 16176, June 4, 1999, 1.

52. *Securities and Exchange Commission v. Redbank Petroleum, et al.*, No. 99-cv-1267 (N.D. Tex. 1999) ("Complaint"), 5–6.

53. Bill Lodge, "Investors Fear They Got Bilked," *Dallas Morning News*, July 26, 1999, 13A.

54. *United States v. Brent A. Wagman*, No. 99-cr-412 (N.D. Tex. 1999) ("Indictment"), 2.

55. Leah Spiro and Geri Smith, "Tax-Haven Whiz or Rogue Banker?" *Business Week*, June 1, 1998, 136.

56. Ibid.

57. David Marchant, "We Expose the Harris Organization's Multi-million Dollar Ponzi Scheme," *Offshore Alert*, March 31, 1998, www.offshorebusiness.com (accessed August 15, 2000).

58. *Marc M. Harris v. David E. Marchant*, No. 98-cv-761 (S.D. Fla. 1998) ("Final Judgement"), 14.

59. Ibid.

60. Jane Bryant Quinn, "Promissory Notes May Promise the Impossible," *Seattle Post-Intelligencer*, December 14, 1999, D1.

61. Florida Office of the Comptroller, "Comptroller Orders Company to Stop Selling Promissory Notes," News Release, November 18, 1999, 1.

62. Todd Robberson, "Area Fugitive Living the Good Life in Panama," *Dallas Morning News*, March 10, 2000, 1A.

63. Bill Lodge, "Fugitive Captured in Panama," *Dallas Morning News*, March 11, 2000, 1A.

64. Ibid.

65. Bill Lodge and Tod Robberson, "Former Promoter Guilty of Swindling Investors," *Dallas Morning News*, May 15, 2000, 29A.

66. *Securities and Exchange Commission v. Redbank Petroleum*, No. 99-cv-1267 (N.D. Tex. 1999) ("Final Judgement as to Brent A. Wagman"), 3.

67. Securities and Exchange Commission, "SEC, State Securities Regulators Announce Promissory Note Enforcement Sweep," News Release, June 1, 2000, 1.

68. California Department of Corporations, "Top Ten Investment Scams for Investors to Avoid," News Release, May 23, 2000, 1.

69. Indraneel Sur, "Sales of Phony Bonds Top State's Fraud List," *Los Angeles Times*, May 24, 2000, C2.

70. Don Bauder, "Too Good to Be True," *San Diego Union-Tribune*, January 15, 2000, C1.

71. Robert Shiller, *Irrational Exuberance* (Princeton, N.J.: Princeton University Press, 2000).

72. Ibid., 42.

73. Ferdinand Pecora, *Wall Street Under Oath* (New York: Kelley Publishers, 1968).

74. Susan Kennedy, *The Banking Crisis of 1933* (Lexington, Ky.: University of Kentucky Press, 1973), 108–128.

## CHAPTER 4

1. Senate Committee on Governmental Affairs, Permanent Subcommittee on Investigations, *Efforts to Combat Fraud and Abuse in the Insurance Industry, Part III,* 102d Cong., 1st sess., July 19, 1991, 81.

2. J. W. Davidson, *Samoa Mo Samoa* (Melbourne, Australia: Oxford University Press, 1967), 48–58. Sylvia Masterman, *The Origins of International Rivalry in Samoa, 1845–1884* (Stanford, Cal.: Stanford University Press, 1934), 117–129.

3. Marc Lifsher, "Insurer Chartered by Phony Country," *Orange County Register,* February 15, 1993, A1.

4. Douglas McLeod, "California Bars Five Insurers," *Business Insurance,* March 29, 1993, 2.

5. California Surplus Lines Association, "Bulletin 567, Re: California Pacific Bankers and Insurance, Ltd. (DOM)," www.sla-cal.org/bulletin/5xx/bulletin567.htm (accessed April 16, 2001).

6. Ibid.

7. McLeod, "California Bars," 1.

8. Ibid.

9. *United States v. Dallas Bessant,* No. 96-cr-177 (E.D. Pa. 1996) ("Presentence Investigation Report"), 4.

10. *United States v. Jeffrey H. Reynolds,* No. 96-cr-003 (N.D. Tex. 1996) ("Indictment").

11. David Pasztor, "Scam Without a Country," *Dallas Observer,* May 2, 1996, 1.

12. The judge tacked on additional eighteen months after Reynolds failed to show up for his prison date.

13. William Barret, "Like Father, Like Son," *Forbes,* April 16, 1999, 46. Tom Curtis, "Jeff Reynolds: Zillionaire," *Texas Monthly,* May 1990, 108.

14. Barret, "Like Father," 46.

15. Charles Boisseau, "What's His Name Now, Mate," *Houston Chronicle,* January 9, 1990, 1.

16. Curtis, "Jeff Reynolds," 110.

17. Ibid.

18. Marc Lifsher, "Twice Burned," *Orange County Register,* August 10, 1993, A1.

19. Susan Will, Henry Pontell, and Richard Cheung, "Risky Business Revisited," *Crime and Delinquency* (1998) 44: 367.

20. Texas Department of Insurance, "Commissioner Stops Illegal Bond Business," Press Release, September 19, 1996, 1.

21. S. P. Dinnen, "Indiana Trying to Expel 'Phantom' Asia Pacific Bank," *Indianapolis Star,* November 9, 1994, E1.

22. Ibid.

23. Michael Wagner, " 'Nation' Waging 'Spiritual War' On State Official," *Sacramento Bee*, February 13, 1995, B1.

24. Pamela Yip, "The Rises and Falls of Leon Hooten III," *Houston Chronicle*, August 26, 1990, 1.

25. Bill Mintz, "Executive May Have Had a Role in Bizarre Scheme," *Houston Chronicle*, September 20, 1996, 1.

26. Yip, "The Rises and Falls," 1.

27. Bill Mintz, "Hooten, Target of FBI Probe, Dies," *Houston Chronicle*, October 12, 1996, 2.

28. Ibid.

29. G. Bruce Knecht, "A 'Nation' in Cyberspace Draws Fire from Authorities," *Wall Street Journal*, February 9, 1999, B1.

30. Richard Leiby and James Lileks, "The Ruse that Roared," *Washington Post*, November 5, 1995, C1.

31. Bob Simon, "Fantasy Island," Transcript, *CBS News: 60 Minutes II* (broadcast April 11, 2000), Dow Jones Interactive Publications Library (accessed April 30, 2000).

32. "The Melchizedek Bible," www.melchizedek.com/nz-bible.htm (accessed February 15, 1998).

33. Ibid.

34. Marc Lifsher, "Insurer Chartered by a Phony Country," *Orange County Register*, February 15, 1993, A1.

35. "Melchizedek Bible."

36. Ibid.

37. David Wessel, "U.S. Accuses Five of Fraud Involving Bank in Marianas," *Wall Street Journal*, January 28, 1986, 1.

38. Ibid.

39. "Melchizedek Bible."

40. William Barret, "Father of His Country," *Forbes*, January 7, 1991, 44.

41. Ibid.

42. "Melchizedek Bible."

43. "Dominion of Melchizedek Embassy (formerly at Austin)," www.melchizedek.com/embassy.htm (accessed January 16, 2001).

44. Ibid.

45. "Dominion of Melchizedek," www.melchizedek.com (accessed February 24, 2000). The term "postmodern state" was first used in a *Washington Post* article (Richard Leiby and James Lileks, "The Ruse that Roared," *Washington Post*, November 5, 1995, C1), but has since been adopted by DOM.

46. Leiby and Lileks, "The Ruse that Roared," C1.

47. "Melchizedek at War with France," www.melchizedek.com/press/war-france.htm (accessed March 29, 1999).

48. "Serbia: Kosovo Albanian Leader Appoints 'Advisory Council' for Negotiations," *BBC Worldwide Monitoring*, March 24, 1998, Dow Jones Interactive Publications Library (accessed April 15, 1998).

49. "Kosovo Republic Officially Recognized by Melchizedek Republic," www.melchizedek.com/press/kosovo.htm (accessed March 29, 1999).

50. Michael Field, "Americans Helping Rotuma to Break Away from Fiji," *Agence France-Presse*, January 31, 2000, Dow Jones Interactive Publications Library (accessed August 7, 2000).

51. Asha Lakhan, "CyberNation Seeks Status of State Within a State," *Agence France-Presse*, February 9, 2000, Dow Jones Interactive Publications Library (accessed August 7, 2000).

52. Michael Field and Asha Lakhan, "Tiny Pacific Island Admits It was Duped in US-based Internet Fraud," *Agence France-Presse*, February 14, 2000, Dow Jones Interactive Publications Library (accessed July 24, 2000).

53. John Shockey, address to the 4th International Financial Fraud Convention in London, May 27, 1999.

54. Terrence O'Hara, "D.C. Home to Shadowy Banking Web," *Washington Business Journal*, February 18, 1991, 1.

55. William Barret, "Bad Bank," *Forbes*, May 27, 1991, 17.

56. Dan Atkinson, "Bogus Bankers May Avoid Charges," *The Guardian*, July 24, 1997, 23.

57. Tony Hetherington, "Mr. Big Cheese of Gouda Is Wanted by the Fraud Squad," *Mail on Sunday* (London), August 16, 1998, 24.

58. "Melchizedek Issues Warning Against BIG International and Swiss Investment Bankers," Press Release, www.melchizedek.com/press/bankwarning.htm (accessed August 7, 2000).

59. United States Office of the Comptroller of Currency, "Special Alert," FIL-92–98, August 26, 1998, 1.

60. *Securities and Exchange Commission v. World Financial and Investment Co.*, No. 99-cv-07608 (E.D.N.Y. 1999) ("Complaint"), 2.

61. Securities and Exchange Commission, *Litigation Release No. 16368*, November 23, 1999.

62. Associated Press, "Offshore Bank in Grenada Draws Scrutiny," *Orlando Sentinel*, April 23, 2000, H8.

63. "Grenada Scam Bank Offers Annual Interest of 250 Per Cent," *Offshore Alert*, February 26, 1999, www.offshorebusiness.com (accessed August 7, 2000).

64. "Massive Banking/Insurance Fraud Exposed," *Offshore Alert*, January 29, 1999, www.offshorebusiness.com (accessed August 7, 2000).

65. The network and its various components have been described in detail in the on-line magazine, *Offshore Alert*.

66. "Proconsul's Dreams Go up in Smoke," *Indian Ocean Newsletter*, September 4, 1999.

67. Michael Allen, "Grenada Banking is Great, but Mr. Brink Is Off to Uganda Now," *Wall Street Journal*, February 29, 2000, A1.

68. Field and Lakhan, "Tiny Pacific Island."

69. Lisa Creffield, "Sham Nation Fleeces Hundred," *South China Morning Post*, July 15, 2000, 10.

70. "Businessman Guilty of $2.2 Million Fraud," *AAP Newsfeed,* June 23, 2000.

71. Bertil Lintner and Andrew Marshall, "Virtual Nation," *Mail on Sunday* (London), February 28, 1999, 6. Bertil Lintner, "Crime: Fantasy Island," *Far Eastern Economic Review,* December 10, 1998, 32.

72. Kitty Calavita, Henry Pontell, and Robert Tillman, *Big Money Crime* (Berkeley: University of California Press, 1997).

73. "Enenkio Atoll Government v. United States," www.enenkio.org/Default_Suit.-pdf (accessed August 20, 2000).

74. Ibid.

75. "A Declaration," www.enenkio.org/declwar.pdf (accessed August 20, 2000).

76. "Government Bond Program," www.enenkio.org/bonds.htm (accessed August 20, 2000). In October 2000, the SEC ordered Moore and the Kingdom of EnenKio to stop selling the bonds (Securities and Exchange Commission, *Litigation Release No. 16780,* October 26, 2000).

77. "Philatelic Products," www.enenkio.org/stamps.htm (accessed August 20, 2000).

78. "Economic Citizenship Program," www.enenkio.org/ecp.htm (accessed August 20, 2000).

79. "Cyber-State Passports on Offer for Kuwait's Stateless People," *Agence France-Press,* February 5, 2000, Lexis-Nexis (accessed August 17, 2000). "Kuwait Scotches Passport Deal with Cyber-State," *Agence France-Press,* February 6, 2000, Lexis-Nexis (accessed August 17, 2000).

80. Tim Hulse, "Prince Lazarus Rules the Waves," *The Independent* (London), May 31, 1998, 4.

81. *Securities and Exchange Commission v. Lazarus R. Long,* No. 99-cv-0257 (E.D. Okla. 1999) ("Exhibit A"), 3.

82. Ruth Sorelle, "Experts Question Freezing of Aborted Fetuses," *Houston Chronicle,* December 22, 1995, 33.

83. Ralph King, "Gray Market," *Wall Street Journal,* January 10, 1996, A1.

84. *Securities and Exchange Commission v. Long* ("Complaint"), 6.

85. "Update," www.new-utopia.com/update.html (accessed January 29, 2000).

86. Ibid.

87. Tom Dubocq, Amy Dricoll, and Martin Merzer, "No Escape," *Miami Herald,* July 25, 1997, 1W.

88. "Spanish Police Smash False 'Virtual Country' of the Web," *Deutsche Presse-Agentur,* April 11, 2000, Dow Jones Interactive Publications Library (accessed April 11, 2000).

89. "Picture Gallery," www.fruitsofthesea.demon.co.uk/sealand/gallery/html (accessed April 7, 2000).

90. "Fact File," www.fruitsofthesea.demon.co.uk/sealand/factfile.html (accessed April 7, 2000).

91. Marjorie Miller and Richard Boudreaux, "A Nation for Fraud and Faux," *Los Angeles Times,* June 7, 2000, A1.

92. John Markoff, "Rebel Outpost on the Fringes of Cyberspace," *New York Times,*

June 4, 2000, 14. Simon McGregor-Wood, "Thank Heavens for Little Worlds," www. abcnews.go.com/sections/tech/DailyNews/sealand000606.html (accessed August 21, 2000).

93. Simon Garfinkel, "Welcome to Sealand. Now Bugger Off," *Wired*, July 7, 2000, www.Wysiwyg://25/http://wired.com/wired/archive/8.07/haven.html (accessed August 21, 2000).

94. United States Department of State, Bureau for International Narcotics and Law Enforcement Affairs, *International Narcotics Control Strategy Report, 1999*, Washington, D.C., March 2000, www.state.gov/www/global/narcots_law/1999_narc_report/mL_intro99.html (accessed August 25, 2000).

95. Marc Harris, "Panama: The New Virtual Nation," www.marc-harris.com/feature/PanamaVirtualNation.htm (accessed June 28, 1998).

96. Department of State, *International Narcotics*.

97. "Economic Citizenship," www.ibuoffshoredominica.dm/ecocit.htm (accessed August 20, 2000).

98. Department of State, *International Narcotics*.

## CONCLUSIONS

1. Marc Lifsher, "Federal Prosecutors Complete Crackdown on Bogus Insurers," *Wall Street Journal*, November 4, 1998, CA1.

2. *Odyssey Re v. Stirling Cooke Browne Holdings Limited*, No. 99-cv-2326 (S.D.N.Y. 1999).

3. Robert Lenzner and Bernard Condon, "In Goldman We Trust," *Forbes*, February 7, 2000, 52.

4. Robert Lenzner, "Passing the Trash," *Forbes*, January 10, 2000, 60.

5. *Reliance Insurance Company v. Unicover Managers*, No. 00/600280 (Supreme Ct., County of New York, New York 2000) ("Complaint"), 3.

6. Robert Merton, "Three Fragments from a Sociologist's Notebooks," *Annual Review of Sociology* 13 (1987): 1-28.

7. John Walton, "Making the Theoretical Case," in *What Is a Case? Exploring the Foundations of Social Inquiry*, Charles Ragin and Howard Becker, eds. (New York: Cambridge University Press, 1992), 124.

8. James Coleman, "Toward an Integrated Theory of White-Collar Crime," *American Journal of Sociology* 93 (1987): 406.

9. Ron Martin, "The New Economic Geography of Money," in *Money and the Space Economy*, Ron Martin, ed. (Chichester, England: John Wiley, 1999), 12-13.

10. Andrew Leyshon and Nigel Thrift, *Money/Space: Geographies of Money Transformation* (London: Routledge, 1997), 132-135.

11. Gordon Clark, "Rogues and Regulation in Global Finance: Maxwell, Leeson and the City of London," *Regional Studies* 31 (1997): 221-236.

12. Testimony of John Garamendi, Commissioner of Insurance, State of California, before the House Committee on Energy and Commerce, Subcommittee on Oversight and Investigations, *Insurance Company Failures*, 102d Cong., 2d sess., April 9, 1992, 299.

13. House Committee on Energy and Commerce, Subcommittee on Oversight and Investigations, *Wishful Thinking: A World View of Insurance Solvency Regulation*, 103d Cong., 2d sess., H. Rprt. 103-R., October 1994, 62.

14. Ibid., 107.

15. Jack Blum, Michael Levi, R. Naylor, and Phil Williams, *Financial Havens, Banking Secrecy and Money Laundering* (United Nations, 1998), 25.

16. Ibid., 68.

17. Bill Maurer, "Law Writing, Immigration, and Globalization in the British Virgin Islands," *Indiana Journal of Global Legal Studies Journal* 2 (1995), 423.

18. Bill Maurer, "Writing Law, Making a 'Nation': History, Modernity, and Paradoxes of Self-Rule in the British Virgin Islands," *Law and Society Review* 29 (1995): 255–286.

19. Peter Evans uses the term "predatory states" to refer to countries like Zaire, which "preys on its citizenry, terrorizing them, despoiling their common patrimony, and providing little in the way of services in return" (Peter Evans, *Embedded Autonomy*, Princeton, N.J.: Princeton University Press, 1995, 45). He also used the term "deviant states" in a later article on the impact of globalization on the state: "Financial markets can easily punish deviant states but in the long run their returns depend on the existence of an interstate system in which the principal national economies are under the control of competent and 'responsible' state actors." Peter Evans, "What Future for the State in a Global Political Economy?" *Swiss Political Science Review* 4 (1998): 1.

20. William Chambliss defines "state-organized crime" as "acts defined by law as criminal and committed by state officials in the pursuit of their job as representatives of the state. Examples include a state's complicity in piracy, smuggling, assassinations, criminal conspiracies, acting as an accessory before or after the fact, and violating laws that limit their activities" (William Chambliss, "State-Organized Crime," *Criminology* 27 (1989): 183).

21. Erving Goffman, *Stigma: Notes on the Management of Spoiled Identity* (New York: Simon and Schuster, 1963).

22. Organisation for Economic Cooperation and Development, "Towards Global Tax Cooperation," (Paris 2000), 10, note 4.

23. Organisation for Economic Cooperation and Development, "OECD Identifies Tax Havens and Potentially Harmful Tax Regimes," Press Release, June 26, 2000, 1.

24. "Rich Nations Can't Stand Competition," *Dow Jones Newswire*, July 26, 2000, Dow Jones Interactive Publications Library (accessed August 23, 2000). "OECD Tax List Called 'Economic Blackmail,' " *Caribbean Update*, August 1, 2000, Dow Jones Interactive Publications Library (accessed August 23, 2000).

25. "Government Reluctant to Act as 'Informer' over Tax Havens," *BBC Summary of World Broadcasts*, July 1, 2000.

26. Eileen McNamara, "Caribbean Leaders Grapple with Threats of Sanctions for Money Laundering," Associated Press, July 3, 2000, Lexis-Nexis (accessed August 23, 2000).

27. Richard Quinney, *The Social Reality of Crime* (Boston: Little, Brown and Company, 1979), 15–18.

28. "Barbados Minister Rejects OECD Report Categorizing Country as a Tax Haven," *BBC Worldwide Monitoring*, July 27, 2000.

29. Ronald M. Sanders, "The OECD Report on 'Harmful Taxation' and its Implications for Small States," www.antigua-barbuda.com/foreignpolicy.html#oecdreport, July 1999 (accessed August 23, 2000).

30. Caribbean Community Secretariat, "OECD Harmful Tax Competition Report: Developed Countries Gain, Caribbean Pain," www.caricom.org/oecdreport.html (accessed September 8, 2000).

31. Gavin Souter, "Bermuda Captive Growth Takes a Breather in 1999," *Business Insurance*, May 1, 2000, 14. United States Department of the Treasury, Financial Crimes Enforcement Network, "FinCen Advisory, Transactions Involving the Cayman Islands," July 2000.

32. Gavin Souter and Sally Roberts, "Top Domiciles Won't Add Taxes; But Bermuda, Cayman Pledge to Comply with OECD Rule," *Business Insurance*, June 26, 2000, 1.

33. Department of the Treasury, "FinCen Advisory," 1.

34. American banks have frequently used offshore banks and trusts to provide financial services to wealthy, often foreign, clients (General Accounting Office, *Money Laundering: Regulatory Oversight of Offshore Private Banking Activities*, GAO/GGD-98-154, June 1998. General Accounting Office, *Private Banking: Raul Salinas, Citibank and Alleged Money Laundering*, GAO/T-OSI-00-3, November 1999. Lucy Komisar, "Fool Me Twice," *The Progressive*, December 1, 1999, 36).

35. Frank Portnoy, *Fiasco: The Inside Story of a Wall Street Trader* (New York: Penguin, 1999), 83.

36. "Global Economic Integration: Opportunities and Challenges," Remarks by Alan Greenspan at a symposium sponsored by the Federal Reserve Bank of Kansas City, Jackson Hole, Wyoming, August 25, 2000. www.federalreserve.gov/BoardDocs/Speeches/2000/20000825.htm.

37. A similar point is made by Eric Helleiner when he argues that states are selective about the types of illicit global finance they choose to crack down on. The United States has focused much of its enforcement efforts on money laundering, while devoting relatively little attention to tax evasion and "capital flight"—"the cross-border movement of financial capital which evades national capital controls." The reason for this, he asserts, is that much of that capital is flowing out of the developing world and into the United States and American financial institutions. They make substantial profits by facilitating this movement (Eric Helleiner, "State Power and the Regulation of Illicit Activity in Global Finance," in *The Illicit Global Economy and State Power*, H. Richard Friman and Peter Andreas, eds. (New York: Rowman and Littlefield, 1999), 53–90).

38. Manuel Castells, "Materials for an Exploratory Theory of the Network Society," *British Journal of Sociology* 51 (2000): 5. John Urry, "Mobile Sociology," *British Journal of Sociology* 51 (2000): 185.

39. Castells, "Materials," 14.

40. Ibid. It is not that physical places have become unimportant but rather their "functional or symbolic meaning depends on their connection to a network rather than on its specific characteristics as localities." Manuel Castells, "Toward a Sociology of the Network Society," *Contemporary Sociology* 29 (2000): 6.

41. Gearoid Tuathail, "Borderless Worlds: Problematizing Discourses of Deterritoriali-

zation in Global Finance and Digital Culture," *Geopolitics* 4 (2000): 2. Held et al. observe, "Under conditions of globalization, 'local,' 'national,' or even 'continental' political, social and economic space is re-formed such that it is no longer co-terminous with established legal and territorial boundaries" (David Held, Anthony McGrew, David Globlatt, and Jonathan Perration, *Global Transformations*, Stanford, Calif.: Stanford University Press, 1999, 29).

42. Richard O'Brien, *Global Financial Integration: The End of Geography* (London: Royal Institute of International Affairs, 1992), 1.

43. R. Martin, "The New Economic Geography of Money," 15–16.

44. United Nations, Commission on Crime Prevention and Criminal Justice, *Implementation of the Naples Political Declaration and Global Action Plan Against Organized Transnational Crime*, 1996, 3, www.uncjin.org/Documents/5comm/2e.htm (accessed November 11, 2000).

45. Ibid.

46. House Committee, *Wishful Thinking*, 69.

47. United Nations, *Implementation*.

48. Ibid.

49. *United States v. Stephen Coker*, No. 94-cr-00128 (S.D. Ala. 1994) ("Superseding Indictment"), 15–34.

50. *United States v. Jerry Brian Lamb*, No. 99-cr-127 (D. Ariz. 1999) ("Indictment"), 2–13.

51. United Nations, *Implementation*.

52. Ibid. See also Phil Williams, "Transnational Criminal Organizations: Strategic Alliances," *Washington Quarterly* 18 (1995): 57.

53. United Nations, *Implementation*.

54. Ibid.

55. Ibid.

56. For a discussion of the concept of loosely coupled organizations, see Richard Ingersoll, "Loosely Coupled Organizations Revisited," in *Research in the Sociology of Organizations* vol. 11, Samual Bacharach, ed. (Greenwich, Conn.: JAI Press, 1993), 81–112.

57. This phrase is borrowed from, Peter Evans, Dietrich Rueschemeyer, and Theda Skocpol, eds., *Bringing the State Back In* (New York: Cambridge University Press, 1985).

58. Thomas Friedman, The *Lexus and the Olive Tree* (New York: Farrar, Straus and Giroux, 1999), 93.

59. Eric Helleiner has argued that the globalization of finance and, specifically, the international trend toward the liberalization of capital controls were not the result of unstoppable technological and market developments. Instead, governments played key roles in encouraging globalization by embracing specific policies that facilitated the process. "As markets became increasingly globalized and liberalization took place in major centers, states found themselves pitched in a war of competitive deregulation in which they sought, as one observer put it, 'to dismantle protectionist financial regimes in order to secure a stake in the emerging global financial marketplace' " (Eric Helleiner, *States and the Reemergence of Global Finance*, Ithaca, N.Y.: Cornell University Press, 1994, 197).

60. Robert Tillman, *Broken Promises: Fraud by Small Business Health Insurers* (Boston: Northeastern University Press, 1998), 168–171.

61. In the mid-1990s, several bills were introduced in Congress that would have allowed MEWAs, in one form or another, essentially to opt out of state regulation. Opponents to one version of the legislation included the National Council of State Legislators, which warned that "the bill . . . opens up an opportunity for scam operators to operate in a netherworld of loose federal standards with little or no meaningful oversight" (Steven Brostoff, "Limited Bill Advances to House," *National Underwriter (Life & Health/Financial Services Edition)*, March 11, 1996, 1). More generally, see Tillman, *Broken Promises*, 171–178.

In California, industry representatives decried the state's regulatory changes regarding surplus lines carriers as characteristic of the "anti-industry approach of regulation" taken by insurance commissioner John Garamendi (National Association of Professional Surplus Lines Office, "California Still Presenting Problems," News Release, November/December, 1995).

62. House Committee on Governmental Affairs, Permanent Subcommittee on Investigations, *Second Interim Report on U.S. Government Efforts to Combat Fraud and Abuse in the Insurance Industry: Problems with the Regulation of the Insurance and the Reinsurance Industry*, 102d Cong., 2d sess., July 1, 1992, 27.

63. House Committee, *Wishful Thinking*, 15.

64. Scot Paltrow, "The Converted: How Insurance Firms Beat Back an Effort for Stricter Controls," *Wall Street Journal*, February 5, 1998, A1.

65. House Committee, *Second Interim Report*, 26.

66. Public Law 102, "Gramm-Leach-Biley Act," 106th Cong., 1st sess. (November 12, 1999).

67. This argument was made by Representative Dingell in a letter to Alan Greenspan in which he warned against some of the provisions of the Gramm-Leach-Biley Act. (John D. Dingell to Alan Greenspan, July 30, 1999). See also United States Department of Treasury, Office of the Inspector General, *Office of the Comptroller of the Currency's Supervision of Banks Selling Insurance*, OIG-00–98, June 27, 2000.

68. General Accounting Office, *Insurance Regulation: Scandal Highlights Need for Strengthened Regulatory Oversight*, GAO/GGD-00–198, September 2000, 18–21.

69. Ibid., 3.

70. Ibid., 46–49.

71. See, for example, Kenichi Ohmae, *The Borderless World* (New York: Harper Business, 1990).

# INDEX

DATE DUE

| | | | |
|---|---|---|---|
| | | | |
| | | | |
| | | | |
| | | | |
| | | | |
| | | | |
| | | | |
| | | | |
| | | | |
| | | | |
| | | | |
| | | | |
| | | | |
| | | | |
| | | | |